KT-211-038

MICHAEL JACKSON'S
MALT WHISKY
COMPANION

DORLING KINDERSLEY
London • New York • Sydney
www.dk.com

MICHAEL JACKSON'S
MALT WHISKY
COMPANION

A DORLING KINDERSLEY BOOK

www.dk.com

Senior Editor
Sharon Lucas

Senior Art Editor
Tim Scott

Managing Editor
Francis Ritter

Managing Art Editor
Derek Coombes

DTP Designer
Sonia Charbonnier

Production Controller
Wendy Penn

Researchers
Owen D. L. Barstow
Lara Brekenfeld

Additional Research
Jürgen Deibel
Bryan Harrel

Fourth edition first published in Great Britain in 1999 by
Dorling Kindersley Limited
9 Henrietta Street, London WC2E 8PS

Copyright © 1989, 1991, 1994, 1999 Dorling Kindersley Limited
Text copyright © 1989, 1991, 1994, 1999 Michael Jackson

All rights reserved. No part of this publication
may be reproduced, stored in a retrieval stystem,
or transmitted in any form or by any means,
electronic, mechanical, photocopying or otherwise,
without the prior written permission of the
copyright owner.

A CIP catalogue record for this book is
available from the British Library.

ISBN 0-7513-0708-4

Reproduced by Colourscan, Singapore
Printed and bound by Mohndruck, Germany

CONTENTS

Before dinner or after? With coffee, chocolate, or a cigar? These are just some of the moments for malt. There are suggestions with every entry...and cigar specifics on page 330.

AUTHOR'S INTRODUCTION
DISCOVERING AND EXPLORING

MY FIRST MALT WHISKY was a 12-year-old, and single. I was 18. We were introduced by a mutual friend in an otherwise undistinguished pub in Edinburgh. Until reaching that height of maturity, I had believed whisky to be something that I did not like. I cannot imagine how I ever held that view. That first kiss of Glen Grant was enough to initiate a lifetime's devotion and exploration.

For decades, the sensuous pleasures offered by malts were virtually a secret. Scotland had more than a hundred distilleries making malt whisky, but almost all of it went into blended Scotches. The handful of distilleries that offered their malt whisky "straight" in the bottle were regarded as a distraction by an industry that had been built on blends. My early researches, carried out as an experienced journalist, were sometimes viewed with a blend – so to speak – of suspicion, amusement, and obstructiveness.

Books by authors such as Barnard, Bruce Lockhart, Daiches, Gunn, and McDowell told me about the process of whisky making, its lore, history, and geography, but little about the taste of the product, which has always been my greatest interest. In the mid 1980s, I committed to print my own best efforts to describe those flavours, and to categorize malts and other whiskies. In doing so, I was given great encouragement by Wallace Milroy and Derek Cooper, both of whom have attempted similar tasks on a smaller scale. My first book on the subject, *The World Guide to Whisky* (published in 1987), was quickly followed by *The Malt Whisky Companion* (1989). No other writer had attempted so thoroughly to describe the taste of individual whiskies, discussed so many, or taken the controversial step of scoring them.

Over the past decade, the astonishing growth in the number of malts available, and the vintages, ages, strengths, and bottlings in which they can be found, has led to each edition of the book being greatly revised and expanded. In both respects, this new edition is the most extensive yet. I have celebrated ten years of *Michael Jackson's Malt Whisky Companion* with a marathon of tasting and note-taking. I hope you will find a page that seems especially appetizing, and raise a glass with me.

Michael Jackson

WHAT'S NEW
THE CHANGING WORLD OF MALTS

S|INGLE MALTS WITH SUSHI…as a digestif…with a cigar…never before have these dazzlingly diverse drinks been explored by the consumer with such zest and interest.

Newly bottled malts constantly appear on the shelves of wine shops and supermarkets, at airports, in bars and restaurants. Some are completely new. Isle of Arran, for example, emerged from a newly built distillery in time to reach the pages of this edition. Other newcomers in recent years are from distilleries whose whisky was never before bottled as a single malt. Some are the first bottlings from the stocks of long-gone distilleries, such as Glen Flagler. Many are very limited editions but they are included for the benefit of enthusiasts who spot one, perhaps at a high price, and wonder whether it might be to their taste. I hope my notes are a help.

TRENDS REFLECTED IN THIS EDITION

Cask strength malts have greatly grown in availability. The strength of whisky in the cask, after maturation, varies according to the extent of natural evaporation during that period. Typically, it will range from the lower 60s to upper 40s, depending upon the period of aging. In almost every case, it will be higher than the standard strengths of 43 or 40, achieved by "reducing" (diluting with water).

Cask-strength bottlings are usually not as thoroughly filtered as malts of conventional strengths, and thus are not stripped of significant flavour elements such as fatty acids. Conventional malts are typically chilled before being filtered, to remove elements that might precipitate, causing haze, when water is added (during reduction, or by the consumer), if ice is added, or if the bottle is kept in the fridge. Connoisseurs do not chill their malts.

Vintage editions are more individualistic (for good or ill) than regular bottlings. A vintage edition contains whisky from just one, identified year, with any variations caused by the harvest, weather, or conditions during maturation. Conventional bottlings contain several ages of the same whisky, to achieve a consistency of flavour. The age on the label is that of the youngest whisky.

Wood finishes are malts that are matured for a conventional period (anything from five to 15 years or more) in one style of wood (usually former Bourbon or sherry casks) then "finished", for a shorter period (typically six months to two years) in another type of barrel, perhaps one that has contained a wine such as port or Madeira, to add a further element of aroma, flavour, and roundness.

THE EVOLUTION OF MALT WHISKY

WILD YEASTS SPONTANEOUSLY cause fermentation of sugars, creating alcohol. This is how alcoholic drinks were empirically discovered. The fruits of warm lands gave up their sugars to make wine, and the grains of cooler regions yielded beer. In distilled form, these become brandy and whisky.

The art of distillation was used by Phoenician sailors (to render sea water drinkable), alchemists, makers of perfumes, and eventually in the production of medicines and alcoholic drinks. To distil is to boil the water, wine, or beer, collect the steam, and condense it back into liquid. This drives off certain subtances (for example, the salt in water) and concentrates others (such as the alcohol in wine or beer).

Distilling may have entered Europe across the Straits of Gibraltar. There are unproven suggestions of the fiery art in Ireland at the beginning of the past millennium. The first indisputable reference in Scotland is from 1494.

The wine or beer is boiled to make steam – which, being wraith-like, may have given rise to the English word "spirit" or German *Geist* (ghost), especially since condensation brings it back to life in a restored (and restorative) form. The "water of life", they call it. (*Vodka,* a diminutive form, in Slavic countries; *aquavit,* in various spellings, in Nordic lands; *eau-de-vie* in French; *usquebaugh,* in various spellings, in Gaelic.) The last became usky, then whisky, in English. All of these terms at first simply indicated a distillate, made from whatever was local.

Like the original vodkas (also grain-based), the first Irish and Scottish barley-malt distillates were flavoured with herbs and spices. By the mid 1700s, a distinction was made in Scotland between these flavoured spirits and "plain malt".

Landseer's The Highland Whisky Still, painted in the 1820s, captures the atmosphere of an early illegal still.

Defining the Drink

Single

The term refers to the whisky being from just one (that is, a single) distillery. The term *single single* is sometimes used to indicate that all the whisky in the bottling came from a single cask. More often, this is called a *single cask* bottling (Balvenie uses the term *single barrel*). Most bottlings of *single malt* contain whisky from several casks and batches. The combining of exclusively malt whisky from different casks is known as a *vatting*. Sometimes they are kept in wood for a further period to marry. So long as it is all malt whisky, from the same distillery, it is a single malt. Even on singles, some distilleries use the less precise term *pure malt*. More often, this term, or simply *malt whisky*, or *vatted malt*, implies that several malt distilleries contributed. Malt whisky is made in a batch process, in a still shaped like a kettle or cooking pot. This *pot still* produces whisky with more flavour than the more modern "patent", continuous, column-shaped still, which is used to make *grain whisky*. The ingredients of grain whisky vary. Although some malt will be used, the dominant grains will be unmalted barley, wheat, or maize. Grain whisky is produced to leaven and lighten blends, but it is also occasionally bottled as *single grain* – something of a novelty.

Malt

Grain that has been steeped in water, partially sprouted, and dried to render it soluble. When the sprouting has reached an optimum point, it is arrested by the drying of the grain in a kiln. The grain used to make malt for whisky in Scotland and Ireland is always barley. In other countries producing malt whisky, this is also usually true. Barley malt is used to make beer, as an ingredient to varying degrees in almost all types of whisky, in milky drinks, baked goods, and syrup-like extracts. The malt used in Scotch whisky was traditionally dried over peat, a local fuel, which imparts the characteristic smokiness. Most Scottish whisky malt is peated to some degree, albeit often very lightly. The place where these procedures happen is known as a maltings. Malt whiskies are often described simply as "malts".

Scotch

Scotland has internationally protected this term. A whisky may not be labelled Scotch unless it is made in that country. If it is to be called Scotch, it cannot be made in England, Wales, Ireland, or anywhere else. Bushmills makes fine malt whiskeys, but they are Irish, not Scotch. Excellent whiskies are made by similar methods in other countries, notably Japan, but they cannot be called Scotches. Nor do they taste the same. The best Scotch whiskies taste of the mountain heather, the peat, the seaweed. They taste of Scotland, more obviously than even Cognac tastes of its region or the best Tequila of its mountain soil.

Whisky

A grain-based distillate in the Scottish and Irish tradition but also made elsewhere in the world – notably North America, where corn (maize) and rye are used to make different local styles. A defining characteristic in all whiskies is the flavour of the grain. While many vodkas and Schnapps are made from grain, they are distilled close to neutrality, or have flavours added, as does gin.

Blended Scotch

The original distillers in Scotland – monks and later farmers – used barley malt, in a pot still. In the 1700s and early 1800s, production was small and irregular, and the notion of "brands" or trademarks was unknown in any industry.

Malt whisky was sold to grocers and wine merchants, who retailed it by the cask at a time when the glass industry had yet to develop mass-produced bottles. Today's bottlings by licensed grocers like Gordon & MacPhail (with their small shop in Elgin, Scotland), and haughtier wine merchants such as Berry Brothers and Rudd, in St James's, London, recall those days.

Johnnie Walker was such a shopkeeper; George Ballantine another; the Chivas brothers were partners in a shop. These merchants dealt with lack of consistency or volume by creating their own house vattings, and these became brands. John Dewar, who went into the business in 1806, was the first person to sell branded whisky in bottles. At first, two or three Highland whiskies might have been blended with a dash of Islay and a filler of Lowland malt, but today a dozen or 20 distillates might be used, perhaps even 30 or 40.

Grain whisky became a distinct element with its production in column stills. They were developed in the 1820s, and widely used by the 1850s. This faster, more industrial process made it possible to produce whisky in much larger quantities, by extending the "agricultural" malt with the "industrial" grain. The resultant blends were also lighter in body and flavour, and perhaps more acceptable to nations unfamiliar with whisky.

The Scots, with their mountainous country and long coastline, are a maritime nation of explorers, traders, and engineers. During the era of exploration and the British empire, they made blended Scotches the most international of spirits.

The best of the blends have great character and complexity, but it is a shame that so many are so similar, and that for so many years orchestrations drowned out the soloists.

The producers of blends have, over the decades, protected their supplies of malt whisky by buying most of the distilleries. Fearing isolation, the handful of independents, most notably Glenfiddich, began seriously to market their whiskies as single malts in the late 1960s and 1970s. What seemed like a lone gamble became an inspiration to others. Blended Scotch is still dominant in volume, but single malts are gaining in sales and commanding far higher prices. The choice is between the orchestra and the soloist.

THE FLAVOURS AND THEIR ORIGIN

T HE TWO SPIRITS MOST OFTEN COMPARED for their regionality are Cognac and single-malt Scotch. In Cognac, the regions of production are contiguous, stretch about 90 miles from one end to the other, and are all in flat countryside. The single malts spread over an area of about 280 miles from one end to the other, from the southern Lowlands to the northern Highlands, from mountain to shore, from the Western Isles to the Orkneys. Cognacs are usually blends, often from more than one region, while a single malt bears the character of just one distillery.

SNOW

The snow that covers the Highland peaks melts to provide water that seeps through fissures in the rock, then emerges into mountain streams before filling the reservoirs of maltings and distilleries. There is melted snow in most bottles of whisky. This is especially true where the Grampian Mountains form a ridge across the biggest land-mass of the Highlands, and small rivers such as the Livet and Fiddich flow into the Spey on their way north to the great inlet known as the Moray Firth. Producers of several types of drink talk in hushed tones of the importance of their water. Nowhere is it more genuinely significant than in single-malt Scotches. The water used in the single malts is usually not treated, and each distillery's supply has its own character, depending upon the local rock and vegetation.

Absolute Scotland: the mountain snow melts, filters through rock, and meets the valley barley. This distillery is Dalwhinnie.

ROCK

Some of the waters are believed to take several hundred years to filter through the mountains before emerging. In 1990, geologists Stephen Cribb and Julie Davison made a study of rock formations in Scotland's whisky regions, and compared them with tasting notes in books on the drink, principally this one. Their findings suggested that the similar tastes in certain whiskies produced near each other might in part be due to the similar rock from which the water rose. For example, in the Lowlands, the crisp, dry Glenkinchie and Rosebank share the same carboniferous rock. The oldest rock is that which supplies water to the Bowmore and Bruichladdich distilleries on Islay, off the west coast of Scotland; it was formed about 600–800 million years ago, and seems to contribute an iron-like flavour. The granite of the Grampians is often credited with the typically soft-water character of the Speyside whiskies. Farther north, sandstone may make for the firmer body of whiskies such as Glenmorangie. Highly individualistic whiskies like Talisker and Clynelish turn out to be based on rock not shared with others.

WATER

The character of the water is influenced not only by the rock from which it rises, but also by the land over which it travels to the distillery. For example, in the Highlands, much of the water used in distilling rises from granite and flows over peat. Water from a mountain stream that flows over rocks may pick up minerals on its journey, adding firmness and crispness to the finished whisky. Some distilleries have water that flows over peaty, mossy, reedy, ferny, or (most often) heathery moorland. This may impart grassy or herbal characteristics. Heather recognizably adds floral and honeyish notes.

Some water flows only over peat, and whiskies may gain peatiness from this; other whiskies have a peaty flavour from the use of the fuel in malting, and some from both sources. The distance the water flows over peat will also be an influence, as will the peat's character.

Water may make its presence felt several times. It is used to steep the grains in the handful of distilleries that have their own maltings, and then again in the infusion that precedes fermentation and distillation. It may also be used to reduce slightly the strength of the spirit off the still before maturation. Some distillers feel they achieve a better maturation if the spirit is reduced in strength by a few percentage points. The distilleries that have their own bottling lines also use the local water to reduce the strength of the whisky at packaging. When a new distillery is planned, a reliable source of good water will be a prime criterion in the choice of a site.

SOIL AND PEAT

The soil will affect not only the water but also the character of the peat. If malting is done at the distillery, local peat will be used in the kilning. The age of the peat deposits, and their degree of grass-root or heather character, will have its own influence on the whisky.

BARLEY

Drinks can be made from any plant that contains fermentable sugars. Among grains, barley was first made into beer. It was especially suited to that purpose because its well-formed husk forms a natural filter. The word barley itself may be an elision of "beer-like". An ancestor of barley, called *bere,* is a traditional grain in the Orkney islands. From beer to whisky is but a small step.

Scotland grows some of the world's best barley for malting, and much of it is cultivated in whisky-producing areas, especially the Lowlands and the stretches where the Spey and other rivers flow over flat, very fertile land to reach the Moray Firth. This coastal rim can have surprisingly long summer days, and cool breezes, though the latter can strengthen worryingly during harvest time, in the later months of summer.

For many years, the local Golden Promise barley was favoured by maltsters and distillers. Its short straw stands up to the wind; it ripens early (in August); and it produces nutty, rich flavours. As the industry has grown, farmers have moved to varieties that give them more grain per acre, and distillers to varieties that yield more fermentable sugars – but these do not necessarily produce such delicious flavours. When Macallan experimentally made one batch with Golden Promise and another with a higher-yield barley, the difference was startling. The lesser variety produced a whisky that was clearly thinner-tasting, "dusty", and almost metallic.

Sometimes a maltster or distiller will check the barley before harvest. He looks for plump, even corns…Golden Promise, growing near Banff.

Microclimate

Although similar yeasts (of broadly the ale type) are used throughout the malt-distilling industry, each tun room (fermentation hall) produces its own characteristics, especially fruity and spicy notes. These may vary according to the material from which the fermenting vessels are made (wood perhaps harbouring its own resident microflora, steel less likely to do so), but it is also influenced by the microclimate in and around the distillery.

Shape of still

Even this has an element of location. Some farmhouse distilleries clearly had stills designed to fit their limited space. Elsewhere, several distilleries in the same valley will have the same shape of still (in much the way that railway stations on the same line may look alike). Obviously, the local coppersmith had his own way of doing things. Distilleries are reluctant to change the shape or size of their stills when wear and tear demands replacement, or when an expansion is planned. The legend is that if a worn out still has been dented at some time, the coppersmith will beat a similar blemish into its replacement, to ensure that the same whisky emerges.

In a tall, narrow still, much of the vapour will condense before it can escape. The condensate will fall back into the still and be re-distilled. This is known as reflux. The result is a more thorough distillation and a more delicate spirit. Because there is far less reflux in a short, fat still, the spirit will be oilier, creamier, and richer. This is just the simplest example of the shape influencing the character of the whisky. Stills vary enormously in size and shape, and the ratio of surface areas to heat, liquid, vapour, and condensate have infinite effects that are not fully understood.

Glenmorangie's pot stills, left, are the tallest in Scotland. The Macallan's stills, above, are the smallest on Speyside.

CLIMATE/TEMPERATURE

A cold location makes for low-temperature spring waters. When very cold water is available for use in the coils that condense the spirit, and the ambient temperature is low, an especially rich, clean whisky is produced. Distilleries in shaded mountain locations are noted for this characteristic. The oak casks used during the maturation of the whisky expand and contract according to the temperature. The greater the local extremes of temperature, the more this happens.

The boat will not quite sail into the still-house, but this shot at Caol Ila shows just how coastal a whisky can be. In this instance, the sea air permeates every corner of the distillery. The narrow seaway outside separates the whisky islands of Islay and Jura.

ATMOSPHERE

This is a very significant factor during maturation. As the casks "breathe", they inhale the local atmosphere. The more traditional type of maturation warehouse has an earth floor, and often a damp atmosphere. The influence of this is especially noticeable in distilleries that are close to the sea. Often, their maturation warehouses are at the water's edge, washed by high seas. Some single malts, especially those from rocky coasts, have a distinctly briny or seaweedy character.

REGIONAL DIFFERENCES

L IKE WINES – and many other drinks – the single malts of Scotland are grouped by region. As with wines, these regions offer a guideline to the style of the product, rather than a rule. Within Bordeaux, a particular Pomerol, for example, might have a richness more reminiscent of Burgundy; similar comparisons can be made in Scotland. The traditional regional divisions – the Lowlands, the Highlands, Campbeltown, and the island of Islay – have their origins in the regulation of licences, but they do also embrace certain typical characteristics of aroma, body, and palate.

THE LOWLANDS

This region is defined by a line following old county boundaries and running from the Clyde estuary to the River Tay. The line swings north of Glasgow and Dumbarton, and runs to Dundee and Perth. There were always relatively few Lowland whiskies, and their numbers have shrunk further in recent years. Auchentoshan and Glenkinchie thrive, but Bladnoch is now yet smaller, while Littlemill, and possibly Rosebank, wait in hope of restoration. Like the region, the Lowland malts suffer from a lack of windswept, buccaneering glamour, yet they can have their own grassy softness. The best have suggestions of lemon grass and maltiness, untempered by Highland heatheriness or coastal seaweed and brine.

Visiting Lowland distilleries: From the centre of Glasgow, it is a cab or bus ride to Glengoyne (phone first). From Edinburgh, it is half an hour's drive, or a little longer by bus, to Glenkinchie.

THE HIGHLANDS

By far the biggest region, the Highlands inevitably embraces wide variations. The western part of the Highlands, at least on the mainland, has only a few, scattered distilleries, and it is difficult to generalize about their character. Some have very exposed locations. If their whiskies have anything in common, it is a firm, dry character, with some peatiness and saltiness. Oban is the best-known. The far north of the Highlands has several whiskies with a notably spicy character, probably deriving from sandstone, clover, and very gentle sea breezes. Glenmorangie is a good example. The more sheltered Eastern Highlands (around Aberdeen) and the Midlands of Scotland, or South Highlands (around Perth), have a number of notably fruity whiskies, among which Aberfeldy is typical.

Visiting Highland distilleries: From Edinburgh, it is a drive of one to two hours to Perthshire distilleries such as Glenturret, Edradour, or Blair Athol.

None of these stretches of the Highlands is officially regarded as a region, but the area between them, known as Speyside, is universally renowned as a heartland of distillation (see over page).

SCOTLAND
The principal divisions are between the distilleries of the Lowlands, the Highlands, and the Islands. Within the Highlands, the valleys of the Spey and adjoining rivers are a distinct region. In the southwest, so is peninsular Campeltown. Among the islands, Islay is accorded special status.

Distilleries
◉ Operating
◎ Mothballed/intermittent production
● Closed
○ Major town or city
▲ Height above sea level (metres)

0   20   40   60   80   100 Kms
0   10 20 30 40 50 60 Mls

ORKNEYS
Scapa○   ●Highland Park

JOHN O'GROATS○

Old Pulteney○

Clynelish○

SPEYSIDE
(See page 18/19)

▲1081
HEBRIDES
NORTHERN HIGHLANDS
Glen Ord○
Glen Albyn○
Glen Mhor○

Findhorn   Spey

Talisker○
SKYE

Balmenach○   ABERDEEN
Drumguish○   1309 EASTERN
▲   HIGHLANDS   Glenury
Lochnagar●   Royal
Glenlochy○   FORT   Dalwhinnie○   Fettercairn○
WILLIAM   Glenesk○
▲1344   Glencadam○   Lochside
Ben Nevis   Blair Athol○   North Port
WESTERN   Aberfeldy○   Edradour○
Tobermory○   HIGHLANDS
MULL   Glenturret○
Oban○

Deanston○   MIDLANDS
Tullibardine○

Loch Lomond○   Glengoyne○
Inverleven○   Littlemill○   Rosebank●   EDINBURGH
Auchentoshan○   Saint
Kinclaith●   GLASGOW   Magdalene●   Glenkinchie○
Arran○   Clyde   LOWLANDS

ISLAY
(See page 20)   CAMPBELTOWN   SCOTLAND   ▲816
Glen○○ Springbank
Scotia   ●Glen Flagler
▲843
Ladyburn●

Bladnoch○

ENGLAND

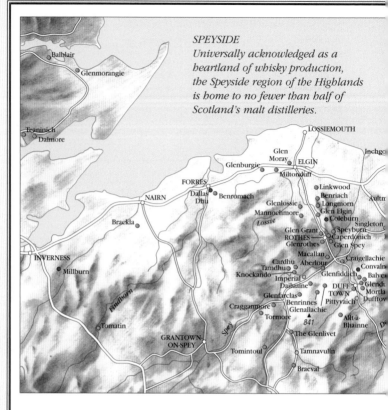

SPEYSIDE
Universally acknowledged as a heartland of whisky production, the Speyside region of the Highlands is home to no fewer than half of Scotland's malt distilleries.

Speyside: This part of the Highlands, between the cities of Inverness and Aberdeen, sweeps from granite mountains down to fertile countryside, where barley is grown. It is the watershed of a system of rivers, the principal among which is the Spey. Although Speyside is not precisely defined, it extends far beyond the one river: it might at its most generous reach from the River Findhorn in the west to the Deveron in the east.

The granite mountains give rise to soft water, which often flows over heathery moorlands. Distillation and maturation tend to be in cool locations. The Speyside single malts are noted in general for their elegance; flowery, heather-honey notes; and sometimes a restrained, fragrant peatiness.

Beyond that, they have two extremes: the big, sherryish type, as typified by The Macallan, Glenfarclas, and Aberlour; and the more subtle style, as shown by Knockando, Glen Grant, or The Glenlivet.

THE GLEN OF THE LIVET: Within Speyside, the Glen (valley) of the river Livet is high, hidden, cool, and so famous that its name has over the years been appropriated by distant distilleries, though this practice is gradually being abandoned as it is misleading. Only one distillery may call itself The Glenlivet. Only Braeval and Tamnavulin are also

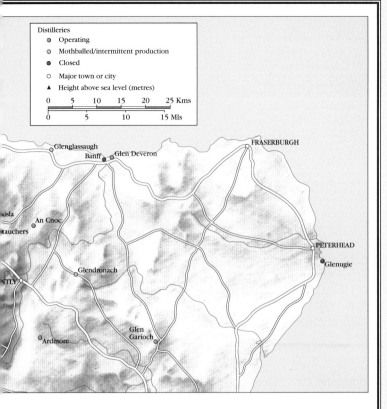

produced in the glen. These are all delicate malts, their character perhaps influenced by the cold, especially during the condensation of vapours and the maturation of the spirit.

Other Glens: It could be more tentatively argued that other glens, such as that of the rivers Fiddich and Lossie, have malts that share certain characteristics. With that in mind, but also as a geographic guide, this book identifies the valley in which each distillery stands. While most of the valleys are popularly deemed to be glens, the term *strath,* meaning a larger valley, is also used.

THE ISLANDS

Traditionally, the Highland region has "claimed" all islands except Islay. Enthusiasts would argue that a specific style of whisky is made, to varying degrees, on all of the islands, most famously on Islay and in the peninsular distilleries of Campbeltown. Some coastal distilleries, most obviously Clynelish, would also be included in this category.

The island character is strongest where malt is made with local peat, as on Orkney, Islay, and occasionally Campbeltown. The peat on these windy islands absorbs other influences, especially briny saltiness on Orkney, and medicinal seaweed on Islay.

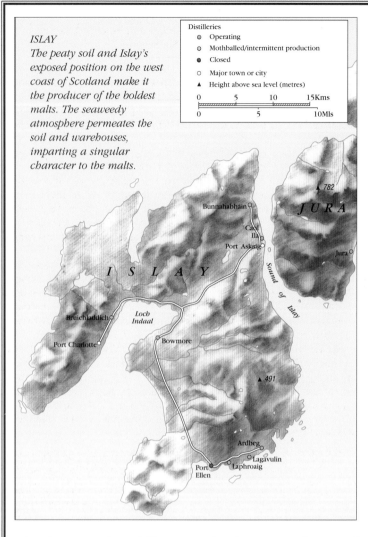

ISLAY

The peaty soil and Islay's exposed position on the west coast of Scotland make it the producer of the boldest malts. The seaweedy atmosphere permeates the soil and warehouses, imparting a singular character to the malts.

Distilleries
- ◉ Operating
- ◉ Mothballed/intermittent production
- ● Closed
- ○ Major town or city
- ▲ Height above sea level (metres)

0   5   10   15Kms

0   5   10Mls

Map labels: Bunnahabhain, Caol Ila, Port Askaig, JURA, Jura, ▲ 782, Sound of Islay, I S L A Y, Bruichladdich, Loch Indaal, Port Charlotte, Bowmore, ▲ 491, Ardbeg, Lagavulin, Laphroaig, Port Ellen

Islay (pronounced eye-luh): Famous for the maritime flavours of malts such as Ardbeg, Lagavulin, Laphroaig, and Bowmore, and for having so many distilleries on a tiny island, only 25 miles long. In recent years, six of its distilleries have been working full-time and a seventh sporadically. Two have been operating their own maltings, while the Port Ellen maltings contributes to all the island's whiskies.

Campbeltown: The Mull of Kintyre is narrow and exposed, and the distilleries at Campbeltown produce distinctly briny whiskies. There were once 30 distilleries. For a time, only one was left in operation: Springbank, making its own famous malt, the peatier Longrow, and recently Hazelburn. Now Glen Scotia has reopened.

THE QUESTION OF AGE

W HISKY MATURES ONLY IN THE CASK, not the bottle. In Scotland and Ireland, the spirit must be aged for three years before it can be called whisky. New distilleries have released pleasant, even enjoyable, whiskies at this age, but most malts benefit from at least eight years, and some two or three times that period. Just as people are not all best at the same age, neither are malts. A grouchy ten-year-old can be a delight in later life, but the opposite can also happen.

Even within a single distillery, the spirit that comes off the still varies slightly between batches, and with the weather. Maturation will be further affected by the type of wood, its history, and condition. Most distilleries have several warehouses, and each may have a slightly different influence. Even the position of the cask within the warehouse will have its effect.

Lighter-tasting malts can lose their freshness, and become overwhelmed by sherry or wood, if they are aged for too long. Bigger, richer whiskies may gain in complexity over longer periods. Occasionally, a distillery will release a 50-year-old. It is a safe bet that the casks were excellent, the conditions perfect, and the whisky regularly monitored to determine whether it was at a peak.

Casks were originally used simply as containers for the freshly distilled spirit. It was originally sold in the cask, and the ability of spirits to develop with age was first appreciated by wealthy customers with cellars full of the liquid gold. Whisky was not systematically aged at the distillery until the late 19th century. Only in recent years has the a scientific approach helped distillers understand the workings of maturation.

Oak staves are steamed and shaped into Bourbon casks, above left. These are briefly charred, above right, before being hand-finished.

SHERRY AND BOURBON

Among the woods used in the production of alcoholic drinks, oak is by far the most widely favoured. It is strong, yet pliable, and makes excellent casks. In theory, all Scotch whisky is aged in oak. In practice, a cask made from chestnut or mahogany very occasionally turns up in a distillery. On the very rare occasions when this happens, no one can remember how the cask was acquired. Although cask acquisitions are monitored carefully today, this was not always the case. Most distilleries have thousands of casks, some acquired 50 or 60 years ago.

Scotland is a mountainous country with plenty of pines but few oaks, and in the early days, wood from England was used, but the forests were soon exhausted. Then the Scots began to take advantage of the English taste for sherry. In the heyday of that fashion, empty casks could be found in great quantity in the English port of Bristol, where merchants bottled sherry from Spain.

Not only were the casks inexpensive, they were found to impart a delicious richness and roundness to the whisky. One producer calls this "a sublime accident". This source of casks diminished when England's stately taste for sherry declined, and even more when Spain became a modern democracy and decided that the bottling of sherry in the growing areas would provide useful jobs for its citizens.

When sherry casks became hard to find, many distilleries moved to Bourbon barrels. The definition of "Bourbon whiskey" requires that it be aged in a new cask; as a robust, sweet, corn-based whiskey, it gains some of its typical character from the caramel flavours, vanillins, and tannins in the wood. (Vanillins are a natural component of wood. Their flavours are similar to those of the vanilla pod). After one fill of Bourbon, such a cask imparts much more delicate flavours to a Scotch malt whisky.

Some distillers refer to new Bourbon barrels as "American oak", and most call a cask of any origin "plain wood" after a couple of fills of whisky. In the past, new wood may have been commonly used, but its flavours, while helpful to Bourbon, tend to overpower a whisky as complex as Scotch.

A bottling of a single malt may contain an orchestration of whiskies from first- and second-fill sherry butts or hogsheads, first- and second-fill Bourbon barrels, and "plain wood", fine-tuned each time to achieve the desired end result.

OTHER "WOODS"

Occasionally, rum casks and port pipes have found their way into whisky warehouses. Springbank briefly had stocks of a sweet, buttery, spicy, minty malt matured in rum casks. In 1993, Gordon & MacPhail released an aromatic, gingery, crisp, oaky malt, aged in a brandy cask, and a very toffeeish example from a port pipe. Both had been laid down in the 1960s. When Glenmorangie released its port-finished whisky in 1994, it also offered an experimental tasting of a very crisp (almost brittle) vintage aged in a Limousin cask intended for Cognac. This was not felt to be a success, and was not marketed. Not every wood works.

WHAT HAPPENS DURING AGING?

Several processes take place during maturation. While the new distillate may have some harsh, "spirity" flavours, these can be lost by evaporation. With the expansion and contraction of the wood, caused by seasonal changes in temperatures, spirit flavours may be exhaled and the natural aromas of the environment taken into the cask: piny, seaweedy, and salty "sea-air" characteristics can all be acquired in this way. Flavours are also imparted by the cask: sherry wood may add the nutty note of the wine; Bourbon barrels can impart caramel flavours, vanillins, and tannins.

American oak is used in the production not only of all Bourbon barrels but also of many sherry casks. Spain also uses its own oak. American oak is finer grained, harder, and slower to mature the whisky. Spanish oak is more resiny. The two oaks are from different families, the Spanish *Quercus robur* or *petraea* being accustomed to the maritime conditions of western Europe, the American *Quercus alba* to the inland environment of its continent.

FINDING THE RIGHT OAK

Perhaps the most important influence on the flavour is that of a very slow, gentle, oxidation of the whisky. While oxygen is regarded as an "enemy" by brewers and some wine makers, because it can cause "stale" flavours, its influence is also a part of the character of Madeira

The Macallan's production director samples sherry in a bodega; the casks labelled "MG" will be used to mature the Macallan malt.

23

wines, for example. The importance of oxidation in the maturation of whisky has been the subject of much recent work by Dr Jim Swan, originally at the Pentlands Scotch Whisky Research Institute (which is owned by the industry), and more recently by his own company.

Dr Swan argues that oxidation increases the complexity and intensity of pleasant flavours in whisky, especially fragrant, fruity, spicy, and minty notes. As in the production of all alcoholic drinks, the flavours emerge from a complex series of actions and reactions. Traces of copper from the stills are the catalyst. They convert oxygen to hydrogen peroxide, which attacks the wood, releasing vanillin. This promotes oxidation, and additionally pulls together the various flavours present. These processes vary according to the region of origin of the wood, and its growth patterns.

This has led distillers to concern themselves not only with the distinctions between sherry and Bourbon wood, and the country in which the trees grew, but also the region. In Spain, where most oak comes from Galicia, trees from mountainous districts are more resiny. In the US, the growth is mainly in Ohio, Kentucky, Illinois, Missouri, and Arkansas. The westerly part of this contiguous region has the poorest soil and the most arid climate, and there the trees have to fight to survive. This optimizes spring growth, which has the most open texture and is the most active in the maturation process.

ALCOHOL CONTENT/PROOF

Alcohol by volume is the easiest measure to understand, and the system that is now standard on labels in many countries throughout the world. The same figure is sometimes referred to as Gay-Lussac. Forty per cent alcohol by volume is the equivalent of 70 proof in the complicated system previously used in Britain, or 80 proof in the American system.

Malt whisky comes off the still at an average strength between the mid or lower 70s and upper 60s, and may be reduced in strength by the addition of water to the mid 60s to stimulate maturation. During aging, it may lose up to 2.5 per cent of its alcohol per year in evaporation. It will emerge from maturation at around 60 or in the 50s or upper 40s ("Cask Strength"), depending upon the duration of aging and the weather. In most cases, the alcohol content is then further reduced to 43 or 40.

Alcohol content is not a measure of quality, but cask-strength whiskies do have their own appeal. "It is like sneaking into a distillery warehouse and tapping a cask," one enthusiast confessed. "There is a sense of whisky direct from the source. I may well add water, but I am the person who decides upon the degree of dilution. That is not determined for me by someone else." The levels of 40 and 43 have evolved as acceptable strengths for several spirits in a number of countries. In Scotch whisky, 40 is the minimum permitted.

A-Z OF
SINGLE MALTS

O VER THE NEXT 294 PAGES is a review, in alphabetical order, of every Scottish malt distillery that has ever witnessed its product in a bottle. These are not "brands" (though their names may be registered); they are actual distilleries: premises at which malt is turned into whisky. Among today's distilleries, only the relatively new Kininvie has not seen its product, a deliciously creamy whisky, bottled. Some of the distilleries reviewed have long closed, but bottlings from their stocks are still being made, or were within recent memory – and therefore may still be on the odd shelf.

Names of distilleries: Some distilleries have been known over the years by several different names. They are listed here by the most recent name on the label of the principal bottlings, though reference may be made in the text to earlier names. If you have bought, or are considering buying, a malt that appears not to be in this book, check the index. If it is not listed there, its name is not that of a distillery. Importers, distributors, and supermarkets often buy malt whisky to bottle under invented names (for example, Glen Bagpipe, Loch Sporran). I have not reviewed these products. The bottle will probably contain whisky supplied by a reputable distiller who happens to have a surplus, but the source could change at any time. The next bottle under the same name might contain an entirely different whisky.

More than 400 malts, especially local examples, line the bar of the Lochside Hotel, in Bowmore, on the island of Islay.

The producers: The parent companies of each distillery at the time of distillation and bottling are listed – in simplified form above the entry. Each parent company has one or more centralized bottling halls serving its entire group of distilleries. The only distilleries with their own bottling lines are Glenfiddich and Springbank. Those two therefore reduce their bottlings with the same water used in production. The others use water with all minerals removed.

Several international drinks-and-foods groups dominate the industry. The first to be formed was the Distillers' Company Limited DCL, which often bottled under the names of its myriad of subsidiary companies. Some distilleries that last operated while part of DCL in the early 1980s nonetheless had their whisky bottled by its successor. This, resulting from the acquisition of DCL and Bell's by Guinness, was called United Distillers, and made some excellent bottlings in the 1990s. That enterprise merged with International Distillers and Vintners in the late 1990s to form Diageo.

Whether the outstanding work of the old United Distillers continues under a marketing-oriented management better known for big international brands remains to be seen. If it did not, that would be a huge setback for single malts, the whisky industry, and ultimately the economy of Scotland.

Other international groups are Allied, initially formed by that brewing group (which gave rise to Carlsberg-Tetley) along with the distilling interests of Long John/Whitbread; Chivas Brothers (part of Seagram); Highland (linked to Rémy-Cointreau); JBB (Jim Beam Brands, resulting from the Kentucky Bourbon distiller's acquisition of Invergordon and Whyte & Mackay); Dewar's (Bacardi); and House of Campbell (Pernod Ricard). Allied has links with the Japanese giant Suntory, which owns the small Bowmore group.

Information and ages and strengths: Some whiskies are bottled without a statement of age. The entry will say "no age statement". If these are inexpensive, it is reasonable to assume that at least some of the whisky in the bottle is younger than eight years. Some very good bottlings balance the liveliness of younger whiskies with the maturity of older ones. If the second line of an entry says, for example, "this bottling contains whiskies of between eight and 16 years", that is based on reliable information, but not necessarily confirmed by the producer. If he were to print an age statement on the label, the "youngest whisky" rule would oblige him to say "eight-year-old", which might sell short a vatting also containing much older whiskies.

The extent of additional information (for example, the type and number of cask, and date of bottling) follows the label of the sample tasted. Whiskies provided to me by distillers as "works in progress" often come in sample bottles simply marked "natural strength from the cask". Until they are bottled for sale, some evaporation may continue, and the exact strength cannot be determined. As a work in progress is by definition unfinished, these are usually not scored.

DISTILLERY OWNERS' SERIES

Whiskies from different distilleries sometimes have labels of almost identical designs. This can be confusing for the neophyte. One reason for similar labels is that owning groups sometimes devise ranges of malts.

When DCL merged with Bell's to become UD, almost all of its distilleries were selling their malt whisky exclusively for blending. The new company decided to promote malts from six distilleries, each highlighting a different region. These were dubbed The Classic Malts. More recently, the same whiskies have been offered with unusual wood finishes as The Distillers Edition. Although each malt in these two families has its own label design, the graphic genre is similar. This still left many UD distilleries without a bottled single malt to offer the consumer. Some of these distilleries had visitor centres, or were in areas popular with tourists. A range with labels showing local Flora and Fauna was developed purely for local sale, though it soon became more widely popular. UD then decided to bottle stocks they still held from distilleries that had closed or even been demolished. These were identified as The Rare Malts, and marketed at prices that reflected their scarcity value. As stocks diminished, this series then began to call upon rare vintages from distilleries still in operation. This was reflected in an extension of the series as Cask Strength Limited Editions.

Similar series of vintage bottlings at the older ages are bottled by other groups, such as Stillman's Dram, from JBB, and Family Silver, from Highland Distillers. In the US, whiskies from Allied have been marketed under the rubric Defenders of the Malt, though they retain their own labels. A second reason for similar labels is the bottling of malts by independents (see over page).

INDEPENDENT BOTTLERS

Vintage 1982
Single Highland Malt Scotch Whisky
Matured in sherry casks for 14 years
Distilled at Benrinnes Distillery
70cl 43%vol

CONNOISSEURS
CHOICE
HIGHLAND
Single Malt Scotch Whisky
DISTILLED AT
BRORA
DISTILLERY
Proprietors: Ainslie & Hathorn (Distillers) Ltd.
DISTILLED
1982
Specially selected, produced
and bottled by
Gordon & MacPhail
Elgin Scotland
Produce of Scotland
70cl 40% vol

PRODUCT OF SCOTLAND
HART
BROTHERS
SINGLE MALT SCOTCH WHISKY
70cl AGED 32 YEARS 44%
DISTILLED DECEMBER 1966 AT
GLEN ALBYN DISTILLERY
INVERNESS SCOTLAND
CASK STRENGTH

The majority of malt distilleries still supply the largest part of their output by the cask, for blending. Those also offering their whisky as a single malt will usually have it packaged at a central bottling hall owned by the parent group, which will also handle the marketing. This is sometimes known as an "official" or distillery bottling.

Others, wishing to concentrate on supplying whisky wholly for blending, leave the bottling of their malt as a single, and sometimes its marketing, to someone else. The tradition survives of wine merchants or licensed grocers offering their own bottlings.

A renowned example is Gordon & MacPhail. This family-owned shop at Elgin, has operated since 1895. While it bottles some malts on behalf of distilleries, it also has a huge collection of casks that it has acquired over the decades and aged in its own warehouses. For this reason Gordon & MacPhail's bottlings of a particular malt have a consistency of style, often with a typical sherry-aged character.

In the boom years for blended Scotches, when the industry largely ignored single malts, many distillers' products were available as singles only through Gordon & MacPhail's range Connoisseurs Choice, or from the Campbeltown bottlers Cadenhead (with shops in Edinburgh and now London. Cadenhead is happy to buy small quantities of whiskies as they become available, so that bottling runs are short and the age or type of cask used may vary greatly. Cadenhead makes a point of not chill-filtering its whisky.

A central figure in the whisky trade is the broker, who buys quantities of malt in cask to sell on to blenders. Sometimes, he may sell to an independent bottler, who will then label the whisky with the name of the distillery where it was made. Some distilleries dislike their names being used on independent bottlings over which they have no control, but may be unable to deny parentage of the whisky.

With the growing interest in malts, established figures in the whisky trade have launched their own bottlings. The best known are Signatory and James MacArthur. Newer names include Adelphi, Hart Brothers, Master of Malt, Murray McDavid, Scot's, and Whisky Castle.

WHAT THE NOTES AND SCORES INDICATE

ABERFELDY 15-year-old, 43 vol, Flora and Fauna
Colour Amber.
Nose Oil, incense, heather, lightly piny and peaty (especially after water is added).
Body Medium, very firm.
Palate Very full flavours. Light peat, barley, fresh, clean touches of Seville orange, rounded.
Finish Sweetness moves to fruitiness, then to firm dryness.

SCORE 77

WHATEVER THE ARGUMENTS about their relative prices, no one denies that a Château Latour is more complex than a mass-market table wine. The fine wines of the whisky world are the single malts. Some malts are made to higher standards than others, and some are inherently more distinctive than their neighbours. This cannot be obscured by the producers' blustery arguments about "personal taste". A tasting note cannot be definitive, but it can be a useful guide: if you are looking for a light, dry malt, do not choose this one, pick the next. If you wanted something rich and sherryish, here is the one for you.

HOUSE STYLE

This is a quick, first, general indication of what to expect from each distillery's products, before looking at the variations that emerge in different ages and bottlings. I also suggest the best moment for each distillery's whiskies (such as before dinner, or with a book at bedtime). These suggestions are meant as an encouragement to try each in a congenial situation. They are not meant to be taken with excessive seriousness.

COLOUR

The natural colour of a malt matured in plain wood is a very pale yellow. Darker shades, ranging from amber to ruby to deep brown, can be imparted by sherry wood. Some distilleries use casks that have been treated with concentrated sherry, and this can cause a caramel-like appearance and palate. Some add caramel to balance the colour. I do not suggest that one colour is in itself better than another, though a particular subtle, or profound, hue can heighten the pleasure of a fine malt. It is, after all, a drink to contemplate. We enjoy food and drink with our eyes as well as our nose and palate.

NOSE

Anyone sampling any food or drink experiences much of the flavour, perhaps without realizing this, through the sense of smell. Whisky is highly aromatic, and the aromas of malts include peat, flowers, honey, toasty maltiness, coastal brine, and seaweed, for example. They are a hugely evocative part of the pleasure.

BODY

Lightness, smoothness, or richness might refresh, soothe, or satisfy. Body and texture (sometimes known as "mouth feel") are distinct features of each malt.

PALATE

In the enjoyment of any complex drink, each sip will offer new aspects of the taste. Even one sip will gradually unfold a number of taste characteristics in different parts of the mouth over a period of, say, a minute. This is notably true of single malts. Some present a very extensive development of palate. A taster working with an unfamiliar malt may go back to it several times over a period of days, in search of its full character. I have adopted this technique in my tastings for this book.

FINISH

In all types of alcoholic drink, the "finish" is a further stage of the pleasure. In most single malts, it is more than a simple aftertaste, however important that may be. It is a crescendo, followed by a series of echoes. When I leave the bottle, I like to be whistling the tune. When the music of the malt fades, there is recollection in tranquillity.

SCORE

The pleasures described above cannot be measured with precision, if at all. The scoring system is intended merely as a guide to the status of the malts. Each tasting note is given a score out of 100. This is inspired by the system of scoring wines devised by the American author Robert Parker. He, in turn, took his lead from American school reports. The pupil gets a mark of 50 for attending the lesson. Beyond that, he is scored for his work. In this book, a rating in the 50s indicates a malt that in my view lacks balance or character, and which – in fairness – was probably never meant to be bottled as a single. The 60s suggest an enjoyable but unexceptional malt. Anything in the 70s is worth tasting, especially above 75. The 80s are, in my view, distinctive and exceptional. The 90s are the greats.

A modest score should not dissuade anyone from trying a malt. People who always drink a favourite, or seek out only the high scorers, miss the pleasure of discovery. Like a tourist guide, this book may help travellers orient themselves, but the confident will then wish to enjoy the ups and downs of new territory. Malt lovers like to explore, compare, and collect. As new bottlings emerge, it is a pleasure that need never end.

ABERFELDY

PRODUCER Dewar's (Bacardi)
REGION Highlands DISTRICT Midlands

ADDRESS Aberfeldy, Perthshire, PH15 2EB TEL 01887-820330
VC Due to open April 2000

L OVERS OF DEWAR'S MAY RECOGNIZE this as its signature malt. The hard water rises from whinstone flecked with iron and gold, and runs through pine, spruce, birch, and bracken. It is piped from the ruins of Pitilie, an earlier distillery, which closed in 1867. The present distillery, built in 1896 and expanded in the 1960s and 1970s, overlooks the raspberry-growing Tay Valley from the Grampian market town and hill resort of Aberfeldy. The distillery, along with Aultmore, Craigellachie, and Royal Brackla, was sold by United Distillers to Bacardi in 1998. For the moment, the bottlings available have not changed.

HOUSE STYLE Firm, oily, cleanly fruity, vigorous, best served in its teens. After dinner or book-at-bedtime.

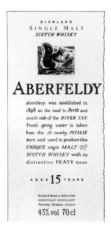

HIGHLAND
SINGLE MALT
SCOTCH WHISKY

ABERFELDY

distillery was established in 1898 on the road to *Perth* and south side of the *RIVER TAY.* Fresh *spring water* is taken from the nearby *PITILIE burn* and used to produce this *UNIQUE single MALT* ⅋ *SCOTCH WHISKY* with its *distinctive* PEATY nose.

AGED **15** YEARS

Distilled & Bottled in SCOTLAND
ABERFELDY DISTILLERY
Aberfeldy, Perthshire, Scotland
43% vol 70 cl

ABERFELDY 15-year-old, 43 vol, Flora and Fauna

Colour Amber.

Nose Oil, incense, heather, lightly piny and peaty (especially after water is added).

Body Medium, very firm.

Palate Very full flavours. Light peat, barley, fresh, clean touches of Seville orange, rounded.

Finish Sweetness moves to fruitiness, then to firm dryness.

SCORE 77

ABERFELDY 14-year-old (bottled 1997), 59.5 vol, Adelphi (cask 942)

Colour Bright greeny gold.

Nose Oily toffee, candied angelica, sweeter. Oranges in boxes.

Body Medium.

Palate Even at a year younger, there is a delicious freshness and sweetness. Clean toffee. Angelica. Moving to oily perfuminess.

Finish Dry, fresh, clean, fruity, leafy, black pepper.

SCORE 77

ABERFELDY 1980 (bottled 1997), 62 vol, Cask Strength Limited Bottling

Colour Pale gold.

Nose Restrained, fragrant, pine, and heather. Drier.

Body Medium, smooth, distinctly oily.

Palate Creamier, nuttier. Hint of orange toffee. Still lively, but two or three years in the cask has brought more tightly combined flavours.

Finish Nutty, late pine. Leafy, peppery, dryness.

SCORE 77

Other versions of Aberfeldy

A Scott's Selection 1978, at 59.3 vol, was powerfully fruity and piney, with a bitter finish. SCORE 75. Gordon and MacPhail's Connoisseurs Choice versions have fractionally less distillery character and more sherry. A 1970 was superseded by a maltier '74, and then by a delicious '75 that seems richer and bigger all round. SCORE 76.

ABERLOUR

PRODUCER Campbell Distillers (Pernod Ricard)
REGION Highlands   **DISTRICT** Speyside

ADDRESS Aberlour, Banffshire, AB3 9PJ
WEBSITE www.aberlour.co.uk

AHUGELY INCREASED RANGE OF BOTTLINGS in various markets has emerged in the past four or five years from this distillery. Once needlessly reticent, it is now responding to its growing appreciation by malt lovers. The village of Aberlour lies in the heart of Speyside malt-distilling country, and the distillery uses soft water that rises from the granite of Ben Rinnes.

Aberlour dates from at least 1826, and was rebuilt in 1879 and 1898. It was expanded in 1945, on its purchase by Campbell Distillers, now owned by Pernod Ricard. Aberlour pioneered the sale of whisky en primeur, and collaborated with the Austrian designer Georg Riedel in the creation of a special glass for single malts.

HOUSE STYLE Soft texture, medium to full flavours, nutty, spicy (nutmeg?), sherry-accented. With dessert, or after dinner, depending upon maturity.

ABERLOUR 10-year-old, 40 vol
Principal version.

Colour Amber.

Nose Malty, spicy, mint-toffee.

Body Remarkably soft and smooth. Medium to full.

Palate Distinctively clinging mouth-feel, with long-lasting flavour development. Both sweetness and spicy, peppery dryness in its malt character. Nutmeg and berry fruit.

Finish Lingering, smooth, aromatic, clean.

SCORE 83

ABERLOUR Antique, no age statement, 43 vol
Contains whiskies of ten to 25 years. Bottled for duty-free stores.

Colour Full amber.

Nose Deeper, oloroso sherry, treacle, raisins.

Body Firmer.

Palate More dryness, cookie-like malt notes, and spiciness.

Finish More complex and spicy, with hints of peat. After dinner.

Score 84

ABERLOUR 100 Proof, no age statement (around 10 years), 57.1 vol
Mainly in duty-free.

Colour Bright orangey amber.

Nose Fresh oak, giving way to light nuttiness and sherry.

Body Firmer, crisper.

Palate Dry oiliness. Delicious, soft fruitiness. (Apricots? Cherries?) Much
more spiciness. Some butterscotch, toffee, and cough-candy. Both robust
(tastes relatively young) and complex.

Finish Big, firm, dry. This version is more of a winter warmer.

Score 84

**ABERLOUR a'bunadh ("The Origin"), no age statement
(a single malt comprising Aberlours from less than 10 to more
than 15 years, vatted together), 59.6 vol**
All sherry-aging, with an emphasis on second-fill dry oloroso. No chill
filtration. Mainly in duty-free and British Isles. In Victorian-style bottle.

Colour Dark orange.

Nose Sherry, mint, pralines. Luxurious, powerful.

Body Full, creamy, textured, layered.

Palate Rich, luxurious, and creamy, with a hint of mint and cherries behind.

Finish Nougat, cherry brandy, ginger, faint smoke. Definitely after dinner.

Score 86

ABERLOUR 12-year-old, all sherry-matured (first-fill dry oloroso), 43 vol
Mainly for the French market.

Colour Full amber.

Nose Nutty, appetizing, relatively fresh, sherry aroma.

Body Medium, soft.

Palate Fresh, soft, malty. Soft licorice, anis, hint of blackcurrant.

Finish Silky, enwrapping, soothing.

SCORE 84

 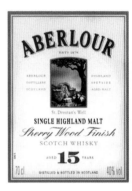

ABERLOUR Cuvée Marie d'Ecosse, 15-year-old, 43 vol
A marriage of Bourbon and sherry-aged Aberlour, for the French market.

Colour Amber.

Nose Malty and toffeeish, developing flowering currant.

Body Medium to full. Silky smooth.

Palate Toffee, licorice, anise, crème brûlée.

Finish Late spiciness and ginger. Long, soothing.

SCORE 83

ABERLOUR 15-year-old, Sherry Wood Finish, 40 vol
A marriage of sherry and Bourbon. Finished in sherry.

Colour Fuller reddish amber.

Nose Roses, candyfloss (cotton candy), slightly buttery.

Body Very firm. Smooth.

Palate Rounded, tightly combined flavours. Beautiful balance of sherryish
nuttiness, anise, and emphatic orange-flower.

Finish Cookies, licorice toffee. Rootiness, spiciness, emphatic mint,
late dryness.

SCORE 84

ABERLOUR 18-year-old, Sherry Wood Matured, 43 vol
100 per cent sherry-aged. Mainly for the North American market.

Colour Bright orangey amber.

Nose Sherryish but dry and slightly oaky. Burnt sugar. Spicy, rounded, teasing.

Body Smooth, nutty.

Palate Well balanced. Spicy, flowery, nutmeg, nutty, fruity. Light, delicate flavours for this distillery and age.

Finish Fresh sherry and oak.

SCORE 84

ABERLOUR 21-year-old, 43 vol
(distillery bottling, numbered edition, cask 32)
Mainly in duty-free and North America.

Colour Bright pale orange.

Nose Sherry, oak, polished leather.

Body Firm, smooth, lightly creamy.

Palate Packed with lively flavours: malt, cookies, fruit, mint.

Finish Spicy, rooty, dry, very long.

SCORE 85

ABERLOUR 30-year-old, 43 vol (bottle 852)
Mainly in duty-free and North America.

Colour Amber.

Nose Polished leather. Tobacco. Cigars.

Body Firm, smooth.

Palate Firmly malty, creamy, licorice, rootiness, hint of smoky peat. Complex and sophisticated. Maturity and finesse.

Finish Surprisingly fresh oak. Sappiness. Log fires. Warming.

SCORE 85

A selection of vintage-dated bottlings

ABERLOUR Distiller's Selection, 1988, 40 vol
Mainly for the Spanish market.

Colour Amber.

Nose Soft but expressive. Bourbon oak. Nuts. Fudge. Citrus.

Body Medium to full. Smooth. Rich.

Palate A dazzling display of fresh malty flavours. Sweetish, but beautifully balanced. Butterscotch, vanilla, orange and lemon, sambuca.

Finish Sticky toffee pudding, balanced by a dryness like crystallized ginger.

SCORE 85

ABERLOUR 1976, 21-year-old, 43 vol (bottle 921 of 3,000)
Matured in first-fill Bourbon casks.

Colour Bright amber.

Nose Quick, assertive malt-honey, then powerful berry fruit at back of nose. Blackberries?

Body Medium, firm, almost crunchy.

Palate Dryish, nutty, toffee, fruit, nutmeg. Lacking in roundness.

Finish Restrained sappy oak. Gingery, warming.

SCORE 83

ABERLOUR 1964, 25-year-old, 43 vol (bottle 5664 of 10,000; 1989)

Colour Full amber.

Nose Richer oak.

Body Medium to full. Firm, smooth, slippery.

Palate Firm, smooth. Very good oaky extract. Hint of vanilla creaminess.

Finish Firm, rounded dryness. Hint of perfuminess.

SCORE 84

ALLT-A-BHAINNE

PRODUCER Chivas (Seagram)
REGION Highlands   DISTRICT Speyside (Fiddich)

ADDRESS Glenrinnes, Dufftown, Banffshire, AB55 4DB

I N GAELIC, ALLT-Á-BHAINNE MEANS "the milk burn", and the distillery lies to the west of the River Fiddich in the foothills of Ben Rinnes, near Dufftown. One of the newer malt distilleries, it is housed in a handsome, tile-hung building commissioned in 1975 to supply malt whisky as a component of the blend Chivas Regal, and it was expanded in 1989. Had Chivas decided from the start to reserve some of the output for bottling as a single, it would have reached a sufficient age in the late 1980s. So far, this has not been done, but casks sold to brokers or blenders have given rise to some independent bottlings from the early 1990s.

HOUSE STYLE Fragrant (dried flowers?), light. Aperitif.

ALLT-A-BHAINNE 13-year-old, The Castle Collection, 43 vol

Colour Pale gold.
Nose Hint of peat. Flowery sweetness, becoming slightly sticky.
Body Light but firm.
Palate Light, sweetish start. Developing flowery and spicy notes.
Finish Light, flowery-spicy, pleasant.

SCORE 73

Other versions of Allt-á-Bhainne

A 12-year-old bottled by James MacArthur in the mid 1990s seemed slightly bigger, no doubt as a result of the cask used. SCORE 74. A 1980 released by Oddbins in 1992 seemed to have enjoyed sherry but was perhaps a little overwhelmed by the sappiness of the oak. SCORE 73.

ARDBEG

PRODUCER Glenmorangie plc
REGION Islay   **DISTRICT** South Shore

ADDRESS Port Ellen, Islay, Argyll, PA42 7DU   **TEL** 01496-302244 **VC**
WEBSITE www.ardbeg.com   **E-MAIL** visitors@glenmorangieplc.co.uk

MAJOR INVESTMENT IN THE REOPENING of this classic waterside distillery was the most exciting news in the malt whisky industry on the eve of the new millennium. There is even a possibility that malting might be restored at Ardbeg. The maltings were unusual in that there were no fans, causing the peat smoke to permeate very heavily. This is evident in older bottlings. The peaty origins of the water are also a big influence in the whisky's earthy, tar-like flavours. Some lovers of Ardbeg believe that an apple-wood, lemon-skin fruitiness derives from a recirculatory system in the spirit still.

The distillery traces its history to 1794. The maltings last worked in 1976–77, though supplies of their malted barley were no doubt eked out a little longer. Ardbeg closed in the early 1980s, but towards the end of that decade began to work again, albeit very sporadically, using malt from Port Ellen. Whisky produced at that time was due to be released as a new, probably less peaty, ten-year-old around the turn of the millennium. The distillery is currently buying an especially heavily peated malt, the impact of which will be seen in bottlings in the course of the next ten years. Various owners and bottlers have over the years made available an astonishing diversity of Ardbegs. On Islay, the Lochside Hotel has been known to offer more than 30 versions at any one time. Overleaf is a selection of relatively recent bottlings.

HOUSE STYLE Earthy, very peaty, smoky, salty, robust. A bedtime malt.

Behind a smart coat of whitewash to its chunky stone buildings, Ardbeg cost its new owners more than £10 million to buy and restore.

ARDBEG 10-year-old (bottled 1993), 40 vol

Colour Fino sherry.

Nose Smoke, brine, iodine dryness.

Body Only medium to full, but very firm. A light heavyweight, with a punch worthy of a higher division.

Palate Skips sweetly along at first, then becomes mean and moody. Bottlings a little variable.

Finish Hefty, lots of iodine.

SCORE 85

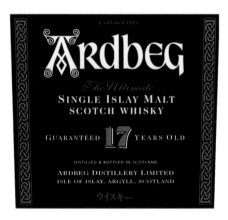

ARDBEG 17-year-old, 40 vol

Colour Full, shimmering, greeny gold.

Nose Assertive, briny, seaweedy, tar-like. Hint of sulphur.

Body Medium, oily. Very firm.

Palate Peppery but also sweet. Cereal grains, oil, gorse. Tightly combined flavours. More mature and rounded, but still robust. Very appetizing.

Finish Oily. Lemon skins. Freshly ground white pepper.

SCORE 86

ARDBEG 18-year-old (distilled 1975 from Ardbeg malt, bottled 1993), 58.1 vol, Cadenhead

Colour Full gold.

Nose Tar. Ropes. Iodine. Slight sulphur. Seaweed.

Body Medium to full. Richly oily.

Palate Malty, sweet, gorse, edible seaweed, pepper.

Finish Pepper, gritty, almost sandy, then very salty indeed.

SCORE 90

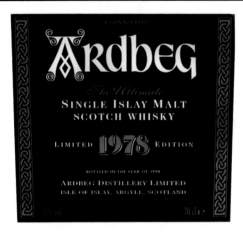

ARDBEG 1978 (bottled 1998), 43 vol

Colour Full gold to bronze.

Nose Seaweedy. Sweet and sour.

Body Big, smooth, firm.

Palate Remarkable flavour development. First, malt and cereal-grain sweetness, with vanilla from Bourbon casks. Then flowery, sourish, seaweed. Finally pepper.

Finish Soothing, long, warming.

SCORE 89

ARDBEG 21-year-old (bottled 1997) , 49.2 vol, Adelphi (cask 453)

Colour Bright gold.

Nose Malt, smoke, gorse, hint of lemon skin.

Body Medium, smooth.

Palate Lemon skin and salt, but surprisingly light, almost thin.

Finish Pepper, peat, and very late fragrant smokiness: the real Ardbeg character emerging at a very late stage.

SCORE 82

ARDBEG 1975 (bottled 1998), 43 vol

Colour Shimmering gold to bronze.

Nose Heathery, rooty, peaty, smoky. Apple-wood barbecue. Leafy bonfires.

Body Big, assertive, but rounded.

Palate Very leafy, sappy, peppery, and mustardy.

Finish Salt, lemon skins, mesquite. Very long indeed.

SCORE 92

ARDBEG 1975, 40 vol, Connoisseurs Choice

Colour Bright gold.

Nose Fresh, sweetish, sea air.

Body Big, firm.

Palate Smooth, sweetish, herbal. Light touches of seaweed and salt. An unusually gentle, restrained bottling.

Finish Perfumy, lightly herbal, soothing.

SCORE 88

ARDBEG Provenance (this example distilled 1974, bottled 1998), 55.8 vol

Colour Full gold to bronze.

Nose Sea air. Seaweed. Oak, rope, leather.

Body Rich and creamy, but dry on tongue.

Palate Huge flavour development. Malty, toffeeish, sweet, fruity. Barbecue wood. Mustard. Salt.

Finish Distinctly sappy, smoky, and very warming.

SCORE 93

ARDBEG 1974, 51.3 vol, Signatory Cask-Strength Series

Colour Bright full gold.

Nose Very assertive. Seaweed, oak, rope, leather.

Body Very oily, but dry on tongue.

Palate Sweet, salty, sandy, peppery, resiny.

Finish Dry, salty, sandy. Slightly woody. Late sandalwood, medicinal note.

SCORE 87

ARDBEG 28-year-old, 54.4 vol, Cadenhead

Colour Dark orange.

Nose Powerful, pungent. Seaweed, oak, rope, leather.

Body Big and oily.

Palate A firm, hard punch of tightly combined flavours. Oaky, creamy (with a splash of water), seaweedy, salty. Only an Islay malt, perhaps solely Ardbeg, could stand up to this degree of woodiness. Some drinkers would find it just too gnarled. Others will love it, if they can find it.

Finish Oak, sandalwood, sand.

SCORE 89

ARDBEG 1967, 49.8 vol, Signatory Cask-Strength Series

Colour Copper-brown.

Nose Polished oak. Sea breezes.

Body Firm. Very smooth indeed.

Palate Intensely earthy, rooty, and dry. Bitter. Woody. Despite all of this, the seaweed and salt still power through. Water seems to enhance the balancing sherry sweetness.

Finish Dry, salty, sandy, gritty. Almost abrasively hot.

SCORE 88

VERY OLD ARDBEG (30 years), 40 vol

Colour Bronze to amber.

Nose Rich, smoky fragrance.

Body Firm, smooth.

Palate Beautiful balance of emphatic malt, peat, smoke, perfumy fragrance, syrupy sherry, and sea. A classic Ardbeg.

Finish Perfumy, warming, caressing, sedative.

SCORE 94

ARDBEG 1963 (bottled 1994), 40 vol, Connoisseurs Choice

Colour Amber.

Nose Firm. Seaweedy.

Body Medium. Gentle.

Palate Astonishingly lively for its age, but well behaved. Peaty, smoky and seaweedy, against a lightly malty, sherryish background.

Finish Perfumy, hint of sherry.

SCORE 90

ARDMORE

Producer Allied Distillers
Region Highlands **District** Speyside (Bogie)

address Kennethmont, by Huntly, Aberdeenshire, AB54 4NH
tel 01464-831213

THE MAGNIFICENT EIGHT COAL-FIRED STILLS at Ardmore produce whisky largely for Teacher's. That company founded Ardmore a century ago. A planned centenary bottling, and visitor facilities, may help it become better known to malt-lovers. This sizable distillery is at Kennethmont, deep in Aberdeenshire barley country.

House style Malty, creamy, robust. After dinner.

ARDMORE 1981, 40 vol, Gordon and MacPhail

Colour Full gold, with amber tinge.

Nose Sherry, cream, cereal-grain oiliness.

Body Distinctly creamy, oily, smooth.

Palate Enjoyably big, no-nonsense, maltiness. Tightly interlocking sweetness and dryness, cereal-grain character, nuttiness, and slight fruitiness.

Finish Cereal-grain, malty dryness.

Score 71

ARDMORE 19-year-old (1978), 59 vol, Cadenhead

Colour White wine.

Nose Faintly flowery and dry.

Body Firm, smooth.

Palate Lightly fudgy, nutty.

Finish Pear skins, flowering currant. Flowery.

Score 69

ARRAN

PRODUCER Isle of Arran Distillers
REGION Highlands   ISLAND Arran

ADDRESS Lochranza, Isle of Arran, Argyll, KA27 8HJ   TEL 01770-830264 **VC**
WEBSITE www.arranwhisky.com   E-MAIL arran.distillers@btinternet.com

T HE NEWEST DISTILLERY IN SCOTLAND. The island of Arran is off the west coast of the Lowlands, sheltered by the Kintyre peninsula (home of the Campbeltown malts). It has granite mountains, peaty land, and good water. The island was once known for its whisky, but passed a century and a half without a legal distillery. The inspiration for a new distillery came after a talk given at the Arran Society in 1992. Industry veteran Harold Currie, a retired managing director of Chivas, organized a scheme in which 2,000 bonds were sold in exchange for whisky from a proposed new distillery. In 1995, the neat distillery, with decorative pagodas, opened at Lochranza, a hamlet on the northern shore of the island. After the minimum period of maturation, Arran offered its first sampling in late 1998. The whisky appears to be maturing very well indeed, and will no doubt rate a far higher score in the future.

HOUSE STYLE Creamy, leafy. Restorative or with dessert.

ISLE OF ARRAN (three years in American oak), 60.5 vol
First historic bottles sold at £100 ($150) each.

Colour Attractive golden yellow.
Nose Creamy, flowery. Very faint, fresh peat smoke.
Body Big, creamy.
Palate Clean, dry, toffee.
Finish Angelica. Surprisingly powerful sweet-lime flavour. Flowery, leafy, faint pine. Developing light dryness.

SCORE 72

Other versions of Arran
A 60.0 per cent sample from a refill sherry butt (tasted as a "work in progress", and therefore not scored) was rich, nutty, sherryish, and creamy. With water, a hint of banana and fragrant smoke emerged.

AUCHENTOSHAN

PRODUCER Morrison Bowmore (Suntory)
REGION Lowlands   DISTRICT Western Lowlands

ADDRESS Dalmuir, Clydebank, Dunbartonshire, G81 4SJ
WEBSITE www.morrisonbowmore.co.uk

CLASSIC EXAMPLES OF LOWLAND MALTS, made by the region's traditional triple-distillation method. They are very light, certainly, but that is the Lowland style. "Light" does not mean lack of character; these are well-defined single malts, with plenty of complexity. If you fancy single malts, but do not care for intensity, Auchentoshan offers the perfect answer: subtlety. For light whiskies, they age surprisingly well, especially in their late teens and early 20s.

The name is pronounced "Och'n'tosh'n", as though it were an imprecation. The distillery lies between the river Clyde and the Kilpatrick Hills, just outside Glasgow. Auchentoshan was founded around 1800, rebuilt after the Second World War, and re-equipped in 1974. A decade later, it was acquired by a private company, Stanley P. Morrison, providing a Lowland partner for their Islay and Highland distilleries, Bowmore and Glen Garioch. The company is now called Morrison Bowmore, and controlled by Suntory of Japan.

HOUSE STYLE Light, lemon grassy, oily. Aperitif or restorative.

AUCHENTOSHAN Select, no age statement, 40 vol

Colour Bright gold.

Nose Oily, with hints of citrus zest.

Body Light, but with some oily mouth smoothness.

Palate Lemon-grass notes. Maltiness – definite, but light. Cleanly sweet.

Finish Light, crisp. Hint of lemon-grass spiciness.

SCORE 78

AUCHENTOSHAN 10-year-old, 40 vol

Colour Bright yellowy gold.

Nose A warm embrace, with perfumes of vanilla, lemon grass, and saddlery.

Body Light but soft, oily.

Palate Zest of lemon, marshmallow, sweet but not cloying.

Finish Longer. Lemon grass, faint ginger, vanilla, perfumy. Soft.

SCORE 83

AUCHENTOSHAN Three Wood, no age statement, 43 vol

This whisky has at least ten years in Bourbon wood, a good year in Oloroso and six months in the hefty Pedro Ximinez. In addition to offering an unusual array of wood characteristics, it fills a gap in Auchentoshan's age range.

Colour Orange liqueur.

Nose Soft. Orange zest, apricot, dates, marshmallow.

Body Oily. Marshmallow-like.

Palate Perfumy, lemon grass, cashews. A delicate interplay of flavours, but the whisky struggles to make itself heard among the woods. Better with little or no water.

Finish Long. Creamy. Raisins. Aniseed. Fresh oak. Sappy dryness.

SCORE 85

AUCHENTOSHAN Selected Cask Vatting, 18-year-old (1978), 58.8 vol

This superb vatting further fills the previous gap in the age range.

Colour Full gold to bronze.

Nose Linseed, saddlery, fresh leather.

Body Smooth, layered, soft.

Palate Linseed, fresh leather, perfumy. A very expressive Auchentoshan.

Finish Clean, lemony, scenty.

SCORE 87

AUCHENTOSHAN 21-year-old, 43 vol

Colour Full, deep gold.

Nose Orange zest, date boxes, cedar, oil.

Body Light to medium, oily, very smooth indeed.

Palate Oily, citrussy, orange peel, lightly spicy, with lots of flavour development. Full of subtleties. More oak character than previous entry. Fresh, with no obtrusive woodiness.

Finish Cedar, vanilla, beautifully rounded and aromatic.

| Score 86 |

AUCHENTOSHAN 22-year-old, 43 vol

Colour Deep gold to amber.

Nose Rich fresh leather.

Body Very firm, smooth, and oily.

Palate Oily, cedary, spicy. Male cosmetics. If soap were edible...

Finish Dry, cedary.

| Score 86 |

AUCHENTOSHAN 25-year-old, 43 vol

Colour Amber.

Nose Leather, oil, oak.

Body Firm, smooth.

Palate Oaky, cedary, oily, lemony.

Finish Slightly woody.

| Score 85 |

AUCHENTOSHAN 31-year-old (distilled 1966), 43.5 vol

Colour Gold to pale amber.

Nose Lemon, oil, cedar. Spicy.

Body Light to medium. Silky.

Palate Oil, lemon – and orange. Fruity toffee. Cookie-like maltiness.
More wood-extract character. Some weakness in the middle.

Finish Soothing. Very long. Cedary dryness and grassy hints of peat
in a very slightly woody finish.

> **SCORE 86**

Some previous bottlings of Auchentoshan

Auchentoshan 12-year-old at 40 vol was more rounded than the 10-year-old, with a deft balance of freshness and maturity. SCORE 86. An 18-year-old at 43 vol was fuller, with a hint of linseed and surprising depth. SCORE 86. An earlier version of the 1966 at 43 vol, labelled "vintage", was paler in colour than the current version, less rounded, but with more distillery character: linseedy, drier, and with lots of flavour development. SCORE 86. An Oddbins 31-year-old came in two bottlings: Cask 2509 was very oily and perfumy, and dryish. SCORE 86. Cask 804 had a reddish walnut colour and was rather woody. SCORE 79.

AUCHENTOSHAN, no age statement, 40 vol

This version is no longer bottled, but may still be found.

Colour Greeny-gold.

Nose Oily, with hints of lemon zest.

Body Light, but with some oily mouth feel.

Palate Lemon-grass notes. Lightly sweet without being sticky.

Finish Light, crisp, quick.

> **SCORE 79**

AULTMORE

PRODUCER Dewar's (Bacardi)
REGION Highlands   DISTRICT Speyside (Isla)

ADDRESS Keith, Banffshire, AB45 3JT
TEL 01542-822762

A FINE MALT IN THE OAKY STYLE that seems to characterize the whiskies made near the Isla (the Highland river, not to be confused with the similiar-sounding western island). This distillery, which is just north of Keith, was built in 1896, and reconstructed in 1971. The malt whisky is a component of the Dewar's blends. The name of an even older associated blending company, John and Robert Harvey, founded in 1770, appears on bottlings released in the 1990s. In 1991, the then-owners, United Distillers, introduced a bottling in their "Flora and Fauna" series. They issued a Rare Malts edition in 1996, and a Cask Strength Limited Bottling in 1997–98. In the latter year, Aultmore was acquired by Bacardi, but no new bottlings have yet appeared.

HOUSE STYLE Fresh, dry, herbal, spicy, oaky. Reminscent of a fino sherry, albeit a very big one. Before dinner.

AULTMORE 12-year-old, 40 vol, John & Robert Harvey

Colour Pale gold.
Nose Big bouquet, fresh, warm, and drily perfumed.
Body Firm.
Palate Light and fruity, developing hints of gentian or quinine.
Finish Crisp, very dry.

SCORE 75

AULTMORE 12-year-old, 43 vol, Flora and Fauna

Colour Very pale.

Nose Flowery, fresh, drily perfumed.

Body Medium, firm.

Palate Begins with a delicate, fruity-perfumy sweetness, developing to a flowery dryness.

Finish Delicate, dry, extraordinarily appetizing.

SCORE 75

AULTMORE 21-year-old (distilled 1974), cask strength, Rare Malts.

Colour Gold.

Nose Stony dryness. Hay. Very faint hint of peat.

Body Very smooth and creamy. Medium.

Palate Creamy flavours, developing to fruity and spicy notes.

Finish Sweetness and dryness. Eucalyptus and gentian. Heady.

SCORE 74

AULTMORE 1983 (bottled 1997), 58.8 vol, Cask Strength Limited Bottling

Colour Bright yellow.

Nose Hay. Earth. Slight peat.

Body Medium to full, rounded.

Palate Creamy, hay-like, stony.

Finish Crisp, dry. Clean spiciness. Appetizing.

SCORE 77

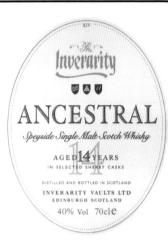

INVERARITY 10-year-old, 40 vol
(An independent bottling of Aultmore.)

Colour Pale gold.

Nose Hint honey, clover. Fresh hay. Grass. Peat.

Body Medium, smooth.

Palate Lively. Clean, light, honey. Flowery. A delicate example of Aultmore.

Finish Flowery, dry. Very light, fresh, peaty smokiness.

SCORE 76

INVERARITY Ancestral, 14-year-old, 40 vol

Colour Amber.

Nose Honey, apricots, nuts, sherry.

Body Medium, drying on tongue.

Palate Delicious honey and oloroso sherry. Some almondy nuttiness. A hint of stony dryness, but the distillery character is somewhat masked.

Finish Honey sweetness and oaky dryness. Hint of peat smoke.

SCORE 75

Further independent bottlings of Aultmore
Aultmore eight-year-old, 60.1 vol, Adelphi: the colour of white wine; aroma flowery and hazelnut; palate lively, light, and grassy, only very faintly spirity; finish sweetish. SCORE 74. Aultmore 1985, 43 vol, Signatory: bright yellow; nose smooth and herbal; body very firm and smooth, perhaps slightly thin; palate fresh, stony, faintly peaty; a classic example. SCORE 77. An earlier 13-year-old from Cadenhead, at 46 vol, had a pale golden colour; a hint of smoke in the nose; a flowery and expressive palate; and a dry finish. SCORE 75.

BALBLAIR

PRODUCER Inver House
REGION Highlands   DISTRICT Northern Highlands

ADDRESS Edderton, Tain, Ross-shire, IV19 1LB
WEBSITE www.inverhouse.com   E-MAIL enquiries@inverhouse.com

BECOMING MORE READILY AVAILABLE since the acquisition of the distillery by Inver House, who have introduced new bottlings. The light spiciness and fresh dryness of the Northern Highland malts is present in definite but delicate form in the various versions of Balblair. They are made using water that has flowed from the piny hillsides of Ben Dearg and over dry, crumbly peat towards the River Carron and the Dornoch Firth. A burn near the distillery feeds Balblair, which is located amid fields at Edderton, close to the Firth and the sea. There is said to have been brewing and distilling in the vicinity in the mid-1700s. Balblair is among Scotland's oldest distilleries. It began in 1790, and the present building dates from the 1870s.

HOUSE STYLE Light, firm, dry. Aperitif when young.

BALBLAIR 5-year-old, 40 vol
Balblair is regarded as a fast-maturing whisky, but the five-year-old might be just too youthful for some malt-lovers. Nonetheless, it has its admirers in the important Italian market. This bottling dates from the previous ownership, when Balblair was strongly associated with the Ballantine blends.

Colour White wine.	
Nose Fresh, slightly sharp and pear-like.	
Body Light.	
Palate Clove-like spiciness.	
Finish Lingers, but not long enough.	

SCORE 70

BALBLAIR "Elements", no age statement, 40 vol

Colour Full gold.

Nose Sea breezes. Slight salt. Barley-malt sweetness.

Body Lean but smooth. Textured.

Palate Teasing, appetizing, balance of slight salt and shortbread-like fresh malt. Faint hint of raspberries.

Finish Plum-skin dryness.

SCORE 76

BALBLAIR 16-year-old, 40 vol

Colour Pale amber.

Nose Nutty. Light, fresh spiciness. Fragrant.

Body Firm, smooth, textured.

Palate Smooth and surprisingly satisfying. Again, the saltiness and shortbread. This time, it is chocolate shortbread.

Finish Toffee apples. Cedary dryness.

SCORE 78

Vintage 1975
Single Highland Malt Scotch Whisky
Matured in oak casks for 21 years
Distilled at Balblair Distillery
on 26.11.75   Bottled 18.9.97
Cask No. 7276   Bottle No. 318 of 635
This whisky has been selected, produced and bottled in
Scotland for and under the sole responsibility of
Signatory Vintage Scotch Whisky Co. Ltd.
70cl   *Edinburgh EH6 6PY Scotland* 56.5%vol

BALBLAIR 1975, 56.5 vol, Signatory

Colour Very pale white wine.

Nose Notably peaty.

Body Light, oily.

Palate Dry, peaty, spicy, fruity, dessert apples.

Finish Dry, somewhat woody, peaty, slightly tannic, green apples.

SCORE 74

Earlier versions of Balblair

Under the distillery's previous ownership, some good bottlings, usually at 40 vol, were made by Gordon & MacPhail. A ten-year-old was raspberryish, with a dry, oily, finish. SCORE 76. A 1964 vintage was more intense, sweetish, with some suggestions of sherry. SCORE 76. A 1957 had a good peatiness, but was on the woody side. SCORE 74.

BALMENACH

PRODUCER Inver House
REGION Highlands   **DISTRICT** Speyside

ADDRESS Cromdale, Grantown-on-Spey, Morayshire, PH26 3PF
WEBSITE www.inverhouse.com   **E-MAIL** enquiries@inverhouse.com

NEWLY THE FLAGSHIP OF INVER HOUSE. Balmenach, an illicit distillery before being licensed in 1824, has contributed to many blends, including Johnnie Walker and Crabbie's. Its first recent bottling as a single malt was a Flora and Fauna edition in 1991, but two years later United Distillers announced that Balmenach was to be mothballed. Four years on, it passed to its present owners, who have not yet made any new bottlings. The distillery is in hilly countryside between the upper reaches of the Spey and the Avon.

HOUSE STYLE Big. Flowery, lightly peaty. Without heavy sherry, an aperitif; with, an after-dinner malt.

SPEYSIDE
SINGLE MALT
SCOTCH WHISKY

Sometime in the early (19th, after *walking*
in the *CROMDALE* hills *with*
his 2 *BROTHERS*, *James M*cGregor settled
and established

BALMENACH

distillery. Spring water from beneath those
same *HILLS* is still used to produce
this *RICH flavoured single MALT SCOTCH
WHISKY* of *exemplary* quality.

AGED **12** YEARS

43% vol   Distilled & Bottled in SCOTLAND.
BALMENACH DISTILLERY, Cromdale, Moray, Scotland.   70cl

BALMENACH 12-year-old, 43 vol, Flora and Fauna

Colour Rich amber-red.	

Nose Huge and deep. Pungent sherry character. Honeyish heather notes.

Body Medium to full. Soft and exceptionally smooth.

Palate Sherryish but dry. Alive with flavours: honey, ginger, bitter herbs, sappy, leafy notes.

Finish Rounded and satisfying.

SCORE 77

DEERSTALKER 12-year-old, 43 vol
(An independent bottling of Balmenach,
from Aberfoyle and Knight, of Glasgow.)

Colour Full greeny gold.

Nose Fragrant, peaty, very flowery, appetizing.

Body Medium, firm, smooth.

Palate Gentle, complex, well balanced. Peaty, flowery, lemon grass, ginger.
Herbal dryness. Appetizing. Without the sherry, the floweriness blossoms.

Finish Firm, smooth, dry, appetizing.

SCORE 79

BALMENACH 15-year-old (distilled 1982, bottled 1997), 63.4 vol, Adelphi

Colour Bright greeny gold.

Nose Flowery, herbal (sorrel?). Buttered parsnips.

Body Medium, dryish on tongue.

Palate Oaky, peaty, flowery dryness. Light malty creaminess.
Honey sweetness. Faint ginger. Falls away somewhat in middle.

Finish Late peat and grassiness.

SCORE 78

BALMENACH 25-year-old (distilled 1972), 43 vol, Hart Brothers

Colour Full gold.

Nose Hint of smokiness. Flowery. Sorrel.

Body Medium to full, firm.

Palate Flowery. Very lightly honeyish. Complex. Very delicate in flavour
for a big-bodied malt of this age.

Finish Light, teasing. Late lemon grass. Faint ginger.

SCORE 79

THE BALVENIE

PRODUCER William Grant and Sons
REGION Highlands **DISTRICT** Speyside (Dufftown)

ADDRESS Dufftown, Banffshire, AB55 4BB **TEL** 01340-820000
WEBSITE www.thebalvenie.com

NEXT DOOR TO GLENFIDDICH. The same company founded both distilleries, in 1886 and 1892 respectively, added Kininvie almost a century later, in 1990, and remains a family firm. The Balvenie whiskies are sweeter and richer: classic examples of the Speyside heather-honey style. The distillery uses barley from the family farm, has its own floor maltings, and its stills have a distinctive, bulbous shape.

In the 1980s, two versions under the name Balvenie Classic were produced. One, without an age statement, was finished in sherry wood (before this technique became fashionable). There was also an 18-year-old Classic without the sherry finish. In 1993 the company dispensed with its flask-shaped bottle in favour of a more robust design, and introduced the versions shown below and on the facing page. In 1997 the Port Wood was added.

HOUSE STYLE The most honeyish of malts, with a distinctively orangey note. Luxurious. After dinner. Ages well.

THE BALVENIE Founder's Reserve, 10-year-old, 40 vol
(90 per cent American oak; 10 per cent sherry.)

Colour Bright gold.
Nose Orange-honey perfume. Musky. Faint hint of peat.
Body Medium.
Palate Honeyed sweetness drying to lightly spicy notes. Very lively. Just a touch of sherry.
Finish A tingly surge of flavours, with lingering, syrupy honey.

SCORE 85

THE BALVENIE Double Wood, 12-year-old, 40 vol
(First- and second-fill Bourbon casks, then 6 to 12 months in sweet oloroso casks.)

Colour Amber.

Nose Sherry and orange skins.

Body Medium, rich.

Palate Beautifully combined mellow flavours: nutty, sweet, sherry, very orangey fruitness, heather, cinnamon spiciness.

Finish Long, tingling. Very warming.

SCORE 87

THE BALVENIE Single Barrel, 15-year-old, 50.4 vol
(All first-fill Bourbon casks.)

Colour Pale gold.

Nose Assertive. Dry, fresh oak. Heather. Rooty. Coconut. Lemon pith.

Body Firm.

Palate Lively. Cedar. Orange-skins, pineapple-like sweetness and acidity.

Finish Very dry. Peppery alcohol.

SCORE 85

THE BALVENIE Port Wood, 21-year-old, 40 vol
(Bourbon casks, then 6-12 months in port pipes.)

Colour Reddish amber.

Nose Perfumy, fruity. Passion fruit. Raisiny. Nutty dryness. Marzipan.

Body Rich.

Palate Very complex. Toffee, creamy, winey, aniseed.

Finish Long, cedary, dry.

SCORE 88

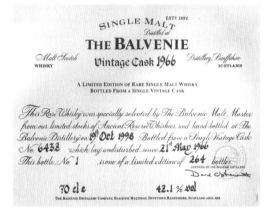

THE BALVENIE Vintage Cask 1966, 42.1 vol (264 bottles)
Colour Full gold to bronze.

Nose Very aromatic. Butter, honey, lemon. Grass. Faint peat.

Body Medium, firm, rounded.

Palate Buttery maltiness. Honey. Orange. Lemon grass. Juicy oak.
A beautifully balanced classic Speyside whisky.

Finish Lemon. Grass. Lightly peaty balancing dryness.

SCORE 88

A 1964 in this range was similar but nuttier and drier. SCORE 88. A 1951 had a dark brown colour and was full of peat and oak-smoke, but still with some malty smoothness underneath it all. Slightly astringent, but bonus points for traditional values and distinctiveness. SCORE 88.

Other versions of The Balvenie
A rare independent bottling by Signatory in 1990, of a 1974 distillate: bright full gold; dry, malty, shortbread aroma; firm, lightly syrupy body; honey, cinnamon, and lemon in palate; smooth, long, rounded, satisfying, warming finish. SCORE 87.

BANFF

PRODUCER DCL
REGION Highlands   **DISTRICT** Speyside (Deveron)

ADDRESS Site at Inverboyndie, on B9139, 1 mile west of Banff

THE HOUSE OF COMMONS was once supplied with whisky from this distillery, in the town of Banff. The distillery dated from at least 1824, was damaged by a bomb in the Second World War, and closed in 1983. It was later dismantled, but left substantial maturing stock. New independent bottlings are still being issued.

HOUSE STYLE Sweet, smoky. Restorative or after dinner.

BANFF 1978, 58.8 vol, Signatory "Silent Stills" series

Colour Bright pale gold.

Nose Fragrant, smoky.

Body Firm, oily, smooth, dry.

Palate Light. Clean. Sweetish start. Becoming smoky.

Finish Peat. Burnt grass.

SCORE 67

BANFF 1976 (21-year-old), 58.2 vol, Cadenhead

Colour Gold, green tinge.

Nose Perfumy, fragrant, burnt grass, peat.

Body Medium, smooth.

Palate Aromatic, oily. Becoming grassy and peaty. Less clean, but drier.

Finish Sweet smokiness. Hint of vanilla.

SCORE 67

BEN NEVIS

PRODUCER Ben Nevis Co (Nikka).
REGION Highlands   DISTRICT West Highlands

ADDRESS Lochy Bridge, Fort William, Inverness-shire, PH33 6TJ
TEL 01397-702476 **VC**

B ECOMING MORE WIDELY AVAILABLE, and in a greater range of bottlings, since this historic Scottish distillery was acquired by the long-established and respected whisky-maker Nikka, of Japan. The distillery, at Fort William, lies at the foot of Scotland's highest mountain, Ben Nevis (1,344m/4,409ft). The peak does not have quite the significance of Fuji, but it is a powerful symbol of Scotland. The distillery was established in 1825 by "Long John" McDonald. The well-known blended Scotch Long John was named after him.

HOUSE STYLE Robust. Waxy fruitiness and floweriness. Oily, a touch of smoke. Restorative or book-at-bedtime.

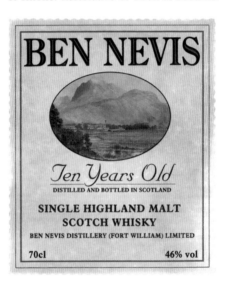

BEN NEVIS

Ten Years Old
DISTILLED AND BOTTLED IN SCOTLAND

**SINGLE HIGHLAND MALT
SCOTCH WHISKY**

BEN NEVIS DISTILLERY (FORT WILLIAM) LIMITED

70cl   46% vol

BEN NEVIS 10-year-old, 46 vol

Colour Warm bronze to amber.

Nose Perfumy, spicy, soft. Waxed fruit. Kumquats. Hard black chocolate.

Body Emphatically big, firm, smooth.

Palate Orange-cream pralines in black chocolate. Belgian toffee wafers.

Finish Orange zest. Pithy dryness. Touch of cigar smoke.

SCORE 77

BEN NEVIS 21-year-old, 60.5 vol, limited edition in decanter

Colour Bronze to amber.

Nose Box of black chocolates.

Body Big, smooth.

Palate Oilier, juicier, chewier, drier.

Finish Robust. Oaky spiciness.

SCORE 77

DISTILLED AND BOTTLED IN SCOTLAND

BEN NEVIS

**SINGLE HIGHLAND MALT
SCOTCH WHISKY**
BEN NEVIS DISTILLERY (FORT WILLIAM) LIMITED
Cask No. 601
DISTILLED IN 1972
BOTTLED IN 1998
70cl 57.4% vol

BEN NEVIS 26-year-old (distilled 1972, bottled 1998), 57.4 vol

Colour Amber.

Nose Black chocolate. Orange flowers.

Body Silky

Palate Clean, fruity toffee. Nuts. Sherry.

Finish Very long. Emphatically smoky and oaky. Beautiful balance.

SCORE 78

BEN NEVIS 1966 (bottled 1998), 51 vol

Colour Bright golden yellow.

Nose Oily.

Body Very oily.

Palate Oily, flowery, surprisingly neutral. Disappointing, like some other Ben Nevis distillates from the 1960s.

Finish Mustardy.

SCORE 62

BENRIACH

PRODUCER Chivas (Seagram)
REGION Highlands   DISTRICT Speyside (Lossie)

ADDRESS Longmorn, Elgin, Morayshire, IV30 3SJ

THE BETTER-KNOWN LONGMORN is next door, and under the same ownership. Both distilleries were built in the 1890s, but Benriach was silent from 1900 until it was rebuilt in 1965.

HOUSE STYLE Cookie-like, with touches of butterscotch. Restorative. A mid-afternoon malt?

**BENRIACH DISTILLERY
EST.1898
A   SINGLE
PURE HIGHLAND MALT
Scotch Whisky**

Benriach Distillery, in the heart of the Highlands,
still malts its own barley. The resulting whisky has
a unique and attractive delicacy

PRODUCED AND BOTTLED BY THE

BENRIACH

DISTILLERY Cº

ELGIN, MORAYSHIRE, SCOTLAND, IV30 3SJ

Distilled and Bottled in Scotland

AGED 10 YEARS

BENRIACH 10-year-old, 43 vol

Colour	Pale, bright gold.
Nose	Light, clean, honey. Flowery dryness.
Body	Light, smooth, textured.
Palate	Pronounced cereal-grain. Oatmeal cookies. Spicy seed-cake.
Finish	Cookie-like, butterscotch sweetness. Then drying and thinning to appetizing, lightly honeyish floweriness. Fresh and well defined.

SCORE 70

Other versions of Benriach

A 12-year-old, at 60.3 vol, from Adelphi, is very oily, but peatier, spicier, and drier. SCORE 71. A 1982, at 60.9 vol, from Gordon & MacPhail, is a solid amber colour; has a sherryish, dry nuttiness; a juicy sweetness reminiscent of barley-sugar candy; and a hint of sweet smokiness. SCORE 77.

BENRINNES

PRODUCER UDV (Diageo)
REGION Highlands   DISTRICT Speyside

ADDRESS Aberlour, Banffshire, AB38 9WN
TEL contact via Dailuaine 01340-872500

THE DOMINANT PEAK among the mountains overlooking the heart of Speyside is Ben Rinnes (840m/2,759ft). It gives its name to a distillery, Benrinnes, which may have been founded as early as the 1820s, and was largely rebuilt in the 1950s. The distillery had a long association with the Crawford blends. Its malt whisky, made by an unusual system of partial triple distillation, had its first official bottling in 1991, in a Flora and Fauna edition.

HOUSE STYLE Big, creamy, smoky, flavoursome, long. Restorative or after dinner.

BENRINNES 15-year-old, 43 vol, Flora and Fauna

Colour Autumnal reddish-brown.

Nose Heavy, almost creamy. A whiff of sherry, then a firm, smoky, burnt-toffee character.

Body Medium to full, firm.

Palate Dry, assertive, rounded. Flavours are gradually unlocked. Hints of licorice, aniseed, vanilla, bitter chocolate, smokiness.

Finish Satisfying, soothing. Faintly sweet and smoky.

SCORE 79

Vintage 1982
Single Highland Malt Scotch Whisky
Matured in sherry casks for 15 years
Distilled at Benrinnes Distillery
on 26.11.82   Bottled 11.3.98
Butt No. 3294   Bottle No.   of 720
*This whisky has been selected, produced and bottled in
Scotland for and under the sole responsibility of
Signatory Vintage Scotch Whisky Co. Ltd
Edinburgh EH8 2Jf Scotland*
70cl   43%vol

BENRINNES 1982, 43 vol, Signatory

Colour Pale amber.

Nose Fresh earth. Peat smoke. Hint of sherryish oak.

Body Creamy.

Palate Decidedly oily, creamy-malty, sherryish, peaty. Beautiful balance.

Finish Long, sweetish, spicy, fresh, expressive. Fruity, then smoky. Lingering.

Score 79

BENRINNES 21-year-old (distilled 1974), 60.4 vol, Rare Malts

Colour Bright gold.

Nose Earthy. Hint of peatiness.

Body Medium, firm.

Palate Oily, nutty, toffeeish, creamy. Developing vanilla, orange, lime.

Finish Delayed, surging finish. Sweetish spicy. Long, lingering, expressive.

Score 79

BENRINNES 22-year-old (bottled 1996), 56.3 vol, Adelphi

Colour Bright gold.

Nose Fresh earth. Peat smoke.

Body Big, creamy, firm, smooth.

Palate Licorice-toffee, becoming grassy, earthy, and peaty.

Finish Flowery, fruity, orange peels, late smoky dryness.

Score 78

Other versions of Benrinnes

A Signatory 1972, at 56.3 vol, is sherryish, packed with flavour, and
beautifully balanced. Score 81. A Connoisseurs Choice 1972, at 40 vol, is
slightly more flowery and smoky, a fresh-tasting delight. Score 80.

BENROMACH

PRODUCER Gordon and MacPhail
REGION Highlands **DISTRICT** Speyside (Findhorn)

ADDRESS Invererne Road, Forres, Moray, IV36 3EB **TEL** 01309-675968 **VC**
WEBSITE www.gordonandmacphail.com

P RINCE CHARLES OFFICIALLY REOPENED THIS DISTILLERY in 1998, exactly a century after its original foundation. Benromach, at Forres, on the river Findhorn, had undergone five years of refurbishment since its acquisition by the renowned merchants Gordon & MacPhail, of Elgin, in the next valley. Only in its very earliest days did the old Benromach make its own bottlings. United Distillers closed the distillery a decade and a half ago, but did subsequently issue one Rare Malts edition, at 20 years old. Apart from that isolated instance, Benromach had for many years been available only in independent bottlings, notably from Gordon & MacPhail. Now, editions from stock bear the proud legend, "bottled by the proprietors".

At its closure, the valuable copper stills had been removed. The new, purpose-built stills are smaller, with a view to producing a fuller, richer spirit. Trial production began in late 1998, so there should be legal, three-year-old whisky by 2001, but the conservative new owners are talking of beginning with a ten-year-old, in 2008.

HOUSE STYLE Assertive, flowery, sometimes creamy.
With dessert or after dinner.

BENROMACH 12-year-old, 40 vol

Colour Full gold.	
Nose Very flowery. Lightly peaty.	
Body Medium. Firm.	
Palate Light, firm, maltiness. Lightly creamy. Hints of apricot, garden mint.	
Finish Flowery. Slightly sharp. Faint peat smoke.	

SCORE 77

Prince Charles receives the Centenary edition from chairman George (left) and Ian Urquhart, of the owning family.

BENROMACH 15-year-old, 40 vol

Colour Bright amber.

Nose Sherry, nuts, flowers.

Body Very creamy.

Palate Creamy, oily, flowery, lightly smoky. Sherryish.

Finish Flowery, nutty, creamy.

SCORE 77

BENROMACH Centenary Bottling, 17-year-old, 43 vol

Colour Deep, full gold.

Nose Very flowery, herbal, smoky, complex, long.

Body Firm, smooth, oily.

Palate Malty background. Richly sherryish. Peachy. Flowery. Lively. Complex.

Finish Nutty, juicy oak, soothing, very long.

SCORE 79

BENROMACH 1982, 63 vol, Gordon and MacPhail "Cask" edition

Colour Chestnut brown.

Nose Polished oak. Rooty peat. Flowers.

Body Big, firm, smooth.

Palate Barley sugar. Toasted nuts. At first, the sherry and oak masks the distillery character. Add water, and a peaches-and-cream fruitiness emerges.

Finish Creamy. Hints of apricot and garden mint.

SCORE 78

Other versions of Benromach

The Rare Malts 20-year-old, bottled in 1998 at cask strength, is creamy, fruity, almondy, and cedary. SCORE 77. A Scott's Selection from the same year, at 52.1 vol, is very flowery, fruity, and dry. SCORE 77. A Cadenhead 1965, bottled at 28 years old (47.6 vol), is heavily sherried and smoky, attenuated with age, but still with a delicate nuttiness and floweriness. SCORE 77.

BLADNOCH

PRODUCER Raymond Armstrong
REGION Lowlands   DISTRICT Borders

ADDRESS Bladnoch, Wigtownshire, DG8 9AB   TEL 01988-402605 VC
WEBSITE www.bladnoch.co.uk

N|EW OWNER RAYMOND ARMSTRONG, from Northern Ireland, made the short hop to the far southwest of Scotland in search of a holiday home. He bought the Bladnoch distillery building with that in mind, then came to feel that it should be returned to its original purpose. Founded as a farmhouse distillery between 1817 and 1825, Bladnoch was mothballed by its then owner United Distillers in 1993, and re-commissioned by Armstrong in 1999. The distillery, at the hamlet of Bladnoch, near Wigtown, is the most southerly in Scotland. The small river Bladnoch flows into the Solway Firth, which forms the border with England.

HOUSE STYLE Grassy, lemony, soft. A classic Lowlander.
Perhaps a dessert malt.

BLADNOCH 8-year-old, 40 vol
This version was bottled during Bell's ownership of the distillery.

Colour Pale yellow.

Nose Grassy, lemony.

Body Very light, but firm.

Palate At first seems very light, but a delicate fruitiness develops.

Finish The citrus character emerges quite strongly in the finish.

SCORE 85

LOWLAND
SINGLE MALT
SCOTCH WHISKY

The *Broad Leaved Helleborine,*
a rare species of *wild orchid*, can be found growing
in the *ancient oak woodland* behind the

BLADNOCH

distillery. The most southerly in *SCOTLAND,*
founded in the *early* 1800's, & the
distillery stands by the *RIVER BLADNOCH*
near *Wigtown.* It produces a *distinctive*
LOWLAND *single MALT WHISKY ~ delicate* and
fruity with a *lemony* aroma and *taste.*

AGED **10** YEARS

43% vol   Distilled & Bottled in *SCOTLAND.*
BLADNOCH DISTILLERY, Bladnoch, Wigtownshire, *Scotland*   70 cl

---

BLADNOCH 10-year-old, 43 vol, Flora and Fauna

Colour Amber.

Nose Hint of sherry, fragrantly fruity, lemony.

Body Fuller, firm.

Palate Lots of development from a sherryish start through cereal-grain grassiness to flowery, fruity, lemony notes.

Finish Again, surprisingly assertive.

SCORE 85

BLADNOCH 1986, 40 vol, Connoisseurs Choice

Colour Gold to peachy.

Nose Slight nutty sherry. Dried citrus skins. Sweet grass.

Body Light but soft.

Palate Orange zest, lemons, faint syrup. Cream. Honey.

Finish Orange zest. Gently gingery balancing dryness.

SCORE 86

BLADNOCH 17-year-old (1980), 57.2 vol, Cadenhead

Colour Gold.

Nose Grassy, dry, herbal, citric.

Body Light but syrupy.

Palate Dry, grassy, leafy. Thin, but still some maltiness emerging.

Finish Dry, herbal. (Bay leaves?)

SCORE 84

Vintage 1980
Single Lowland Malt Scotch Whisky
Matured in oak casks for 17 years
Distilled at Bladnoch Distillery
on 30.6.80   *Bottled 3.98*
Cask No. 89/531/28   Bottle No. 392 of 430
*This whisky has been selected, produced and bottled in
Scotland for and under the sole responsibility of
Signatory Vintage Scotch Whisky Co. Ltd.*
70cl   *Edinburgh EH6 5PY Scotland*   43%vol

BLADNOCH 1980, 43 vol, Signatory

Colour Full gold.

Nose Very fresh. Lemony. Sherbety.

Body Syrupy.

Palate Smooth malt. Clean, fresh, lemon. Classic Bladnoch.

Finish Pastry-like grainy dryness.

SCORE 85

BLADNOCH 22-year-old (distilled 1974, bottled 1996), 54.3 vol, Adelphi (cask 282)

Colour Full gold.

Nose Slightly cedary, grassy, earthy, allspice.

Body Light but smooth.

Palate Grassy, some herbal subtleties, dry.

Finish Herbal, dry. Late rooty bitterness.

SCORE 84

Other versions of Bladnoch

The 1986 Connoisseurs Choice reviewed on the previous page replaces a 1984, also at 40 vol, from the same bottler. That, too, was lemony, but perhaps more toffeeish and luscious: a very good example of Bladnoch as a dessert malt. For a light whisky, Bladnoch ages very well. SCORE 85. A 28-year-old from Cadenhead, at 42.5 vol, was still surprisingly citric, but with lots of dry grassiness. SCORE 85. From the same bottler, a 34-year-old (distilled 1958, bottled 1993), 43.5 vol, was very oaky, but still with malt and vanilla-lemon notes. SCORE 84.

BLAIR ATHOL

PRODUCER UDV (Diageo)
REGION Highlands **DISTRICT** Midlands

ADDRESS Pitlochry, Perthshire, PH16 5LY
TEL 01796-482003 **VC**

BLAIR IS A SCOTTISH NAME, referring to a tract of flat land or someone who originates from such a place. Blair Castle is the home of the Duke of Atholl. The village of Blair Atholl ends with a double "l", while the distillery prefers to keep it single. The distillery is nearby at the inland resort of Pitlochry, known for its summer theatre. The well-designed, beautifully maintained distillery, overgrown with ivy and Virginia creeper, traces its origins to 1798, though it has been sympathetically expanded several times. Its malt whisky is extensively used in the Bell's blends. Without being huge in body, it stands up well to sherry.

HOUSE STYLE Redolent of shortbread and ginger cake. Spicy, nutty.
A mid-afternoon malt?

BLAIR ATHOL 8-year-old, 40 vol
This Bell's bottling is now hard to find.

Colour Pale gold.

Nose Fresh and very clean, with a suggestion of ginger
or shortbread.

Body Light to medium.

Palate Dryish start. Aromatic. Hints of butterscotch and ginger.

Finish A little more gingery in its smooth, round finish.

SCORE 75

BLAIR ATHOL
COMMEMORATIVE
LIMITED EDITION
1 7 9 8 ❧ 1 9 9 8

BLAIR ATHOL 12-year-old, 43 vol, Commemorative Limited Edition
A much more sherryish version.

Colour Distinctively deep. Orange liqueur.

Nose Very complex. Fragrant, candied orange peels,
dried fruit, cinnamon.

Body Medium, silky.

Palate Walnuts. Sweetish. Cakey. Faint treacle or molasses.

Finish Very smooth, round, soothing, lightly smoky.
Very sophisticated for its age. Blair Athol matures quickly, gaining
perfuminess, sweetness, richness, spiciness, complexity, and length.
The sherry helps to emulsify the elements.

SCORE 77

BLAIR ATHOL 18-year-old 56.7 vol, Bicentenary Limited Edition

Colour Full peachy amber (but less dark than the 12-year-old).

Nose Very delicate, finessed, orange and cinnamon.

Body Bigger and firm.

Palate Dates. Raisins. Dried figs. Moist cake. Butter.

Finish Toasty. The slightly burnt crust on a cake.

Score 78

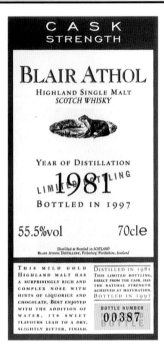

BLAIR ATHOL 1981 (bottled 1997), 55.5 vol,
Cask Strength Limited Bottling

Colour Deep, bright orange-red.

Nose Oakier and smokier, but appetizingly so.

Body Medium, firm, smooth.

Palate Delicious, clean toffee. Firm, slightly chewy. Pronounced black treacle. Lively. Hints of banana, orange, lemon. Faint fragrant smokiness.

Finish Ginger, toasty oak.

SCORE 78

BLAIR ATHOL 1973, 55 vol, Signatory Cask Strength Series

Colour White wine.

Nose Lightly smoky. Lightly fruity.

Body Light to medium, textured.

Palate Lemony, syrupy, lightly smoky.

Finish After a palate that seems to lack complexity, a very long finish. Starts flowery and fruity, with suggestions of an almost-ripe pear or dessert apple. Develops to buttery shortbread. Then a late, surprising hit of gingery warmth.

SCORE 74

BOWMORE

PRODUCER Morrison Bowmore (Suntory)
REGION Islay   **DISTRICT** Loch Indaal

ADDRESS Bowmore, Islay, Argyll, PA34 7JS   **TEL** 01496-810441 **VC**
WEBSITE www.morrisonbowmore.co.uk

T HE VILLAGE OF BOWMORE is the "capital" of Islay, and its famous distillery a justifiably popular centre for visitors. The distillery, founded in 1779, is kept in beautiful condition – but not to be confused with the local school, which has decorative pagodas. In both geography and palate, the whiskies of Bowmore are between the intense malts of the south shore and the gentlest extremes of the north. Their character is not a compromise but an enigma, and tasters have found it difficult to unfold its complexity. The water used rises from iron-tinged rock, and picks up some peat from the earth as it flows by way of the River Laggan, through moss, ferns, and rushes, to the distillery. While the peat higher on the island is rooty, that at Bowmore is sandier. The company has its own maltings, where the peat is crumbled before it is fired to give more smoke than heat. The malt is peated for a shorter time than that used for the more intense Islay whiskies. About 30 per cent of the whisky is aged in sherry. The distillery is more exposed to the westerly winds than others, so there may be more ozone in the complex of aromas and flavours.

HOUSE STYLE Smoky, with leafy notes (ferns?) and sea air. Younger ages before dinner, older after.

In this copper-domed mash tun, the barley malted at Bowmore and the island's peaty water meet and infuse on the way to becoming whisky.

BOWMORE Legend, no age statement, 40 vol
A light, young version, identified in some markets as an eight-year-old.

Colour Full gold.

Nose Peaty, smoky, very appetizing.

Body Light but textured.

Palate Firm, a touch of iron, leafy, ferny, peaty. Earthy sweetness. Flavours very singular. A fresh, young whisky, but no obvious spiritiness.

Finish Sweet, then salty.

SCORE 80

BOWMORE 12-year-old, 43 vol

Colour Amber.

Nose More salt, seaweed, and smoke than at 10 years.

Body Medium. Lightly syrupy.

Palate Persistent sherry sweetness. Spicy, heathery, seaweedy, salty. Very complex, with lots of flavour development.

Finish Remarkably long and salty.

SCORE 87

BOWMORE Cask Strength, no age statement, 56 vol
Vatting of whiskies in mid teens.

Colour Sunny, yellow-gold.

Nose Sea air. Cereal-grain oiliness. Nutty. Malty sweetness. Syrupy. Scenty.

Body Medium, substantial, smooth.

Palate Earthy dryness. Some tasters have found "wet wool". Others find it carbolic. Lively. Flavours not very well integrated.

Finish Orange peels. Leafy. Ferns. Peaty.

SCORE 81

BOWMORE Darkest, no age statement, 43 vol

Whisky in its mid teens, but from superb sherry casks.

Colour Attractive, refractive, deep amber to tawny.

Nose Smoky. Floral. Hessian. Sea air. Fresh, delicious, appetizing, complex.

Body Medium to full. Satiny.

Palate Perfumy start. Flowering currant. Nutty. Dry, black-treacle maltiness.

Finish Smooth. Polished stone. Hard, salty, licorice.

SCORE 91

BOWMORE Mariner, 15-year-old, 43 vol

Colour Full gold to amber.

Nose Fresh leather. Ferns. Powerful sea air. Notably dry.

Body Medium to full. Firm, smooth.

Palate Clean, smooth, satiny maltiness. Sweet sherry notes. Developing to crisp leafiness, then sea-saltiness.

Finish Sweet, juicy maltiness, moving to very lively, appetizing sea-salt.

SCORE 87

An earlier 15-year-old, bottled in a limited edition without an age statement as Bowmore Bicentenary, had a fruitier, flowering currant accent. SCORE 87.

BOWMORE 17-year-old, 43 vol

Colour Full gold to bronze.

Nose Smoothly aromatic. Nutty malt. Smoky. Medicinal Islay character.

Body Light to medium. Smooth. Firm.

Palate Rounded, firm, malty, dry creaminess. Tightly combined flavours.

Finish Leafy, ferny, malty, sandy, smoky, slightly astringent.

SCORE 86

BOWMORE 21-year-old, 43 vol

Colour Full gold, amber-red tinge.

Nose Very aromatic. Fragrant, distinct smokiness. Leafy bonfires.

Body Medium to full. Soft. Malty. Honeyish.

Palate Clean, honeyed malt, developing to lavender and flowering currant. Full-flavoured, complex, and beautifully balanced.

Finish Lively, quick, vanilla sweetness, and sea air.

SCORE 90

BOWMORE 25-year-old, 43 vol

Colour Pale amber.

Nose Lovely balance of appetizing, barley-sugar maltiness, sweet leafy bonfires, and fresh sea air. Long.

Body Full, firm, rounded.

Palate Lightly but definitely oily, nutty, marzipan.

Finish Starts light but lingers. Toasted nuts. Salted nuts. Sea air. Then late peanut-brittle toffee character.

SCORE 89

BOWMORE 30-year-old, 43 vol

Colour Pale amber.

Nose Clean, dry maltiness and appetizingly fragrant smokiness. Lavender. Salt.

Body Light to medium, very smooth.

Palate Soft, heathery. Very complex and spicy. Lots of lavender.

Finish Surprisingly lively licorice and aniseed. Very late woody, rooty, smoky notes. Very distinctive.

SCORE 88

BLACK BOWMORE 1964, 50 vol
A limited edition. No longer being bottled, but still prized where
it can be found.

Colour Unusually dark. Reddish-brown, with black olive tinges.

Nose Lots of sherry. No excessive oakiness. Earthy, smoky, medicinal.

Body Medium, firm.

Palate Very sweet sherry notes, oaky, earthy, peaty. Astonishingly flowery.
Sweetness and dryness. With a dash of water, endless complexities emerge.

Finish Cough linctus. Licorice. Very big and extremely long.

SCORE 90

BOWMORE 40-year-old, 42 vol
After 20 years in a first-fill oloroso sherry hogshead, this sprung a leak and
was re-racked for the same period in American oak. A stolen decanter of
this whisky was famously held to ransom in Canada in 1999.

Colour Full, refractive, gold.

Nose Herbal. Sea air.

Body Light, firm, smooth.

Palate Malty, fresh pine nuts, sagebrush, herbal.

Finish Astonishingly lively. Licorice and aniseed. Rooty, ferns, grass,
lemon grass. Lemons. Lemon pith. Very long.

SCORE 91

Vintage 1974
Single Islay Malt Scotch Whisky
Matured in an oak cask for 23 years
Distilled in the village of Bowmore
on 26.8.74   Bottled 15.12.97
Cask No. 2105   Bottle No.   of 270
*This whisky has been selected, produced and bottled in
Scotland for and under the sole responsibility of
Signatory Vintage Scotch Whisky Co. Ltd.*
70cl   *Edinburgh EH6 8RJ Scotland*   49.2%vol

BOWMORE 1974, 49.2 vol. Signatory

Colour Pale primrose yellow.

Nose Malty. Toffeeish. Hard toffee. Stony. Leafy.

Body Light on tongue. Smooth.

Palate Light, dry, maltiness. Ferns. Leafy. Cut grass. Hay. Faint sulphur.

Finish Light, dry, oaky. Salty. Sea air.

SCORE 80

BRACKLA

PRODUCER Dewar's (Bacardi)
REGION Highlands   DISTRICT Speyside (Findhorn Valley)

ADDRESS Royal Brackla Distillery Cawdor, Nairn, Inverness-shire, IV12 5QY
TEL 01667-402002

NEWLY ACQUIRED BY DEWAR'S, who have not yet issued any bottlings of Brackla as a single malt. The distillery is on the estate of Cawdor, not far from Nairn, and was founded in 1812. In 1835, Brackla became the first distillery to receive the royal warrant. Brackla has twice been rebuilt, and was extended in 1970. A Flora and Fauna bottling was released in 1993–94, and a Rare Malts edition in 1998.

HOUSE STYLE Fruity, cleansing, sometimes with a dry, hot finish. A refresher or a pousse-café.

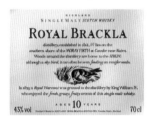

ROYAL BRACKLA 10-year-old, 43 vol, Flora and Fauna

Colour Pale gold.

Nose Smoky, slightly sulphurous, burnt, molasses.

Body Medium, drying on the tongue.

Palate Starts malty and sweet, becoming robustly fruity, then spicy notes.

Finish Cedary, smoky.

SCORE 74

ROYAL BRACKLA 1979, 43 vol. Signatory

Colour Very pale white wine.

Nose Light, fresh, sweetish, fruity, melony.

Body Lightly creamy.

Palate Refreshing. Clean, soft, fresh dessert apple and honeydew. Faint cream.

Finish Weak, dryish, faint cedar.

SCORE 69

From the same bottler, a 1975 at 58.6 vol was a great deal more impressive, with an appetizing balance of restrained fruit and big spiciness. SCORE 75.

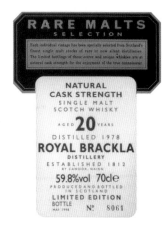

ROYAL BRACKLA 1979 (17 years in refill sherry), 46 vol, Murray McDavid

Colour Pale gold.

Nose Honeydew melon. Flowery. Fragrant.

Body Medium, drying on tongue.

Palate Creamy flavours, but very light. Apple, melon. Sweetish. Refreshing, restorative.

Finish Light. Dessert apples. Cleansing.

SCORE 72

ROYAL BRACKLA 20-year-old (bottled 1998), 59.8 vol, Rare Malts

Colour Bright gold.

Nose Flowery, melony, gingery.

Body Rich, syrupy.

Palate Very sweet. Honey. Anis.

Finish Warming. Late angelica, pepper, cedary dryness. Slightly astringent.

SCORE 75

ROYAL BRACKLA 1974, 40 vol, Connoisseurs Choice

Colour Bright gold.

Nose Melon. Flowery.

Body Medium, creamy.

Palate Light, oily, flowery, melony.

Finish Angelica, pepper. Restrained. Warming.

SCORE 74

BRAEVAL

PRODUCER Chivas (Seagram)
REGION Highlands   DISTRICT Speyside (Livet)

ADDRESS Chapelton, Ballindalloch, Banffshire, AB37 9JS

ORIGINALLY CALLED BRAES OF GLENLIVET. Brae is Scottish Gaelic for a "hillside" or "steep bank". Against a mountain ridge, this distillery is perched on a stream that feeds the River Livet. It was built in 1973–74, and expanded in 1975 and 1978. Its name was changed to avoid confusion with The Glenlivet, owned by the same company. Its whisky is intended as a component of the Chivas Regal blend.

HOUSE STYLE Light, sweet, honeyish, with a zesty finish. Aperitif.

BRAES OF GLENLIVET 21-year-old (1977), Madeira Wood, 43 vol, Hart Brothers

Colour Sunny, full gold.
Nose Toffee, honey, orange-flowers.
Body Medium, slightly chewy.
Palate Soft, honeyed. Creamy. Orange-flowers. Clean. Beautifully combined.
Finish Winey, spicy, gingery, zesty.

SCORE 77

Other versions of Braeval

A ten-year-old Braes of Glenlivet, at 43 vol, from Master of Malt, has a white-wine colour; a fruity, honeyed floweriness; and a hint of peat. SCORE 76. A 1987 Braes of Glenlivet, at ten years old and 61.7 vol, from Cadenhead, has a white-wine colour; a fresh, flowery nose; a light body; a honeyish palate, with notes of butter; and a gingery finish. SCORE 75. A 1979 Braes of Glenlivet, at 58.1 vol, from Signatory, has a deep amber to tawny colour; a fruity-flowery nose, with a hint of peat; a toffeeish palate; and a juicy, oaky finish. SCORE 76.

BRUICHLADDICH

PRODUCER JBB
REGION Islay   **DISTRICT** Loch Indaal

ADDRESS Bruichladdich, Islay, Argyll, PA49 7UN

WHEN PUFFS OF STEAM BROKE BRUICLADDICH'S recent silence for a week or two – experimentally making a notably peatier spirit than usual – one Islay enthusiast thought a new Pope had been chosen. "That beauty across the loch" is how another local referred to Scotland's most westerly, workable distillery. Bruichladdich (pronounced "Brook Laddie") is on the north shore of Loch Indaal. Its water rises from iron-tinged stone, and flows lightly over peat. The stills have tall necks, producing a relatively light, clean spirit. Unlike the other Islay distilleries, Bruichladdich is separated from the sea, albeit only by a quiet, coastal road. Its lightly tasty whisky is a good introduction to Islay malts. The distillery was founded in 1881, rebuilt in 1886 and, despite an extension in 1975, remains little changed. Some independent bottlers call the whisky Lochindaal. An unrelated distillery of that name, long closed, vestigially survives a couple of miles further west at Port Charlotte.

HOUSE STYLE Light to medium, firm, hint of passion fruit, salty.
Very drinkable. Aperitif.

BRUICHLADDICH 10-year-old, 40 vol

Colour Pale gold.

Nose Very flowery, heathery, lightly seaweedy, emphatically salty.

Body Light to medium, smooth and firm.

Palate Firm and dry at first, with a touch of iron. Slight oiliness, and a suggestion of peat. Becoming maltier and sweeter, with touches of heather. Very slightly spirity.

Finish Long, with a range of subtle flavours.

SCORE 77

LOCHINDAAL 10-year-old, 43 vol
Bruichladdich whisky in an independent bottling named after the loch.

Colour Full yellowy gold.

Nose Very dry, woody, corky, medicine bottles.

Body Light but smooth.

Palate Sweetish vanilla, oak, woody, corky, iodine.

Finish Flowery, seaweedy, peppery.

SCORE 76

A 17-year-old, 43 vol, rendering Loch Indaal as two words, is a Master of Malt bottling. It is greeny-gold, cleanly medicinal, with a salty finish. Score 77.

BRUICHLADDICH 1986 (bottled 1997, refill sherry), 46 vol, Murray McDavid

Colour Pale gold.

Nose Faint peat smoke. Sea breezes.

Body Light but firm maltiness.

Palate Hint of passion fruit. Late fragrant smokiness, and hint of seaweed.

Finish Dry. Hint of passion fruit. Delicate interplay of flavours.

SCORE 78

BRUICHLADDICH 12-year-old (distilled 1986, bottled 1998), 57.5 vol, Adelphi (cask 660)

Colour Bright gold.

Nose Lightly peaty.

Body Smooth, malty.

Palate Slight fruit. Grassy, peaty. Falls away towards finish.

Finish Delayed explosion of pepper seaweed.

SCORE 77

A Scott's Selection from the same year, at 57.2 vol, was softer, sweeter, and fruitier. SCORE 76.

BRUICHLADDICH 15-year-old, 40 vol

Colour Old gold.

Nose Intense. Drier, flowery, seaweedy, salty.

Body Firm, smooth, lightly oily.

Palate Flowery, seaweedy, salty. Flavours very well combined and rounded. An easily drinkable yet satisfying malt. Has benefited from the extra five years.

Finish Long, warming, salty.

SCORE 78

BRUICHLADDICH 21-year-old, 43 vol

Colour Full gold.

Nose Intense, complex, appetizing.

Body Medium, very firm.

Palate All the flavours intensify. Big maltiness in the middle, developing to powerful salt. For a relatively gentle whisky, a surprising lack of woodiness at this age.

Finish Complex, dry, salty, appetizing.

SCORE 79

BRUICHLADDICH 26-year-old, 45 vol, Stillman's Dram

Colour Full gold to amber.

Nose Spicy (some tasters have found mace), fruity, sherry, lightly toasty oak, sea air.

Body Medium, very smooth.

Palate Light oak, malt, salt, passion fruit, sherry sweetness. Flavours tightly locked together.

Finish Lightly toasty oak, seaweed, salt and pepper.

SCORE 77

Other versions of Bruichladdich

A 25-year-old (1968), at 53.8 vol, from Cadenhead, is flowery and complex. SCORE 78. A 1968, at 52.9 vol, in Signatory's 10th anniversary series, is sherryish, malty, and salty, with a distinct smoky fragrance in the finish. SCORE 79. A 1965, at 53.5, from Gordon & MacPhail, is even more sherryish, with lots of oak and smoke. SCORE 78.

BUNNAHABHAIN

PRODUCER Highland Distillers
REGION Islay   **DISTRICT** North Shore

ADDRESS Port Askaig, Islay, Argyll, PA46 7RP   **TEL** 01496-840646
WEBSITE www.blackbottle.com

AMONG THE ISLAY MALTS, Bunnahabhain (pronounced Boona'havn, meaning ("mouth of the creek") is by far the lightest in palate, but its body has a distinctive, light oiliness. It has a faint, flowery, nutty hint of peatiness, a whiff of sea air, and a character that is quietly distinctive. The distillery, established in 1881 and expanded in 1963, is set around a courtyard in a remote cove. A kerb has been built to stops visitors' cars from rolling into the sea. A ships' bell, salvaged from a nearby wreck, hangs from the wall. It was at one time used to summon the manager from his home if he were urgently needed. The distillery's water rises through limestone, and because it is piped to the distillery, it does not pick up peat on the way. The stills are large, in a style that the industry refers to as onion-shaped. The whisky plays an important part in the Cutty Sark blends. Recently, Bunnahabhain has emphasized its role in Black Bottle, a blend containing all the Islay malts.

HOUSE STYLE Fresh, sweetish, nutty, herbal, salty. Aperitif.

BUNNAHABHAIN 12-year-old, 40 vol

Colour Gold.
Nose Remarkably fresh, sweet, sea-air aroma.
Body Light to medium, firm.
Palate Gentle, clean, nutty-malty sweetness.
Finish Very full flavour development. A refreshing quality.

SCORE 77

HIGHLAND DISTILLERS

THE FAMILY SILVER

LIMITED BOTTLING

MALT SCOTCH WHISKY

PRODUCT OF SCOTLAND

EVERY ONCE IN A WHILE, *and entirely at their discretion*, THE BOARD OF DIRECTORS at *Highland Distillers authorise a special limited edition of a vintage malt whisky that, to the nose of the MASTER DISTILLER, has reached the peak of perfection. This bottle contains such an exclusive vintage - savour it as you would a* RARE HEIRLOOM *that has been passed down to you.*

BUNNAHABHAIN

VINTAGE **1968** RESERVE

70cl

DISTILLED AND BOTTLED BY
HIGHLAND DISTILLERS PLC.
PERTH, SCOTLAND

40% Vol.

BUNNAHABHAIN 1968, 40 vol, The Family Silver

Colour Attractive pale walnut.

Nose Fragrant sea air and polished wood.

Body Firm, creamy.

Palate Depth of flowery nuttiness and creamy flavours.

Finish Delightful teasing subtlety of nuttiness and gently salty sea air.

SCORE 79

BUNNAHABHAIN 1963, 43 vol

Colour Deep shiny gold.

Nose Slightly saltier than the 1968.

Body Firm, lightly creamy.

Palate Full of flavour, beautifully balanced between restrained oakiness, nuttiness, and saltiness.

Finish Almondy, salty. Faint hint of edible seaweed, as in Japanese cocktail snacks.

SCORE 80

Other versions of Bunnahabhain

A Gordon & MacPhail 1988, at 40 vol, balances the distillery character with toastiness and ginger-marmalade sherry notes, suggesting a breakfast whisky for the truly decadent. SCORE 77. A Signatory 1980, at 43 vol, is grassier, with some peat and faint seaweed. SCORE 76. A 1977, 55.6 vol from the same bottler is richly sherryish and nutty, still with a late saltiness. SCORE 78. A Murray McDavid 1979 (bottled 1996), 46 vol, is light and flowery, with very fresh sea air. SCORE 76.

CAOL ILA

Producer UDV (Diageo)
Region Islay **District** North shore

ADDRESS Port Askaig, Islay, Argyll, PA46 7RL
TEL 01496-840207 Distillery has shop

MUCH MORE READILY AVAILABLE in recent years. Its qualities as a single malt, long appreciated by connoisseurs, seem to have become more apparent to the distillery's owners. The name, pronounced "cull-eela", means "Sound of Islay". The Gaelic word "caol" is more familiar as "kyle". The distillery is in a cove near Port Askaig. The large windows of the still-house overlook the Sound of Islay, across which the ferry chugs to the nearby island of Jura. Behind the distillery, a hillside covered in fuschias, foxgloves, and wild roses rises toward the peaty loch where the water gathers. It is quite salty and minerally, having risen from limestone. The distillery was built in 1846, reconstructed in 1879, and brusquely modernised in the 1970s. Its whisky has been a component of Johnnie Walker Swing, Bell's, and for many years the export blend Bulloch and Lade.

House style Oily, olive-like, junipery. A wonderful aperitif.

CAOL ILA 12-year-old, 40 vol, Bulloch and Lade bottling

Colour Pale, white wine.
Nose Peaty, seaweedy, fruity.
Body Light, but very firm, becoming slightly syrupy.
Palate Peaty, peppery, spicy, olive-like.
Finish Peppery, warming.

SCORE 77

ISLAY
SINGLE MALT *SCOTCH WHISKY*

CAOL ILA

distillery, built in 1846 is situated near *Port Askaig* on the *Isle of Islay.* Steamers used to call twice a week to collect *whisky* from this remote site in a cove facing the *Isle of Jura.* Water supplies for mashing come from *Loch nam Ban* although the sea provides *water* for condensing. Unusual for an *Islay* this *single MALT SCOTCH WHISKY* has *a fresh aroma* and *a light yet well rounded* flavour.

AGED **15** YEARS

43% vol Distilled & Bottled in SCOTLAND. CAOL ILA DISTILLERY Port Askaig, Isle of Islay, Scotland 70 cl

CAOL ILA 15-year-old, 43 vol, Flora and Fauna

Colour Fino sherry, bright.

Nose Aromatic, complex.

Body Light, very firm, smooth.

Palate Rounder, with the flavours more combined.

Finish Oily and warming enough to keep out the sea.

SCORE 80

CASK STRENGTH

CAOL ILA
ISLAY SINGLE MALT
SCOTCH WHISKY

YEAR OF DISTILLATION
LIMITED **1981** BOTTLING
BOTTLED IN 1997

63.8%vol   70cle

Distilled & Bottled in SCOTLAND
Caol Ila Distillery, Port Askaig, Isle of Islay, Scotland

THIS PALE GOLD ISLAY MALT HAS A FRAGRANT NOSE WITH A STRONG PEAT BACKGROUND. BEST ENJOYED WITH THE ADDITION OF WATER, IT HAS A FULL SHORT FLAVOUR WITH TRACES OF SALT, AND AN UNUSUAL PEPPERY KICK IN THE FINISH.
THIS LIMITED BOTTLING, DRAWN FROM THE CASK, HAS THE NATURAL STRENGTH ACHIEVED AT MATURATION.

BOTTLE NUMBER
01578

CAOL ILA 1981 (bottled 1997), 63.8 vol, Cask Strength Limited Bottling

Colour Bright limey yellow.

Nose Fragrant peat smoke, juniper, seaweed. Very appetizing.

Body Firm, oily.

Palate Assertively oily, junipery. Late surge of peaty dryness. Very dry.

Finish Wonderfully long and warming.

SCORE 82

CAOL ILA 20-year-old (bottled 1996), 57.86 vol, 150th Anniversary Edition

Colour Orange.

Nose Sweet seaweed. Juniper. Pine nuts.

Body Medium, smooth, rounded.

Palate Enormously complex and distinctive. Nutty, appetizingly seaweedy, peppery, salty. Tightly combined flavours. Beautifully balanced.

Finish Sherry, toasty oak, seaweed, lemon skin, pepper.

SCORE 85

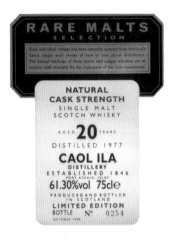

CAOL ILA 20-year-old, 61.3 vol, Rare Malts

Colour Full greeny gold.

Nose Powerfully aromatic. Roasted peppers. Olives. Salt.

Body Medium but gentle, oily, soothing.

Palate Oily. Roasted peppers, olives, lemon juice.

Finish Dry, junipery, vine leaves, stemmy. Intense, expressive.

SCORE 82

CAOL ILA 21-year-old, 61.3 vol, Rare Malts

Colour Attractive, subtle pale gold.

Nose Very fresh. Sea air.

Body Medium, oily, smooth.

Palate Astonishingly fresh. More sea air. Almost a sandy taste Fresh seaweed. Sweet and dry, olivey. Sustained development of flavours.

Finish Big, long. Expressive. Smoky fragrance. Appetizing. Oaky dryness.

SCORE 82

Some independent bottlings of Caol Ila

SCOTCH MALT WHISKY SOCIETY, 8-year-old (distilled 1989, bottled 1998), 60.4 vol, cask 53.34

Colour Pale gold.

Nose Big, aromatic, soapy, seaweedy, dry, appetizing.

Body Light, firm.

Palate Oily, olives, baked aubergines. Sensuous in its robust youthfulness.

Finish Assertively smoky, tar-like, and peppery.

SCORE 78

A bottling from the same vintage, also eight years old, also at cask strength, from Cadenhead, was very similar, possibly fractionally more oaky. SCORE 78. A third, but a 46 vol, from Murray McDavid, had a creamy oiliness and more fruity character. SCORE 77.

CAOL ILA 1981, 62.7 vol, Gordon & MacPhail "Cask" edition

Colour Bright greeny gold.

Nose Seaweedy, appetizing.

Body Light, firm.

Palate Dry, classically junipery, sandy. Slightly thin.

Finish Crisp punch of seaweed and pepper.

SCORE 80

The same bottler's 40 vol version of a 1981 was more sherried, leafy, tobacco-like, and peaty. SCORE 77. A 1982, at 43 vol, from Signatory, was very pale, but again very tobacco-like. SCORE 77.

CAOL ILA 21-year-old (distilled 1976), 58.1 vol, Adelphi (cask 8093)

Colour Bright greeny gold.

Nose Fresh, grassy. Sea air. A walk on the dunes.

Body Firm, lightly oily.

Palate Sweet, grassy maltiness, moving to gentle sea air and seaweed.

Finish Sweetish, late tobacco.

SCORE 79

A 1974, bottled in 1995, at 46 vol, from Murray McDavid, is fragrant and junipery, with an oily finish and a great deal of finesse. SCORE 81.
A 1974 at 60.4 vol, from Signatory is also very oily, sweetish with lots of sea air and gorse, and an appetizingly peppery finish. SCORE 80.

CAPERDONICH

PRODUCER Chivas (Seagram)
REGION Highlands   DISTRICT Speyside (Rothes)

ADDRESS Rothes, Morayshire, AB38 7BN

P|ARTNER TO THE RENOWNED GLEN GRANT. The two distilleries, under the same ownership, are across the street from one another in the whisky town of Rothes. This little town on the Spey has five distilleries. Caperdonich, founded in 1898, was rebuilt in 1965 and extended in 1967. From the start, it has been a back-up to Glen Grant. When young, the malts of both distilleries are light and fragrant in their bouquet, medium-bodied, and nutty-tasting. Of the two, Caperdonich is perhaps a dash fruitier and slightly more smoky. It, too, is a component of the Chivas Regal blend. Chivas seems recently to have been keeping a tight control on stocks of its malts. Although there are current bottlings of Caperdonich from independents, they are of very old vintages. Some malt-lovers would dismiss them for an overpowering oakiness; others would love them for their sherry and intensity.

HOUSE STYLE Dried fruits, smoky. After dinner.

CAPERDONICH 1977, 57 vol, Cadenhead

Colour Remarkably deep. Garnet.

Nose Fruity, distinctly raisiny. Cloves. Very dry.

Body Firm, smooth.

Palate Dried fruits. Raisins. Dates. Georgian brandy. Woody. Smoky.

Finish Spicy, gingery, oaky, extremely smoky.

SCORE 75

SINGLE CASK SCOTCH MALT WHISKY		
DATE DISTILLED	Feb 67	
DATE BOTTLED	Sept 98	*"Muscovado*
AGED IN OAK	31 yrs	*sugar and*
PROOF STRENGTH	85.4° 48.8% vol e	*Friars Balsam"*
CONTENTS BY VOL	70 cl	PRODUCED &
		BOTTLED IN SCOTLAND

SCOTCH MALT WHISKY SOCIETY, 31-year-old (distilled 1967, bottled 1998), 48.8 vol, cask number 38.6

Colour Chestnut to mahogany.

Nose Smokier, oakier, but still raisiny.

Body Medium, firm, very smooth indeed.

Palate Hard treacle-toffee. Figs. Dense sherry.

Finish Cough syrup.

SCORE 75

Vintage 1966
Single Highland Malt Scotch Whisky
Matured in sherry casks for 30 years
Distilled at Caperdonich Distillery
on 16.3.66
Cask No. 633 Bottle No.   of 303
This whisky has been selected, produced and bottled in
Scotland for and under the sole responsibility of
Signatory Vintage Scotch Whisky Co. Ltd.
70cl *Edinburgh 2008 EH6 Scotland* 53.4%vol

CAPERDONICH 1966, 53.4 vol, Signatory Cask Strength Series

Colour Garnet to ruby.

Nose Fruitier. Again, raisins and dates.

Body Medium to full, rounded.

Palate Dates, figs, soothingly medicinal.

Finish Tasty, then oaky and smoky.

SCORE 76

Earlier versions of Caperdonich

A Cadenhead 14-year-old at 60.5 vol, made available in 1994, was paler but still verging on woodiness. SCORE 75. A Connoisseurs Choice 1968, at 40 vol, released around the same time, was fruity and coconut-like. SCORE 73.

CARDHU

PRODUCER UDV (Diageo)
REGION Highlands   DISTRICT Speyside

ADDRESS Aberlour, Banffshire, AB38 7RY
TEL 01340-872555 **VC**

ONE OF SEVERAL WOMEN who were key figures in the industry, Elizabeth Cumming rebuilt this distillery in 1872 (at the time, it was at least half a century old). Her family were long involved in the fortunes of the Johnnie Walker blends, of which Cardhu malt whisky is the soft heart. In more recent years, a Cumming had a role in the introduction of the present Cardhu as the first widely available single malt from what is now UDV. In 1998, a Rare Malts edition was released. Independent bottlings can occasionally be found, sometimes using older spellings of the name. Cardhu is on a hillside near the Spey, in the heart of malt-whisky country.

HOUSE STYLE Light, smooth, sweetish, delicate.
An easy-drinking malt.

CARDHU 12-year-old, 40 vol

Colour Pale.

Nose Light, appetizing, hints of greengage, and the gentlest touch of smoke.

Body Light and smooth.

Palate Light to medium in flavour, with the emphasis on malty sweetness and vanilla.

Finish A lingering, syrupy sweetness, but also a rounder dryness with late hints of peat, although again faint.

SCORE 72

Other versions of Cardhu
The Rare Malts 25-year-old (distilled 1973), at 60.5 vol, has a richer, marshmallow maltiness, a suggestion of crystallized fruit, and a hint of tangerine in the finish. SCORE 76.

CLYNELISH

PRODUCER UDV (Diageo)
REGION Highlands   DISTRICT North Highlands

ADDRESS Brora, Sutherland, KW9 6LR
TEL 01408-623000 **VC**

ACLASSIC CASE OF A COASTAL MALT having a slightly "island" character. The location is the fishing and golfing resort of Brora, which gave its name to a distillery established in 1819 by the Marquess of Stafford. Across the road is its successor, Clynelish. Between the late 1960s and early 1980s, the two both operated, the older one using an especially highly peated malt. Clynelish uses a medium peating. The malt from the older distillery may still appear from independent bottlers or retail chains.

HOUSE STYLE Seaweedy, spicy. With a roast-beef sandwich.

CLYNELISH 14-year-old, 43 vol, Flora and Fauna

Colour Pale gold.
Nose Sea, perhaps seaweed, and peat.
Body Medium to full, smooth. Visibly oily.
Palate Starts malty (sweetish when water is added), becoming fruity-spicy (mustard?), with notes of seaweed and salt.
Finish Remarkable, lingering spiciness. Stays very fresh, with an emphatic mustard flavour. Reminiscent of mustard and cress. A tremendously appetizing malt.

SCORE 81

CLYNELISH 1982 (bottled 1997), 57.7 vol, Cask Strength Limited Bottling

Colour Bright greeny gold.

Nose Restrained seaweed, oily, gunmetal.

Body Medium. Very firm.

Palate Oily. Mustardy. Grainy. Seaweedy acidity and sweetness. Flavours more tightly combined than in similar Flora and Fauna edition, but big in finish.

Finish Pepperiness, seaweed, and saltiness.

SCORE 81

BRORA 21-year-old (distilled 1977), 56.9 vol, Rare Malts

Colour Bright gold.

Nose Appetizing. Fresh sea air. Salty. Seaweed on rocks. Fragrant, smoky.

Body Oily, tar-like, chewy.

Palate Very spicy indeed. Stinging flavours. Lots of flavour development. Grassiness. Gorse. Flowering currant. Sweet mustard.

Finish Pepper. Hot mustard. Grainy. Cumin.

SCORE 85

Earlier Rare Malts from Brora have included a more flowery 1975. SCORE 84. There was also a wonderfully seaweedy, medicinal 1972. SCORE 86.

CLYNELISH 22-year-old (distilled 1972), 58.95 vol, Rare Malts

Colour Lemony.

Nose Fresh, restrained for a Clynelish. Spicy, grassy, briny.

Body Firm, oily.

Palate Starts gently. Big maltiness. Molasses-like peatiness. Grassy and cress-like. Toasty, buttery, salty.

Finish A late, big hit. Peppery, sandy, warming.

SCORE 82

Some independent bottlings of Clynelish/Brora

CLYNELISH 9-year-old (distilled 1989), 61.6 vol, Adelphi, cask 6081

Colour Very pale gold.

Nose Very flowery. Soft for a relatively young example.

Body Light, smooth.

Palate Flowery. Cress. Pepper. Salt. Delicate interplay of flavours. A lovely, flowery aperitif.

Finish Lightly seaweedy. Late sweetness.

SCORE 80

BRORA 1982 40 vol, Connoisseurs Choice, 40 vol

Colour Full, bright, yellowy gold.

Nose Powerful. Gorse in a sea mist.

Body Very firm.

Palate Salsify, aparagus, edible cactus, juicy cucumber. Very unusual. Both refreshing and appetizing, though rather weak in the middle.

Finish Oily, olivey, peppery.

SCORE 79

CLYNELISH 1983, 43 vol, Signatory

Colour Very pale white wine.

Nose Light seaweed and sea air.

Body Lightly silky.

Palate Light, refreshing, weak in the middle, developing some peppery notes.

Finish Peppery, light, fruity seaweed, sea-salt, pepper. Very late, mustardy dryness, and heat.

SCORE 78

AN CNOC

Producer Inver House
Region Highlands   **District** Speyside (Isla/Deveron)

address Knock by Huntly, Aberdeenshire, AB5 5LJ
website www.inverhouse.com   **e-mail** enquiries@inverhouse.com

A N CNOC IS SCOTTISH GAELIC for "The Hill". The full name of the distillery, in Gaelic, is Cnoc Dubh ("Black Hill"). In English, this is rendered as Knockdhu, not be confused with another wholly unrelated distillery, Knockando ("Little Black Hill"). There was probably no thought of confusion when these two distilleries were established, both in the 1890s, as their original purpose was to produce whisky for blending, rather than as single malt.

Knockdhu was built in 1894 to supply malt for the Haig blends, and closed in 1983. Only after its acquisition by its present owners, and its reopening, did official bottlings, albeit on a small scale, begin to be issued in the 1990s.

House style Creamy and fruity. A dessert malt?

AN CNOC 12-year-old, 40 vol
Colour Pale gold.
Nose Very aromatic, smooth, fruity. Pineapple?
Body Light but very smooth.
Palate Smooth, creamy, vanilla notes. Very soft note of fruit. Very drinkable and enjoyable.
Finish Creamy, oaty. Sweet herbs.

SCORE 75

CNOC DHU/KNOCKDHU 21-year-old, 57.5 Limited Edition

Colour Fractionally fuller gold.

Nose Appetizingly perfumy but restrained and smooth. Perhaps a pineapple that has not been peeled or cut. Some grassy, peaty-smoke notes.

Body Very creamy.

Palate Deep, soft, rounded marshmallow maltiness, restrained fruit, grass and peat-smoke fragrance. Beautifully balanced.

Finish Fruit zest. Spicy. Smoky fragrance.

SCORE 77

KNOCKDHU 20-year-old (distilled 1978, bottled 1998), 59.7 vol, Adelphi, cask number 1889

Colour Greeny gold.

Nose Lightly fruity, more flowery.

Body Lightly syrupy.

Palate Vanilla, cream, pineapples.

Finish Lemon, coriander, balancing dryness.

SCORE 76

Other versions of Cnoc Dhu/Knockdhu
Using the English spelling, a 1974, at 40 vol, from Connoisseurs Choice, is similar to the official 21-year-old. It has a good long finish, but is heavily sherried for a relatively delicate malt. SCORE 75.

COLEBURN

PRODUCER DCL/United Distillers
REGION Highlands   **DISTRICT** Speyside (Lossie)

ADDRESS Longmorn by Elgin, Moray, IV38 8GN

T HE USHER'S BLENDED SCOTCHES once relied heavily upon whisky from this distillery. Coleburn was built in 1896, and closed in 1985, the year before its owners DCL were subsumed into United Distillers. In 1992, its licence was cancelled, and there have been proposals to redevelop the site as housing.

HOUSE STYLE Dry, fruity. Aperitif.

Vintage 1983
Single Highland Malt Scotch Whisky
Matured in oak casks for 14 years
Distilled at Coleburn Distillery

70cl   43%vol

COLEBURN 1983, 43 vol Signatory

Colour Bright limey-lemony yellow.

Nose Very fruity, syrupy, slightly resiny. Dried lemon peels.

Body Lightly syrupy, oily.

Palate Slight dry toffee. Lemony, sherbety, powdery.

Finish Dryish, slightly gummy.

SCORE 68

COLEBURN 1978, 19-year-old, 59.1 vol, Cadenhead

Colour Full yellow.

Nose Fruit skins.

Body Oily.

Palate Oily, cereal grain, grassy. Hint of peaty smokiness.

Finish Dryish. Gummy. Hint of lemon grass or orange zest.

SCORE 67

CONVALMORE

PRODUCER DCL (owner William Grant and Sons)
REGION Highlands   **DISTRICT** Speyside (Dufftown)

ADDRESS Dufftown, Banffshire, AB55 4BD

THE BUCHANAN'S BLENDS once relied heavily on whisky from this distillery, which was founded in 1894. Like many distilleries, it had a disastrous fire, in 1909. (Not only is whisky itself highly inflammable, so are its vapours exhaled by casks in the warehouses.) It was rebuilt in 1910, with the novel addition of a continuous column still intended to produce malt whisky. This experiment was not deemed a success, and ended at the time of the First World War. The distillery was modernised in 1964–65, but mothballed a couple of decades later by its then owners DCL. Their successors UDV still notionally have the right to issue a Convalmore whisky, but there have been only independent bottlings. In 1992, the premises were acquired by William Grant and Sons, owners of nearby Glenfiddich and Balvenie, as warehousing.

HOUSE STYLE Malty, syrupy, fruity, biggish. After dinner.

CONVALMORE 1983, 43 vol, Signatory

Colour Full gold.

Nose Very pleasant, sweetish, traditional malt whisky. Malty, with a whiff of peat smoke, and a touch of sherry.

Body Medium. Firm.

Palate Lightly malty. Hint of cocoa butter. Falls away in middle.

Finish Dryish, lightly nutty, and sherryish.

SCORE 70

CONVALMORE 1981, 40 vol Connoisseurs Choice

Colour Yellowy gold.	
Nose Oily.	
Body Medium. Oily.	
Palate Oily, falls away in middle.	
Finish Hint of honey.	

SCORE 67

Less malty sweetness and spiciness than the 1969 vintage. SCORE 68.

CONVALMORE 1960, 40 vol, Gordon and MacPhail. Released in 1999 as part of a new "Rare Old" series

Colour Rich lemony gold.
Nose Aromatic. Oily. Very "clean" smoke.
Body Medium, Oily. Clean.
Palate Begins with a good malt background. Distinctly oily. Again, lightly smoky.
Finish Light malt. Hint of honey. Yet more oiliness. Hint of sulphur. Clean peatiness. Warming. Long.

SCORE 70

Previous bottlings of Convalmore
A 30-year-old, at 46.5 vol, from Cadenhead, was fruitier, with honey and heather. SCORE 75.

CRAGGANMORE

PRODUCER UDV (Diageo)
REGION Highlands   **DISTRICT** Speyside

ADDRESS Ballindalloch, Banffshire, AB37 9AB

ONE OF THE FINEST SPEYSIDE MALTS, recently also issued with a ruby port finish (in a limited Distiller's Edition). Cragganmore is less widely known than might be expected, though it has gained a wider appreciation in recent years as one of UDV's six "Classic Malts". The distillery, founded in 1869–70, is very pretty, hidden in a hollow high on the Spey. Its water, from nearby springs, is relatively hard, and its spirit stills have an unusual, flat-topped shape. These two elements may be factors in the complexity of the malt. The usual version, from re-fill sherry casks, some more sherried independent bottlings, and the new port finish, are each in their own ways almost equal delights. Cragganmore is a component of Old Parr.

HOUSE STYLE Austere, stonily dry, aromatic. After dinner.

CRAGGANMORE 12-year-old, 40 vol

Colour Golden.

Nose The most complex aroma of any malt. Its bouquet is astonishingly fragrant and delicate, with sweetish notes of cut grass and herbs (thyme perhaps?).

Body Light to medium, but very firm and smooth.

Palate Delicate, clean, restrained, with a huge range of herbal, flowery notes.

Finish Long.

SCORE 90

CRAGGANMORE 1984, Double Matured, 40 vol
Finished in ruby port.

Colour Pale amber.

Nose Heather honey. Scented. Beeswax. Hessian.

Body Firm, smooth. Fuller.

Palate Flowery. Orange blossom. Sweet oranges. Cherries. Port.

Finish Flowery, balancing dryness. Warming. Soothing.
Connoisseurs might miss the austerity of the original – or enjoy the
added layer of fruity, winey, sweetness.

SCORE 90

CRAGGANMORE 1976, 53.8 vol, Gordon and MacPhail

Colour Pale gold.

Nose Fragrant, lightly peaty, grassy, nutty, herbal.

Body Medium, very smooth.

Palate Complex, restrained, with rooty, licorice notes.

Finish Long, more licorice, enveloping.

SCORE 89

A 1976 Connoisseurs Choice, at 40 vol (bottled 1999), had a superb
interplay of sherry, malt, fragrant peat smoke, and spicy perfuminess.
SCORE 90.

CRAIGELLACHIE

PRODUCER Dewar's (Bacardi)
REGION Highlands   DISTRICT Speyside

ADDRESS Craigellachie, Banffshire, AB38 9ST
TEL 01340-881212 or 881228

AT THE VERY HEART OF SPEYSIDE, where the Fiddich meets the Spey, and the district's main roads cross – between Dufftown, Aberlour, and Rothes – the village of Craigellachie has a bridge, designed by the great Scottish engineer Thomas Telford, a cooperage, and two distilleries. The one called simply Craigellachie stands to the southeast of the Spey; northwest is Macallan. Craigellachie is pronounced "Craig-ella-ki" – the "i" is short. Its full-flavoured, malty-fruity whisky is a component of the White Horse blends. The distillery was founded in 1891 and rebuilt in 1965.

HOUSE STYLE Sweet, malty-nutty, fruity. After dinner.

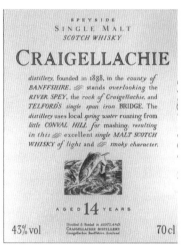

CRAIGELLACHIE 14-year-old, 43 vol, Flora and Fauna

Colour Old gold.

Nose Fragrant. Lightly smoky. Plenty of sweet, crushed-barley maltiness.

Body Medium.

Palate Starts sweet, slightly syrupy, and malty, then becomes nutty, developing a very fruity, Seville-orange character.

Finish Orangey, lightly smoky, aromatic, warming.

SCORE 75

CRAIGELLACHIE 13-year-old, 59.2 vol, Adelphi (cask number 3783)

Colour Bright gold.

Nose Sweet, malty, nutty, buttery.

Body Medium but rich.

Palate Creamy, nutty. Lacks complexity, but delicious.

Finish. Light, clean, fruitness. Orange zest. Quick.

SCORE 75

CRAIGELLACHIE 1982 (bottled 1997), 62.7 vol, Scott's Selection

Colour Primrose.

Nose Very fresh. Dessert apples. Grass. Clean smokiness.

Body Creamy.

Palate Clean, fresh apple, fruitiness. Nuttiness. Grassy smokiness.

Finish Fragrant, clean smokiness.

SCORE 76

A 40 vol from the same year, bottled by Gordon & MacPhail, was superbly balanced, with a more peaty smokiness and the faintest suggestion of sherry. SCORE 78.

CRAIGELLACHIE 1981, 43 vol, Signatory

Colour White wine.

Nose Fragrant. Restrained dessert apples, grass, and fragrant smokiness.

Body Oily.

Palate Cereal-grain oiliness. Very oily. Perfumy. Soapy.

Finish Flowery. Dessert apples again.

SCORE 75

Other versions of Craigellachie

A 1973 (22-year-old) Rare Malts edition, at cask strength, begins with crushed barley, moving to fudgy nuttiness and peanut brittle. SCORE 77. A 19-year-old, at 43 vol, from Master of Malt, is distinctly firm and very nutty. SCORE 76.

DAILUAINE

PRODUCER UDV (Diageo)
REGION Highlands **DISTRICT** Speyside

ADDRESS Carron, Banffshire, AB38 7RE
TEL 01340-872500

BETWEEN THE MOUNTAIN BEN RINNES and the River Spey, at the hamlet of Carron, not far from Aberlour, the Dailuaine ("Dal-oo-ayn") distillery is hidden in a hollow. The name means green vale, and that accurately describes the setting. It was founded in 1852, and has been rebuilt several times since. It is one of several distilleries along the Spey valley that once had its own railway halt for workers and visitors – and as a means of shipping in barley or malt and despatching the whisky. A small part of the Speyside Line still runs trains for hobbyists and visitors, at the Aviemore ski resort, and Dailuaine's own shunting locomotive has appeared there under steam, but is now preserved at Aberfeldy, a distillery formerly in the same group. Most of the route from the mountains to the sea is now preserved for walkers, as the Speyside Way. Dailuaine's whisky has long been a component of the Johnnie Walker blends. It was made available as a single malt in the Flora and Fauna series in 1991, and later in a Cask Strength Limited Edition.

HOUSE STYLE Firmly malty, fruity, fragrant. After dinner.

SPEYSIDE
SINGLE MALT *SCOTCH WHISKY*

DAILUAINE

is the GAELIC for "the green vale". The *distillery*, established
in 1852, lies in a hollow by the *CARRON BURN* in *BANFFSHIRE*. This
single Malt Scotch Whisky has a *full bodied fruity* nose and a *smoky* finish.
For more than a *hundred years* all *distillery* supplies were despatched by
rail. The steam *locomotive* "DAILUAINE NO.1" was in use
from 1939 – 1967 and is *preserved* on the *STRATHSPEY RAILWAY*.

AGED **16** YEARS

43% vol Distilled & Bottled in *SCOTLAND* DAILUAINE DISTILLERY Carron, Aberlour, Banffshire, Scotland 70 cl

DAILUAINE 16-year-old, 43 vol, Flora and Fauna
Colour Emphatically reddish-amber.
Nose Sherryish but dry, perfumy.
Body Medium to full, smooth.
Palate Sherryish, with barley-sugar maltiness, but balanced by a dry cedar or oak background.
Finish Sherryish, smooth, very warming, long.

SCORE 76

DAILUAINE 1980 (bottled 1997), 63.0 vol, Cask Strength Limited Edition

Colour Bright deep orange. Very distinctive.

Nose Lightly smoky. Orange marmalade. Sherry. Oak.

Body Medium to full. Smooth.

Palate Sherryish. Firm maltiness. Surge of peat smoke. Oak.

Finish Oaky, dry, earthy, peppery.

SCORE 77

DAILUAINE 1973, 22-year-old, 60.92 vol, Rare Malts

Colour Full gold.

Nose Distinctly peaty.

Body Light to medium. Very smooth.

Palate Long-lasting flavours. Tightly combined barley-sugar sweetness and flowery dryness. Less sherried and big than the above, but with more distillery character.

Finish Fruity, perfumy. Violets?

SCORE 77

DAILUAINE 1974, 40 vol, Connoisseurs Choice

Colour Full gold to pale amber.

Nose Fruity, spicy. Long, complex.

Body Full, smooth, cleanly syrupy.

Palate Syrupy, cinnamon-toffee, nutty, sherryish, oaky, earthy.

Finish Soft spiciness. Flowery. Grassy. Earthy.

SCORE 77

A 1971 from the same bottler was richer, sweeter, and fruitier, with less distillery character. SCORE 74.

DALLAS DHU

PRODUCER DCL
REGION Highlands **DISTRICT** Speyside (Findhorn)

ADDRESS Forres, Morayshire, IV36 2RR
TEL 01309-676548 **VC**

THE NAME MEANS "BLACK WATER VALLEY". This Dallas accommodates a hamlet rather smaller than its indirect descendant in Texas (named after US Vice-president George Mifflin Dallas, who seems to have been of Scottish origin). The Dallas Dhu distillery was established in 1899. Despite a fire in 1939, it does not appear to have changed greatly. Latterly, its whisky appeared in the Benmore blends and vattings, and as Dallas Mhor single malt. The distillery closed in 1983 and reopened to the public in 1988, under the aegis of Scotland's Historic Buildings and Monument Directorate. There are no plans to restart production, but the later batches continue to appear in independent bottlings.

HOUSE STYLE Silky, honeyish, sometimes chocolatey. After dinner.

DALLAS DHU 1979, 40 vol, Gordon & MacPhail

Colour White wine.

Nose Peaty, flowery, dry.

Body Light to medium, but silky smooth.

Palate Fresh apple, white chocolate, malt.

Finish Smooth, flowery.

SCORE 78

An earlier ten-year-old at 40 vol from the same bottler had some sherry aging, helping unfold a dark-chocolate richness. It is now to hard find. SCORE 80.

DALLAS DHU 19-year-old (distilled 1978), 43 vol, Master of Malt

Colour Bright greeny-gold.

Nose Peaty. Grassy. Hint of apple. Cream.

Body Lightly creamy.

Palate Very clean. Honeyish. Flowery. Dry.

Finish Honeyish dryness, moving to grass and peat.

SCORE 79

DALLAS DHU 21-year-old (distilled 1975), 61.9 vol, Rare Malts

Colour Old gold.

Nose Orange blossom. Honey. Musk. Heathery. Peat smoke.

Body Smooth, light on the tongue, syrupy.

Palate Orange zest, crème brûlée, burnt sugar.

Finish Slightly chewy, treacle toffee. Late warmth. Long.

SCORE 81

DALLAS DHU 1978, 59.8 vol, Signatory "Silent Stills" series

Colour Full gold.

Nose Much more complex. Smoky, fragrant, flowery. Nutty malt.

Body Medium. Creamy.

Palate Flowery, creamy, white chocolate.

Finish Touch of black chocolate. Toasted nuts. Lightly smoky.

SCORE 79

A 1974, at 59.8 vol, from the same bottler is also gold, but grassier, spicier, smokier, and oakier. SCORE 80.

Other versions of Dallas Dhu

An Oddbins 24-year-old, at 60.6 vol, had a full gold colour, a smoky aroma, a sweet maltiness, and a big, peppery, oaky finish. SCORE 81.
A Connoisseurs Choice 1971, at 40 vol, was complex, with some sappy oakiness and a very long finish. SCORE 85. A Cadenhead 30-year-old, at 53.3 vol, was slightly woody on the nose, full in palate, with concentrated honey flavours and a flowery finish. SCORE 80.

THE DALMORE

PRODUCER JBB
REGION Highlands   DISTRICT Northern Highlands

ADDRESS Alness, Morayshire, IV17 0UT
TEL 01349-882362

T HE "CIGAR MALT", a rich whisky intended to accompany a fine Havana, is a fashion-conscious new product from this old-established distillery. Dalmore was once owned by a distinguished local family, the Mackenzies, friends of James Whyte and Charles Mackay, who created a famous name in blended Scotch.

The Dalmore distillery, said to have been founded in 1839, bears a passing resemblance to a country railway station. Its offices are panelled with carved oak that once graced a shooting lodge. The soft, full-bodied water comes from the River Alness, which flows through forest. The wash stills have an unusually conical upper chamber and the spirit stills are cooled with a water jacket – another distinctive feature. There are two pairs of stills, identical in shape but different sizes. The warehouses are by the waters of the Cromarty Firth. About 85 per cent of the whisky is matured in Bourbon casks, mainly first-fill, the rest in sweet oloroso and amontillado, but it is all married in sherry butts.

HOUSE STYLE Rich, flavourful, orange marmalade. After dinner.

THE DALMORE 12-year-old, 40 vol

Colour An attractive amber hue.

Nose Arousing, with fruit (orange marmalade?), malt, and sherry.

Body Medium to full. Velvet-smooth.

Palate Rich, with gradual restrained flavour development. Malty sweetness, bittersweet orange, spiciness (anise?), perfuminess, heather, light peat; even a faint, salty tang of the sea.

Finish Remarkably long.

SCORE 79

THE DALMORE CIGAR MALT, 43 vol.
A marriage of Dalmore whiskies between ten and 20 years old,
mainly in the mid teens.

Colour Dark orange.

Nose A soft, rounded smokiness. Suggestions of black chocolate
and orange creams.

Body Firm, smooth.

Palate Rich, rounded. A hint of rum butter, then dryish and firm. Hard
caramel toffee. Hint of burnt sugar. Faint smoke. Never cloying. With the
cigar, a complement rather than a contrast.

Finish Light, smoky, wood bark, ground almonds, dryness. Scores points
for originality and for balance.

SCORE 81

THE DALMORE 21-year-old, 43 vol

Colour Pale orange.

Nose Soft, perfumy, fruity.

Body Silky.

Palate A distinctly finessed and elegant interpretation. Very well combined,
complex flavours. Orange, chocolate, flowers, late spices, hint of smoke.

Finish Light touch of citrus. Whiff of smoke.

SCORE 80

THE DALMORE 26-year-old, cask strength, Stillman's Dram

Colour Amber to orange.

Nose Appetizing smoke and orangey sherry.

Body Medium, textured.

Palate At this age, Dalmore emerges as a good, solid, traditional malt. Big flavours, in clean hits: maltiness, pronounced smokiness, and sea notes.

Finish Smoky, oaky, salty.

SCORE 80

From the same series, a 29-year-old had a fractionally darker colour; a remarkably similar character overall; perhaps a slightly woodier finish. SCORE 80. A 30-year-old was quite different in colour, very pale for a Dalmore; quite syrupy and rich in palate; with oak and char in the finish. SCORE 77.

THE BOTTLERS 30-year-old (distilled 1966), 54.1 vol (cask 6869)
An independent bottling for the retailer Whiskies of the World.

Colour Bronze.

Nose Distinct sea character.

Body Soft, slightly syrupy.

Palate Very sweet, orangey, perfumy. Fragrantly smoke dryness for balance.

Finish Lightly nutty.

SCORE 78

THE DALMORE 50-year-old, 52 vol
Occasional bottlings. Some have contained proportions of far older whiskies, dating to 1868. The enjoyment is in the pleasure of tasting history. A whisky of this age has more memory than muscle. (Available at the Sheraton Hotel, Edinburgh.)

Colour Chestnut.

Nose Astonishingly, the fruit is still discernible. Perfumy, polished oak. Quickly moving to surprisingly fresh smokiness and oakiness.

Body Has lost some fullness with age. Thin but silky.

Palate Orange, lemon pith, flowering currant, sap, oak, smoke.

Finish Caramelized charred oak.

SCORE 82

Earlier versions of The Dalmore
An 18-year-old Cullicudden bottling, at 54.8 vol, was pale, syrupy, and heathery, with a salty finish. SCORE 75. A 30-year-old, at 54.5 vol, from Cadenhead, was orangey and rather woody. SCORE 75.

DALWHINNIE

PRODUCER UDV (Diageo)
REGION Highlands DISTRICT Speyside

ADDRESS Dalwhinnie, Inverness-shire, PH19 1AB
TEL 01540-672219 **VC**

THE HIGHEST DISTILLERY IN SCOTLAND, at 326m (1,073ft). Dalwhinnie has the Monadhlaith Mountains to one side, and the Forest of Atholl, the Cairngorms, and the Grampians to the other. Its name is Gaelic for "meeting place". The village of the same name stands at the junction of old cattle-droving routes from the west and north down to the central Lowlands. Much whisky smuggling went on along this route. The distillery was called Strathspey when it opened in 1897. Stretching a point, it can regard itself as being on Speyside, although it is 25 miles or more away to the north. Its whisky has traditionally been an important component of the Buchanan blends, and it represents the Highlands in United Distillers' "Classic Malts" range.

HOUSE STYLE Lightly peaty. Cut grass and heather honey. Clear flavours against a very clean background. Aperitif.

DALWHINNIE 15-year-old, 43 vol

Colour Bright gold.

Nose Very aromatic, dry, faintly phenolic, lightly peaty.

Body Firm, slightly oily.

Palate Remarkably smooth, long-lasting flavour development. Aromatic, heather-honey notes give way to cut-grass, malty sweetness, which intensifies to a sudden burst of peat.

Finish A long crescendo.

SCORE 76

DALWHINNIE 15-year-old, Natural Cask Strength, 56.1 vol, limited edition for the distillery's centenary

Colour Gold.

Nose Slightly grassier, smokier.

Body Firm, textured.

Palate Slightly drier, peatier. Good, firm, oily, malty middle. Then honey (especially when water is added) and vanilla. Beautifully highlights the natural distillery character.

Finish Fresh herbs. Long.

SCORE 77

DALWHINNIE 1980 Double Matured, 43 vol
Oloroso finish.

Colour Sunny gold to bronze.

Nose Oloroso, licorice, rooty, grassy.

Body Firm, rounded.

Palate Very sweet, toffeeish start. Honey. Lemons. Long flavour development to peatiness, cut grass, vanilla, and fresh oak. Beautiful interplay and balance. The sherry sweetness seems, by contrast, to accentuate the usually light peatiness of Dalwhinnie.

Finish Very long. Cut grass, peat, smoke, oak.

SCORE 79

Earlier versions of Dalwhinnie
A 1970, at 40 vol, from Connoisseurs Choice, had emphatic peat but also syrupy maltiness. SCORE 76. A 27-year-old, at 45.5 vol, from Cadenhead, was sweeter and grassier, but still peaty. SCORE 76. A 17-year-old, at 57.8 vol, from the Scotch Malt Whisky Society, was robust in flavours, with both a sweet, syrupy maltiness and rough grassiness towards its long finish. SCORE 76.

DEANSTON

PRODUCER Burn Stewart
REGION Highlands   **DISTRICT** Midlands

ADDRESS Deanston, near Doune, Perthshire, FK16 6AG   **TEL** 01786-841422
WEBSITE www.wallace-malt.co.uk/

THIS DISTILLERY IS IN THE HIGHLANDS, but only by a few miles – it is at Doune, southwest of Perth. The town, known in the 17th century for the manufacture of pistols, later had a cotton mill, designed in 1785 by Richard Arkwright and extended in 1836. The mill was driven by the waters of the River Teith. The supply of good water apparently contributed to the decision to turn the building into a distillery at a time when the whisky industry was doing very well. It opened as the Deanston distillery in 1965–66, with the vaulted weaving shed serving as a warehouse. The distillery prospered during the 1970s, but closed during the difficult mid 1980s. At the time it was owned by Invergordon. With the growth of interest in single malts in the late 1980s and early 1990s, Deanston was bought by the blenders Burn Stewart, and more versions of this pleasant whisky became available.

HOUSE STYLE Light, slightly oily, nutty, accented toward a notably clean, malty sweetness. Restorative.

DEANSTON 12-year-old, 40 vol

Colour	Very pale, greeny-gold. Fino sherry.

Nose	Linseed oil.

Body	Light, smooth, soothing.

Palate Light, very clean. Lightly malty, drying in finish. Also reminiscent of a lightly nutty, dry sherry.

Finish Again, very light, but a touch of nuttiness. In character, less of a Highland malt than a very good Lowlander.

SCORE 70

DEANSTON 16-year-old, 55 vol, Cadenhead

Colour Very pale greenish-gold.

Nose Grassy.

Body Light, firmer.

Palate Sweetish start, toffeeish, nutty, becoming grassy, with bittersweet notes.

Finish Dry, herbal. Flowery. Rhododendrons?

SCORE 71

DEANSTON 17-year-old, 40 vol

Colour Markedly fuller. Bright bronze.

Nose Linseed oil, grass, cereal grain, barley sugar.

Body Light to medium.

Palate Cereal grain, more emphatically nutty. Slightly creamy.

Finish Nutty, appetizing.

SCORE 71

DEANSTON 25-year-old, 40 vol

Colour Bronze.

Nose Cereal grain, nutty.

Body Medium, very smooth.

Palate Cereal grain, nutty, some sweetness.

Finish Touch of creaminess.

SCORE 71

DRUMGUISH

PRODUCER Speyside Distillery Company
REGION Highlands   **DISTRICT** Speyside

ADDRESS Tromie Mills, Glentromie, Kingussie, PH21 1HS   **TEL** 01413-530110
WEBSITE www.speysidedistillery.co.uk **VC** By appointment

ONE OF THE NEWEST DISTILLERIES in Scotland, having made its first spirit in 1991, though the handsome, gabled, stone building intentionally looks a hundred years old. Its opening was the realization of a dream for its owner, George Christie, who had planned it for three or four decades, his progress on the project ebbing and flowing with the fortunes of the industry. One of his earlier essays was a vatted malt, popular in the United States, under the name Glentromie. His distillery is near Kingussie, at Drumguish, where the tiny river Tromie flows into the highest reaches of the Spey. His company takes its name not only from its location but also from a distillery called Speyside that operated in Kingussie between 1895 and 1910.

HOUSE STYLE Oily, nutty, lightly peaty. Aperitif.

DRUMGUISH, no age statement, 40 vol

Colour Full gold.

Nose Flowery. Dry, lightly peaty. Very nutty indeed.

Body Medium, soft. Oily-creamy.

Palate Creamy richness, quickly developing to an oily nut character, and a sweetish dried-grass note that recalls great Scotch whiskies of the past.

Finish Cookies. Toasted marshmallows. Faintly kirsch-like, dry fruitinesss.

SCORE 73

An edition called Speyside Millennium, tasted as a work in progress, was paler, richer, yet nuttier, and fruitier.

DUFFTOWN

PRODUCER UDV (Diageo)
REGION Highlands   **DISTRICT** Speyside (Dufftown)

ADDRESS Dufftown, Keith, Banffshire, AB55 4BR

THE EARL OF FIFE, JAMES DUFF, laid out this handsome, hilly little town of stone buildings in 1817. It lies at the confluence of the Rivers Fiddich and Dullan on their way to the Spey, and is pronounced "Duff-ton". There are seven malt distilleries in the town, of which only one appropriates Dufftown as its name. This distillery and Pittyvaich, its next-door neighbour, were both owned by Bell's until that company was acquired by United Distillers, now UDV. Dufftown's stone-built premises were a meal mill until 1896, but they have since sprouted a pagoda, and were twice expanded in the 1970s. Dufftown's malt is a good, no-nonsense Highland whisky.

HOUSE STYLE Aromatic, dry, malty. Aperitif.

Like many distilleries exaggerating their proximity to the most famous whisky glen, Dufftown has recently dropped the suffix.

DUFFTOWN 8-year-old, 40 vol
A Bell's bottling that is now hard to find.

Colour Full, golden.
Nose Lightly aromatic, with hints of smoke and plenty of malty dryness.
Body Medium, rounded, firm, and dryish.
Palate Seems to promise more than it delivers. Again, suggestions of smoke and a lot of malty dryness.
Finish A lingering viscosity on the tongue, but not a great deal of flavour.

SCORE 70

DUFFTOWN 10-year-old, 40 vol
Another Bell's bottling.

Colour Full, golden.

Nose A little more of everything. Very well-rounded.

Body Much more viscosity.

Palate Quite syrupy.

Finish Lacks flavour development.

SCORE 71

DUFFTOWN 15-year-old, 43 vol, Flora and Fauna

Colour Pale golden.

Nose Assertively aromatic.

Body Lightly syrupy.

Palate Malty, on the dry side, becoming flowery.

Finish Lingers, but very light.

SCORE 71

MURRAY McDAVID

Speyside single malt
Scotch whisky from

DUFFTOWN
DISTILLERY
Distilled in 1979

There is a saying that goes "Rome was
built of seven hills and Dufftown stands on
seven stills". This small highland town
where the rivers Fiddich and Dullan join,
became a major distilling centre during the
late 19th century. The distillery was
founded in 1896 on Kininvie farm mill.
It draws the traditional water from nearby
Jock's Well. The single malt produced is
classic Speyside flavoured with its long
aging in Old Therese casks.

Cask Ref:	
Distilled:	
Bottled:	AUGUST 1997
Cask Type:	REFILL SHERRY WOOD

SELECTED AND BOTTLED IN SCOTLAND BY
Murray McDavid Ltd. Glasgow & London
SW3 1RB

70cl   46% VOL

DUFFTOWN 1979 (bottled 1997, refill sherry), 46 vol, Murray McDavid

Colour Full amber.
Nose Toast. Marmaladey sherry.
Body Medium, firm, oily.
Palate Butter, honey, oranges. Toasty and grainy. Sesame-seed bagels.
Finish Smoky. Slightly burnt and astringent.

SCORE 74

A version distilled and bottled in those years, but with more sherry, at 57.1 vol, from Cadenhead, had an attractive, dark orange colour; a big aroma of oak, toast, orange, and cinnamon; a syrupy body; and a very fruity palate, finishing with dry malt and lots of sappy oak. SCORE 72.

DUFFTOWN 1976, 20-year-old, cask strength, Rare Malts

Colour White wine.
Nose Heather honey. Very honeyish.
Body Medium, firm.
Palate Lively, fruity, perfumy. Flapjacks. Shortbread. Fudge.
Finish Ginger cookies. Sweetish smokiness.

SCORE 73

DUFFTOWN 1975, 21-year-old, cask strength, Rare Malts

Colour Vinho verde.
Nose Honey. Honeydew melon. Glace cherries. Waxy. Lipstick.
Body Creamy, firm.
Palate Remarkably fudgy. Treacle toffee.
Finish Very gingery. Sweet, "leafy bonfires" smokiness.

SCORE 72

EDRADOUR

Producer Campbell Distillers (Pernod Ricard)
Region Highlands   **District** Midlands

address Pitlochry, Perthshire, PH16 5JP
tel 01796-472095 **VC**

THE SMALLEST DISTILLERY IN SCOTLAND, clearly showing its origins as a farm. Edradour likes to trace its history back to the beginning of legal whisky production in the Highlands in 1825, although the present distillery is believed to have been founded in 1837. The distillery, at the hamlet of Balnauld, above the town of Pitlochry, is secreted by the hills. It is reputed to have enjoyed much American custom during Prohibition. One story maintains that it was later indirectly owned for a period by the Mafia.

Its water rises through granite and peat. Edradour uses local barley and its stills are the smallest in Scotland, which must contribute to the distinctive richness of the malt. Stills much smaller would not be permitted by Customs and Excise, for fear that they could be hidden from the law. At one stage, Edradour's whisky was quite evident in a creamy, spicy, vatted malt called Glenforres. In the late 1980s, a ten-year-old Edradour was introduced as a single malt.

House style Minty, creamy. After dinner.

This classically pretty distillery is hidden in a glen. The approaching visitor crests a hill, and suddenly there it is in the hollow below.

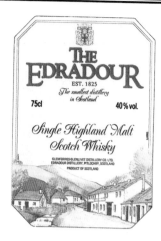

EDRADOUR 10-year-old, 40 vol

Colour Full golden.

Nose Peppermint, sugared almonds, hint of sherry, spicy-smoky notes.

Body Remarkably creamy texture for a relatively light malt.

Palate Minty-clean, creamy, malty.

Finish Mellow, warming.

SCORE 81

EDRADOUR 1976, 54 vol, Signatory Cask Strength Series

Colour Full gold to bronze.

Nose Garden mint, grass, and peat.

Body Decidedly creamy.

Palate Very creamy-tasting. Slightly buttery.

Finish Late, lively, spiciness.

SCORE 81

An earlier Signatory bottling, a 1968, at 46 vol, was nuttier, more flowery, and drier. SCORE 80.

EDRADOUR 1973, 40 vol, Gordon & MacPhail

Colour Bronze.

Nose More sherry character.

Body Light, but smooth and rounded.

Palate More nutty maltiness. Astonishingly creamy.

Finish Warming, enveloping, long.

SCORE 85

FETTERCAIRN

PRODUCER JBB
REGION Highlands   **DISTRICT** Eastern Highlands
ADDRESS Distillery Road, Laurencekirk, Kincardineshire, AB30 1YE
TEL 01561-340244 **VC**

THE VILLAGE OF FETTERCAIRN is near the glen of the North Esk. The distillery, founded in 1824, was rebuilt around the turn of the century, and extended in 1966. Its whisky is an important contributor to the Whyte and Mackay blends.

HOUSE STYLE Lightly earthy, nutty. Easy drinking or aperitif.

OLD FETTERCAIRN 10-year-old, 43 vol

Colour Very full gold.

Nose A hint of sherry. Nutty. Faint peat. Slight burnt note. Wet wool.

Body Light, smooth, silky.

Palate Nutty dryness and a toffeeish (but elusive, light, and clean) sweetness, beautifully balanced. Some tasters have found a hint of rhubarb.

Finish Gentle, with a clean sweetness, becoming perfumy. Lingering.

SCORE 77

OLD FETTERCAIRN 26-year-old, 45 vol, Stillman's Dram

Colour Deep gold.

Nose Very elegant sherry.

Body Light to medium. Very soft.

Palate Clean, juicy sherry almost masks the distillery character.

Finish Sherry. Faint earthiness and peat. Very delicate.

SCORE 78

GLEN ALBYN

PRODUCER DCL
REGION Highlands   **DISTRICT** Speyside (Inverness)

ADDRESS Telford Street, Inverness, Inverness-shire, IV3 5LD

THE CITY OF INVERNESS IS REGARDED as the capital of the Highlands. Despite its being on the western edge of the Speyside region, a distillery there might just squeeze into the appellation. On a former brewery site, Glen Albyn was founded by a Provost (Mayor) of the city in 1844. It had a waterside position on the Caledonian Canal basin. For half a century the distillery was owned by the blenders Mackinlay. DCL were the proprietors at its closure in 1983. It has since been demolished to make way for a supermarket, but new bottlings are still being issued from stock.

HOUSE STYLE Light. Fruity, flowery, dry. Aperitif.

GLEN ALBYN 19-year-old (distilled 1978), Hart Brothers

Colour Bright lemony yellow.

Nose Fragrant. Very light fruit, equally restrained peat, and faint ozone.

Body Light. Firm.

Palate Surprisingly fresh. Very restrained sweet apple.

Finish Flowery, herbal, earthy, peaty.

SCORE 72

Other versions of Glen Albyn

A 1977, at 43 vol, from Signatory, had a white-wine colour; ozone in the nose; a lightly refreshing, flowery palate; and a resiny, oaky finish. SCORE 71. A 1973, at 40 vol, from Connoisseurs Choice, had a balance of nutty sherry. SCORE 74. A 1972, at 40 vol, from Connoisseurs Choice, was very similar. SCORE 74.

GLENALLACHIE

PRODUCER Campbell (Pernod Ricard)
REGION Highlands   DISTRICT Speyside

ADDRESS Aberlour, Banffshire, AB38 9LR

G|LENALLACHIE IS IN THE HEART OF SPEYSIDE, near Aberlour. A dam and a small waterfall soften the exterior of the functional, modern distillery building. It was built in 1967 primarily to contribute malt to the Mackinlay blends.

The distillery was temporarily closed in the late 1980s, then acquired and reopened by Campbell Distillers at the end of the decade. Since then, its whisky has been used in the Glen Campbell blends, fast growing and especially popular in France. Earlier vintages as a single malt are still being issued by independent bottlers. Glenallachie (pronounced "Glen-alec-y") has only a modest reputation, but is a good example of a subtle, delicate, flowery Speysider.

HOUSE STYLE Complex, subtle, delicate. Aperitif.

GLENALLACHIE 12-year-old, 40 vol
A Mackinlay bottling that is now difficult to find. A graceful
pre-dinner companion.

Colour Very pale.

Nose Hint of peat. Fragrant. Lightly malty.

Body Light but firm.

Palate Beautifully clean, smooth, and delicate.

Finish Starts sweet and develops towards a long, perfumy finish.

SCORE 76

Other versions of Glenallachie
A 1985, at 43 vol, from Signatory, has a white-wine colour; a very faint,
fruity aroma; a light body; a pears-and-pepper palate; and a dry, faintly
astringent finish. SCORE 72.

GLENBURGIE

PRODUCER Allied Distillers
REGION Highlands **DISTRICT** Speyside (Findhorn)

ADDRESS Forres, Morayshire, IV36 0QX
TEL 01343-850258

I N THE WATERSHED OF THE FINDHORN, at Alves, between Forres and Elgin. This distillery produces a whisky that contributes to the Ballantine blends. There have been official releases of Glenburgie as a single malt in the distant past, but only independent bottlings can be found today. The Gordon & MacPhail label refers to proprietors J.G. Stodart, an early component of Ballantine's parent Allied.

The distillery traces its history to 1810, and on its present site to 1829. It was extended after World War II, at a time when many malt whiskies were in short supply. At that time, some Allied distilleries were being given additional stills of a different design to extend their range. These "Lomond" stills, with a column-shaped neck, produced an oilier, fruitier malt. The whisky from Glenburgie's Lomond stills was named after Willie Craig, one of the company's senior managers. Those stills were removed in the early 1980s.

HOUSE STYLE Oily, fruity, herbal. Aperitif.

GLENBURGIE 1968, 40 vol, Gordon & MacPhail

Colour Deep gold to amber.

Nose Polished oak. Deep fruitiness. Raisins. Hint of burnt currants.

Body Oily, firm.

Palate Waxy citrus skins. Almonds. Cream. Vanilla. Leafy.

Finish Very herbal, spicy, and cinnamon-like.

SCORE 69

A 1966, at 61.2 vol, from the same bottler, was similar but with a slightly astringent finish. SCORE 69. An earlier 1966, at 57.6 vol, had a balance of citrus and spice. SCORE 70. An eight-year-old, also from Gordon & MacPhail, at 40 vol, was more citrussy. SCORE 69.

GLENBURGIE 1975, 56.6, Signatory

Colour Deep gold.

Nose Spicy.

Body Oily, creamy.

Palate Leafy, herbal, spicy, almondy.

Finish Slightly bitter.

SCORE 68

GLENCRAIG 1970, 40 vol, Connoisseurs Choice

Colour Bright gold.

Nose Dry but powerfully fruity (tropical fruit? Guava perhaps?), especially after a dash of water has been added.

Body Firm, oily.

Palate Some syrupy sweetness, then a pear-brandy dryness.

Finish Very long, dry, and slightly woody.

SCORE 68

GLENCADAM

PRODUCER Allied Distillers
REGION Highlands   **DISTRICT** Eastern Highlands

ADDRESS Brechin, Angus, DD9 7PA
TEL 01356-622217

THE ROMANTICALLY NAMED "CREAM OF THE BARLEY" blend, from Alexander Stewart and Son, an Allied company, leans heavily on this distillery. That seems appropriate, as Glencadam is a notably creamy malt. As a single, it is available only in independent bottlings. The neat little distillery, at Brechin, was founded in 1825 and modernized in 1959. The very soft water is piped an astonishing 30 miles from Loch Lee, at the head of Glen Esk.

HOUSE STYLE Creamy, with a suggestion of berry fruits.
With dessert, or after dinner.

GLENCADAM 1987, 40 vol, Connoisseurs Choice

Colour Full gold.
Nose Fragrant. Very clean. Apple blossom. Berry fruits in a honey glaze.
Body Full, creamy.
Palate Astonishingly cream-like flavour. Strawberry shortcake.
Finish Buttery. Satisfying. Faint orange-peel dryness.

SCORE 69

Other versions of Glencadam

A 1976, at 57 vol, from Signatory, is a yet fuller gold, more flowery, with vanilla and very pronounced strawberry. SCORE 72. A 1974, 40 vol, Connoisseurs Choice was smokier and more buttery (pancake-like?). SCORE 68.

GLEN DEVERON

PRODUCER William Lawson (Bacardi)
REGION Highlands   **DISTRICT** Speyside (Deveron)

ADDRESS Banff, Banffshire, AB45 3JT
TEL 01261-812612

A NOVICE WISHING TO LEARN the true aroma and taste of malt could do worse than spend a few evenings with a 12-year-old Glen Deveron. This is a clean, uncluttered, malty whisky that is very easy to drink and enjoy. It takes its name, and its distilling water, from the river Deveron. The distillery is at the point where the glen of the Deveron reaches the sea, at the old fishing town and former spa of Macduff. On the other side of the river is the town of Banff. At a stretch, this is the western fringe of Speyside. The distillery was built in 1962 and extended in 1966 and 1968. Its malt whisky is an important component of the William Lawson blends. This company, through the international Martini and Rossi group, is now part of Bacardi. The whisky appears under the name Macduff in some independent bottlings.

HOUSE STYLE Malty. Sweet limes in older versions. Restorative or after dinner.

GLEN DEVERON 12-year-old, 40 vol

Colour Gold.
Nose Faint hints of sherry. Rich, sweet, fresh maltiness.
Body Light to medium, but notably smooth.
Palate Full, very clean, delicious maltiness.
Finish Malty dryness. Quick but pleasantly warming.

SCORE 75

Macduff bottlings

MACDUFF 1987, 40 vol, Connoisseurs Choice

Colour Bright gold.

Nose Malty. Toffee. Faint lemon grass.

Body Syrupy.

Palate Malty. Marshmallows. Lemon jam.

Finish Lemon-zest dryness. Slight junipery bitterness. Hints at what is to come in the Cadenhead version below.

SCORE 74

MACDUFF 1978, 57.8 vol, Cadenhead

Colour Bright greeny gold.

Nose Sweet lime juice.

Body Syrupy.

Palate Sweet lime juice. Oily. Remarkably aromatic, perfumy, juniper-like flavours. Gin and lime? Very unusual, but enjoyable.

Finish Refreshing.

SCORE 74

Vintage 1978
Single Highland Malt Scotch Whisky
Matured in sherry casks for 17 years
Distilled at Macduff Distillery
on 25.8.78 *Bottled 5.96*
Butt no. 4459 *Bottle no.* *of 576*
This whisky has been selected, produced and bottled in Scotland for and under the sole responsibility of Signatory Vintage Scotch Whisky Co. Ltd.
70cl *Edinburgh EH6 8PY Scotland* 58.8%vol

MACDUFF 1978, 58.8 vol, Signatory

Colour Pale oak.

Nose Dry malt.

Body Dense, dryish, syrup.

Palate Maple syrup. Lemon juice.

Finish Lemon zest.

SCORE 73

GLENDRONACH

Producer Allied Distillers
Region Highlands **District** Speyside (Deveron)

address Forgue, by Huntly, Aberdeenshire, AB5 6DB
tel 01466-730202 **VC**

T HE ODD BAR OR STORE still offers the interesting comparison between two 12-year-old Glendronachs. The "Original" was matured in second-fill casks, the majority having once held Bourbon, the minority sherry. The additional version was clearly identified on the label as being wholly aged in sherry wood. Neither has been bottled for some time, having been replaced by The Glendronach Traditional, which is intended to marry the virtues of each. A recent addition is the 15-year-old wholly aged in sherry casks. Where sherry is employed, its use has been very assertive, and this has offended more than one critic. The sherry is toffeeish and caramelly, but fresh and juicy – not woody and astringent. The distillery, founded in 1826, is in barley-growing country on the eastern fringes of the Speyside region, at Forgue, near Huntly. Glendronach still has its own floor maltings, and coal-fired stills. Its whisky is also a component in the malty Teacher's blends. The distillery is not currently working, but is maintained to an operational standard.

House style Smooth, big, with a teasing sweet-and-dry maltiness. Sherry-friendly. After dinner.

The Glendronach distillery is set in rich, Aberdeenshire farming country.

GLENDRONACH Traditional, 12-year-old, 40 vol

Colour Bright, full amber. Very attractive.

Nose Sweetish sherry notes, lots of malt, some heather.

Body Medium to full. Very smooth, slight chewiness.

Palate Light but definite sherry, a touch of oak, malt, heather, and faint peat. Very well balanced.

Finish Long. Spicy. Dry maltiness.

SCORE 77

GLENDRONACH Original, 12-year-old, 43 vol

Colour Gold.

Nose Dry, with a hint of sherry and lots of maltiness.

Body Medium to full. Very smooth and slightly syrupy.

Palate Well balanced by heathery dryness.

Finish Big development of flavour, with clean, fruity, perfumy notes.

SCORE 75

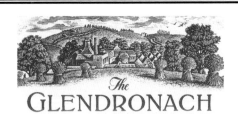

GLENDRONACH Matured in sherry casks, 12-year-old, 40 vol

Colour Full amber.	

Nose Intense sherry (sweet oloroso?).

Body Very rich and luscious.

Palate A good balance of sherry character and maltiness. Some caramel-like sweetness, although by no means overpowering.

Finish Very long, with some dryness.

SCORE 77

GLENDRONACH 15-year-old, 100% sherry casks

Colour Full amber.

Nose Sweet, raisiny, sherry, balanced by polished oak and sweetish, fragrant, peat smoke.

Body Rich and smooth.

Palate Oaky. Dry maltiness. Crunchy toffee. Buttery.

Finish Licorice-toffee, sherry notes.

SCORE 79

GLENDRONACH 18-year-old, 43 vol
(There has also been a peatier limited edition at 19 years old)

Colour A bright, extremely deep amber.

Nose Very heavily sherried. Burnt-toffee dryness. Hint of smoke.

Body Smooth, slightly drying.

Palate Starts with burnt-toffee dryness, moves to malty sweetness, then to sherry.

Finish Long, smooth, warming, with some toffeeish dryness.

SCORE 78

GLENDRONACH 1975, 57.7 vol, Signatory

Colour Bright, full gold.

Nose Dry and grassy, then creamy and malty.

Body Creamy but firm.

Palate Creamy, buttery.

Finish Leafy, peaty, long, warming.

SCORE 76

GLENDULLAN

PRODUCER UDV (Diageo)
REGION Highland   **DISTRICT** Speyside (Dufftown)

ADDRESS Dufftown, Banffshire, AB55 4DJ

A ROBUST BOTTLING FOR THE DISTILLERY'S ANNIVERSARY, a Flora and Fauna edition, and no fewer than four Rare Malts versions have brought some overdue attention to Glendullan. This distillery, established in 1897–8, has had its moments of glory, notably the supply of its whisky in the early 1900s to King Edward VII, an honour that was for some years proclaimed on its casks. In 1919, it became part of Macdonald and Greenlees, later subsumed into DCL and UDV. Its whisky is an important contributor to the Old Parr blends, especially popular in Japan. A new stillhouse was added in 1972, and run in parallel with the old one until 1985, during which period much of the output from the two was probably vatted. The older distillations seem firmer and more austere; the more recent lighter but more herbal and fruity. The name derives from the river Dullan; no marketing executive would have devised anything so unjustly close to "dull one" or such a quaint label as the one below.

HOUSE STYLE Perfumy, fruity, dry, chilli-like, oily, big.
Put it in a hip flask.

GLENDULLAN 12-year-old, 43 vol
Macdonald and Greenlees bottling. Now hard to find.

Colour Amber.

Nose Some sherry, malty, lightly perfumy and fruity.

Body Medium to full. Smooth, firm, and silky.

Palate Powerful, dry and malty, with perfumy, fruity notes developing.

Finish Firm, long, peppery, warming.

SCORE 75

GLENDULLAN 12-year-old, 43 vol, Flora and Fauna

Colour Almost white, with just a tinge of gold.

Nose Light, dry maltiness. Hint of fruit.

Body A hard edge, then silky.

Palate Dry start, becoming buttery, malty, nutty, perfumy, and lightly fruity.

Finish Extraordinarily perfumy and long.

SCORE 75

GLENDULLAN 16-year-old (bottled 1998), 62.6 vol, Centenary Bottling

Colour Deep gold to amber.

Nose Perfumy. Floral. Polished oak.

Body Rich, creamy, clinging.

Palate First, a long taste of clotted cream, then a fat, nutty dryness.

Finish Long. Dusty. Lemon grass. Chilli.

SCORE 78

GLENDULLAN 1981 (bottled 1997), 60.4 vol, Scott's

Colour Full primrose.

Nose Dry maltiness. Lemon grass. Floral. Polish. Leather.

Body Soft, smooth, on the light side.

Palate Buttery, creamy, maltiness, moving to fruity hint of chilli.

Finish Light, late, lemon-grass fruitiness and a crisp
punch of pepper.

SCORE 75

Rare Malts versions of Glendullan

22-year-old (distilled 1972, bottled 1995), 62.6 vol: Full gold; fragrant but
restrained in aroma; firm, dry, austere, and steely at first, becoming leafy
and sweeter; finishing sweet, heathery, and big. SCORE 77.

23-year-old (distilled 1972, bottled 1996), 62.43 vol: Yellowish; heathery
floweriness and malty sweetness in aroma; chewy maltiness in a clean,
rounded, satisfying, soothing palate; big, sweet, and heathery in the
finish. SCORE 78.

23-year-old (distilled 1973, bottled 1997), 58.8 vol: Bright golden yellow; big
bouquet of dried flowers and pressed heather; oaty creaminess in the
palate; dryish heather, honey, and peaches in the finish. SCORE 78.

23-year-old (distilled 1974, bottled 1998), 63.1 vol: Amber-red tinge; very
flowery and pot-pourri-like aroma; peanut brittle, toffee, and malt in the
palate; heather, garden mint, and tea in the finish. SCORE 77.

Earlier bottlings
A 22-year-old, at 46 vol, from Cadenhead, had a dry aroma; sweetness
and perfume in the palate; and a perfumy, warming finish. SCORE 74.

GLEN ELGIN

PRODUCER UDV (Diageo)
REGION Highlands **DISTRICT** Speyside (Lossie)

ADDRESS Longmorn, Morayshire, IV30 8SS
TEL 01343-547891

WHERE THE RIVER LOSSIE approaches the town of Elgin, there are no fewer than eight distilleries within a few miles. Glen Elgin is not the nearest to the town, but it is close enough. There are some excellent whiskies in this stretch of country, and the sweetish Glen Elgin is one of them. The distillery was founded in 1898–1900, and rebuilt and extended in 1964. The malt is an important component of the White Horse blended whisky. "White Horse Distillers" appears in small type as a corporate name on bottlings of Glen Elgin. A version at around 12 years old, but with no age statement, has been sold mainly in Japan. It is to be hoped that the distillery is more active in the single malts market in the future. Elgin is also worth a visit for Gordon & MacPhail's whisky shop – and 13th-century cathedral ruins.

HOUSE STYLE Honey and tangerines. Restorative or after dinner.

GLEN ELGIN, no age statement, 43 vol

Colour	Medium gold.
Nose Heather honey.	
Body Light to medium.	

Palate Dryish flowery start; becoming sweet, honeyish, clean, and malty; developing a dash of tangerine-like fruitiness.

Finish Smooth, becoming drier again, with late notes of smoke and sherry.

SCORE 76

Other versions of Glen Elgin

A 1978, at 50.4 vol, from Signatory, has a pale primrose colour; a lemony, flowery aroma; a smooth body; a delicious, clean, and honeyish palate, sweetish at first, with a late, very light smokiness in the finish. SCORE 78.
A 1970, at 43 vol, from Hart Brothers, has a fuller gold colour; a similarly flowery aroma; a bigger, firmer body, but a lighter honey palate; and a spicier dry finish. SCORE 78. A Cadenhead 22-year-old, at 50.1 vol, had a greeny-gold colour; a powerful heather-honey aroma; a smooth body; a sweet, honeyish palate; and a drier, fruity finish. SCORE 76.

GLENESK

PRODUCER UDV (Diageo)
REGION Highlands DISTRICT Eastern Highlands

ADDRESS Kinnaber Road, Hillside, Montrose, Angus, DD10 9EP

AT THE MOUTH OF THE SOUTH ESK RIVER, at Montrose. Over the years, a confusion of names have been used for this establishment, employing various prefixes to the word Esk. At times it has also been known as Hillside. It began as a flax mill, converted in 1897 by a wine merchant to be become a malt distillery. At one later stage it made only grain whisky. Its career was intermittent, even by the standards of a cyclical industry. From the mid 1960s to the mid 1980s, it was again a significant malt distillery, contributing to the famous blend VAT 69, made by William Sanderson, part of DCL and later United Distilleries. William Sanderson bottlings of Glenesk Single Malt at 12 years old can still occasionally be found. In recent years, there have been several bottlings under the Hillside name in the Rare Malts series. The distillery closed in 1985. Its relatively modern maltings, on an adjacent site, still operates. That is now owned by the firm of Paul's, the independent maltsters.

HOUSE STYLE Fresh, clean, dry. Aperitif.

GLENESK 12-year-old, 40 vol

Colour Full gold.

Nose Dry maltiness. Aromatic. Some restrained, balancing sweetness.

Body Light to medium, soft, smooth.

Palate Soft and pleasant. Dry maltiness, with some balancing notes of restrained sweetness.

Finish An aromatic, dry maltiness throughout makes for an unusual, clean, and fresh malt.

SCORE 66

HILLSIDE, 25-year-old (distilled 1969), 61.9 vol, Rare Malts

Colour Bright, pale greeny-gold.

Nose Vanilla.

Body Light, firm.

Palate Sweetish start. Then dry maltiness. Dried apricot and dried banana.

Finish Slightly resiny, herbal, and salty. Crisp. Fresh.

SCORE 69

Earlier Rare Malts as Hillside

A 1970 25-year-old had more obvious notes. SCORE 68. A 1971 at the same age veered towards apricot and pear. SCORE 68. A 1973 was more toffeeish. SCORE 69. The whisky develops fruity complexity and maltiness with age, but has not been helped by a pulpy, matchwood note – presumably from tired casks.

Glenesk 1984, 40 vol, Connoisseurs Choice

Colour Full gold.

Nose Cedary, resiny.

Body Light to medium. Soft, smooth.

Palate Sweet start, moving to dried bananas.

Finish Creamy, spicy.

SCORE 67

GLENFARCLAS

Producer J. and G. Grant
Region Highlands **District** Speyside

address Ballindalloch, Banffshire, AB37 9BD **tel** 01807-500257 **VC**
website www.glenfarclas.co.uk **e-mail** J&BGrant@glenfarclas.demon.co.uk

AMONG THE HANDFUL OF truly stand-alone distilleries in Scotland, Glenfarclas is the most assertive of its independence, by far the longest-established, and the best-known to connoisseurs. Its whiskies are in the top flight among Speysiders, though they do not enjoy the wider popular reputation of some similar examples from this region.

From the river Spey, it is about a mile to Glenfarclas ("Valley of the Green Grass"). The distillery is near the village of Marypark. Behind it, heather-covered hills rise towards Ben Rinnes, from which the distillery's water flows. Barley is grown in the surrounding area. The distillery belongs to a private, family-owned company, J. and G. Grant. The family is not connected (except perhaps distantly) to any of the other whisky-making Grants, and does not own any other distilleries or bottlers. Glenfarclas traces its history to 1836, and has been in the family since 1865. Although some of the buildings date from that period, and the reception room has panelling from an ocean liner, the equipment is modern, and its stills are the biggest in Speyside.

House style Big, complex, malty, sherryish. After dinner.

GLENFARCLAS 105, no age statement, 60 vol
Known as 105º, and is eight to ten years old. A very youthful version for such a big malt, but it wins points for firm-muscled individuality.

Colour Full gold to bronze.
Nose Robust: butterscotch and raisins.
Body Full, heavy.
Palate Very sweet, rich nectar, with some honeyish dryness.
Finish Long, and warmed by the high proof. Rounded.

Score 88

GLENFARCLAS 10-year-old, 40 vol
Elegant and quite dry for a Glenfarclas.

Colour Full gold.

Nose Big, with some sherry sweetness and nuttiness, but also smokiness at the back of the nose.

Body Characteristically firm.

Palate Crisp and dry at first, with the flavour filling out as it develops.

Finish Sweet and long.

SCORE 86

"Eagle of Spey" is a less sherried, lighter-bodied, slightly fruitier, drier, smokier counterpart in some export markets. SCORE 79.

GLENFARCLAS 12-year-old, 43 vol
For many devotees, the most familiar face of Glenfarclas.

Colour Bronze.

Nose Drier, with a quick, big attack.

Body Firm, slightly oily.

Palate Plenty of flavour, with notes of peat smoke.

Finish Long, with oaky notes, even at this relatively young age.

SCORE 87

"Meadhan" is a much less sherried, light-tasting, slightly peaty counterpart in some markets. SCORE 78.

GLENFARCLAS 15-year-old, 46 vol

Many enthusiasts feel that this age most deftly demonstrates the complexity of this malt. Certainly the best-balanced Glenfarclas.

Colour Amber.

Nose Plenty of sherry, oak, maltiness, and a hint of smokiness – all the elements of a lovely, mixed bouquet.

Body Firm, rounded.

Palate Assertive, again with all the elements beautifully melded.

Finish Long and smooth.

SCORE 88

GLENFARCLAS 17-year-old, 43 vol

Mainly available in the Far East.

Colour Full amber.

Nose Fuller sherry. Light, fragrant smokiness. Clean oak.

Body Firm, rounded.

Palate Firm at first, then a surge of buttery notes in the middle, moving to fruity dryness.

Finish Touch of almonds and bitter chocolate.

SCORE 88

GLENFARCLAS 21-year-old, 43 vol

Colour Amber.

Nose More sherry. Butter. Sultana-like fruitiness. Sweet lemon juice on a pancake. Greater smokiness, as well as a dash of oak. All slowly emerges as distinct notes.

Body Big, firm.

Palate Immense flavour development. Raisiny, spicy, gingery.

Finish Remarkably long, with lots of sherry, becoming sweetish and perfumy.

SCORE 89

GLENFARCLAS 25-year-old, 43 vol

More of everything. Perhaps a touch woody for purists, but a remorselessly serious after-dinner malt for others.

Colour Dark amber.

Nose Pungent, sappy.

Body Big, with some dryness of texture.

Palate The flavours are so tightly interlocked at first that the whisky appears reluctant to give up its secrets. Very slow, insistent flavour development. All the components gradually emerge, but in a drier mood.

Finish Long, oaky, sappy. Extra points out of respect for idiosyncratic age.

SCORE 88

GLENFARCLAS 30-year-old, 43 vol

Colour Refractive, bright amber.

Nose Oaky, slightly woody.

Body Very firm.

Palate Nutty and oaky.

Finish Oaky, sappy, peaty.

SCORE 87

GLENFARCLAS 40-year-old, 54.7 vol (Millennium Edition)

Colour Deep amber, with a yellowy suggestion of a gibbous moon.

Nose Oaky.

Body Medium to full. Very firm.

Palate Oaky start, with nutty maltiness and raisiny sweetness fighting through. Tightly locked flavours open with a dash of water.

Finish Peat. Log fires. Oak.

SCORE 87

Some vintage bottlings of Glenfarclas

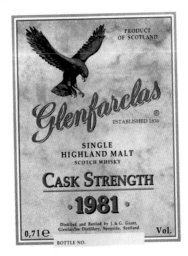

1981, Cask Strength, 53.4 vol

Lovely, warm, amber colour; appetizingly nutty aroma; and smooth richness of sherry, fruit, and malt, with a clingy, lightly peat-tinged finish.
Score 89.

1979 (bottled February, 1998), 43 vol

Pale amber; nutty, perfumy aroma; soft, sweet, complex palate; sherry and butter in the finish. Score 88.

1979, Cask Strength, 57.1 vol

Warm amber; clean, nutty aroma; smooth, rich; delicious licorice flavours; very long, big, spicy, dry, warming finish. Score 89.

June 1978 (bottled August, 1998), 43 vol

Pale amber; aroma of polished leather; lovely interplay of dry and sweet; maltiness; faint grassy peat in finish. Score 88.

1978 "Maria Stuart" edition, 45.5 vol
Full, walnut colour; appetizing oak, and some peat in the aroma;
superb interplay of oak, sherry, maltiness, and peatiness. The dryness
seems to win, then a late, fruity sweetness prolongs the struggle. A very
complex whisky for lovers of older ages. SCORE 90.

September 1973 (bottled August, 1998), 43 vol
Old gold; peaty aroma; oily, buttery; smooth; late sweetness; some vanilla;
firm, warm finish. SCORE 87.

1966 (bottled 1997), 46 vol
Bronze; fragrant, sweetish aroma; peaty, spicy palate; very warm,
spicy finish, with some sweetness. SCORE 89.

Independent bottlings of Glenfarclas
Glenfarclas does not encourage independent bottlers, but some have
managed to locate supplies. Cadenhead in 1993 released a 13-year-old
(distilled in 1980), 59.6 vol, smoothly oily, with a robust, tasty interplay of
peat, malt, and spiciness. SCORE 86. The same bottler in 1997 issued a
17-year-old, 58.5 vol, from the same year. This is very complex, beautifully
balanced, and spicy. SCORE 87. In the same year, Cadenhead bottled a
25-year-old, 53.4 vol, distilled in 1972. It is drier, peatier, and oakier, but
again with the characteristic sweet finish. SCORE 87. None is overtly sherried,
so they offer a truly different expression of this flavoursome malt.

GLENFIDDICH

PRODUCER William Grant and Sons
REGION Highlands **DISTRICT** Speyside (Dufftown)

ADDRESS Dufftown, Banffshire, AB55 4DH
WEBSITE www.glenfiddich.com **TEL** 01340-820000 **VC**

THE GLEN OF THE RIVER FIDDICH gives its name to the biggest-selling single malt whisky in the world. The Glenfiddich distillery lies on the small river whose name it bears, in Dufftown. The name Fiddich indicates that the river runs through the valley of the deer. Hence the company's emblem, a stag.

This justifiably famous distillery was founded in 1886–87, and is still owned by the original family as a limited company. As a relatively small enterprise, it faced intense competition from bigger companies during the economic boom after the Second World War. Rather than relying on supplying whisky to blenders owned by the giants, it decided in 1963 to widen the availablity of its whisky as a bottled single malt. An industry dominated at the time by blended Scotches regarded this as foolishness. The widely held view was that single malts were too intense, flavoursome, or complex for the English and other foreigners.

The vision and persistence of the company was in more than one sense single-minded. It was an example and precedent, without which few of its rivals would have been emboldened to offer themselves as bottled single malts. Devotees of the genre owe a debt of gratitude to Glenfiddich.

The early start laid the foundations for the success of Glenfiddich. Its fortunes were no doubt further assisted by its being, among malts, one of the less challenging to the palate. Glenfiddich in its usual form (no age statement, but said to be eight years old) is very easily drinkable: a light, smooth malt with a hint of fruitiness. It used to be labelled "Special Old Reserve" (the latter word is a favourite of Glenfiddich's), but the suggestion of great antiquity has been dropped in recent years.

Devotees of malts who are ready for a greater challenge will find much more complexity in the longer-matured versions, including a recent innovation: a Glenfiddich that is aged for 15 years then vatted in a solera system. In 1991, nine casks of a 50-year-old were bottled. These were sold in London at around US $5,000 each, but one fetched US $70,000 in an auction in Milan. For its age, the whisky was surprisingly rounded and chocolatey, without excessive oakiness.

A much newer product is Glenfiddich Malt Whisky Liqueur. The malt whisky is used as the basis for a sweetened, flavoured drink, with notes of brown sugar, honey, and lemons.

The Glenfiddich distillery is full of character. Much of the original structure, in honey-and-grey stone, remains beautifully maintained, and the style has been followed in considerable new construction.

Glenfiddich also led the way in the industry by being the first to have a visitor centre. Some may be argue that this is for tourists rather than purists, but no visitor to this part of the Highlands should miss it.

A truly traditional element is the use of coal-fired stills. The stills are small, and the whisky is principally aged in plain oak, although about ten per cent goes into sherry casks. Whisky aged in different woods is married in plain oak. Glenfiddich likes to describe its malt as "Château-bottled". The distillery is unusual in that it has its own bottling line on the premises. The only other malt distillery with bottling facilities on site is Springbank (see entry).

Adjoining the Glenfiddich site, William Grant also owns The Balvenie (established 1892) and newish (1990) Kininvie malt distilleries. Kininvie is little more than a basic stillhouse. Its rich, creamy malt goes into the Grant's blends, but has not been bottled as a single. Elsewhere in Scotland, it has the Girvan grain distillery (see Ladyburn).

HOUSE STYLE When young, a dry, fruity aperitif; when more mature, a raisiny, chocolatey after-dinner malt.

The handsome, steeply pitched roofs and traditional pagoda shape of distillery maltings at the Glenfiddich distillery.

GLENFIDDICH Special Reserve, no age statement, 40 vol

Colour Very pale, white wine.

Nose Light, fresh but sweet, appetizing, fruity, pear-like.

Body Light, lean, firm, smooth.

Palate Dryish, pear-like, more fruitiness as flavour develops. A dash of water releases a hint of smokiness and some sweet, malty notes.

Finish Restrained, aromatic.

> SCORE 75

GLENFIDDICH Classic, no age statement, 43 vol
This version is no longer bottled, but may still be found.

Colour Pale gold.

Nose Softer. Dry maltiness, pear-skins, slight sherry, and faint smokiness.

Body Firm, smooth.

Palate Smooth. Dry maltiness balanced by restrained sweetness, with slight smokiness. Flavours tightly combined.

Finish Smooth, dry.

> SCORE 76

GLENFIDDICH 15-year-old Cask Strength, 51 vol
Especially available in duty-free.

Colour Full gold.

Nose Soft, light, peat smoke.

Body Smooth, lightly creamy.

Palate Smooth. Hazelnut. Light cream. Dry maltiness.

Finish Tasty, appetizing. Grassy notes and peat smoke.

> SCORE 80

GLENFIDDICH 15-year-old Solera Reserve, 40 vol

Colour Bright gold.

Nose Chocolate. Toast. Hint of peat.

Body Light but very smooth indeed.

Palate Suave. Silky. White chocolate. Pears in cream. Cardamom.

Finish Cream. Hint of ginger.

SCORE 78

GLENFIDDICH Excellence 18-year-old, 43 vol

This version is becoming harder to find with the success of the Ancient Reserve (see below).

Colour Gold.

Nose Fragrant, flowery.

Body Very smooth and well rounded.

Palate Mellow, developing sweeter, spicier notes.

Finish Dryish, lengthening to spicy, herbal (gentian?), peaty firmness.

SCORE 79

GLENFIDDICH Ancient Reserve, 18-year-old, 40 vol

A proportion of the whisky in this version is older than the age on the label, with a slight accent toward first-fill sherry (butts, rather than hogsheads, and made from Spanish oak rather than American), and earth-floored, traditional warehouses.

Colour Old gold.

Nose Richer.

Body Softer.

Palate More mellow and rounded, soft and restrained. Scores points for sophistication and sherry character.

Finish Nutty. A flowery hint of peat.

SCORE 78

A 43 vol version with the same name, in a ceramic decanter, seems smoother and maltier. Perhaps more vanilla from American oak? SCORE 77. This interpretation is hard to find.

GLENFIDDICH Superior Reserve, 18-year-old, 43 vol
This version, in a gilded decanter, seems to be the most sherryish version.

Colour Full gold.

Nose Very soft. A good dash of sherry, and some ginger spiciness.

Body Medium, smooth.

Palate Silky, chocolatey.

Finish Soft spiciness.

SCORE 79

GLENFIDDICH 21-year-old, 43 vol
This version, in a Wedgwood decanter, is no longer bottled, but may still be found.

Colour Full gold, fractionally darker.

Nose Hint of sherry?

Body Surprisingly full.

Palate Complex, with both sweetness and dryness. Bitter-chocolate and dried fruit, slightly burnt. Eventually the dry notes are more assertive, with a hint of peat.

Finish Still gentle, but longer.

SCORE 81

GLENFIDDICH 30-year-old, 43 vol
This version, in a crystal decanter, is no longer bottled, but may still be found.

Colour Full gold, fractionally darker still.

Nose Notes of sherry, fruit, chocolate, and ginger.

Body Soft, full, some viscosity.

Palate More sherry, raisins, chocolate, ginger. Luxurious.

Finish Unhurried, with chocolatey notes and gingery dryness.

SCORE 86

Independent bottlings of Glenfiddich
Like many distillers, Glenfiddich discourages independent bottlers. Its interesting policy is to add a tiny token amount of The Balvenie to any Glenfiddich sold in cask and presumed to be destined for blending. This therefore cannot be sold as Glenfiddich. It is some years since an independent bottling of Glenfiddich was sighted. A 30-year-old issued in the mid 1990s by Cadenhead was a little woody, rooty, and almondy, but had plenty of character and some sherry. SCORE 77.

GLEN FLAGLER

PRODUCER Inver House
REGION Central Lowlands **DISTRICT** Central Lowlands

ADDRESS Towers Road, Moffat, Airdrie, Lanarkshire, ML6 8PL
WEBSITE www.inverhouse.com **E-MAIL** enquiries@inverhouse.com

Silent Stills

SINGLE
LOWLAND MALT
SCOTCH
WHISKY

24 YEARS OLD
Distilled at
GLEN FLAGLER DISTILLERY
Distilled 10.11.72 Bottled 15.5.97
Cask No. 228444 Bottle No. of 230
70cl   52%vol

Bottled in Scotland by
Signatory Vintage Scotch Whisky Co. Ltd. Edinburgh EH6 5PY

A FLEETING PRESENCE THAT REAPPEARS from time to time like a ghostly spirit. Two malt whiskies were produced, under the names Glen Flagler and Killyloch, in different sets of stills, and a grain whisky called Garnheath in a third, at a complex at Moffat, near Airdrie, from 1965. These were some of the shortest-lived distilleries in the history of Scotch whisky. The modern complex, in former paper mills, was intended to support the Inver House blend, then owned by Publicker, of Philadelphia, but was hit by one of the industry's cyclical downturns. Killyloch ceased production in the early 1970s, Glen Flagler and Garnheath in the mid 1980s, and the distilleries were dismantled. A management buy out created a new company, under the name Inver House, based on the same site. The company has since been acquiring malt distilleries elsewhere and has several blends, including Catto's and Hanker Bannister.

Glen Flagler was briefly the brand name of a single malt from the distillery. Both it and Killyloch later manifested themselves as vatted malts. In the 1990s, when they seemed to have been lost forever, the independent bottler Signatory located very small stocks of both singles, and issued them. From a short-lived, industrial-style distillery, the two, especially Glen Flagler, are surprisingly interesting malts. Both are enjoyable – though their greater interest is to collectors.

HOUSE STYLE Glen Flagler a spicy, perfumy restorative or aperitif. Killyloch grainier and sweeter, with dessert. Both have Lowland characters, though these are more obvious in Killyloch.

GLEN FLAGLER 24-year-old (distilled 1972, bottled 1997), 52 vol

Colour Bright yellow.

Nose Grassy. Linseed. Young leather.

Body Medium, firm. Soapy dryness.

Palate Lemony, oily, peaty.

Finish Dry. Late, warming, pepperiness.

SCORE 70

GLEN FLAGLER 1970 (bottled 1995), 52 vol, Signatory
This rare sample was past its best.

Colour Full amber.

Nose Peaty, scenty (violets?), very dry.

Body Thick.

Palate Lemony, grassy, dusty.

Finish Woody, dusty. Enjoyable, peppery warmth.

SCORE 63

KILLYLOCH 1972, 22-year-old, 52.6 vol

Colour Warm bronze.

Nose Vanilla. Cornflour pudding.

Body Light to medium, lapping on the tongue.

Palate Sweet. Nutty. Sliced almonds.

Finish Lemon curd. Lemon rind. Lemon zest.

SCORE 69

GLEN GARIOCH

PRODUCER Morrison Bowmore (Suntory)
REGION Highlands **DISTRICT** Eastern Highlands

ADDRESS Old Meldrum, Inverurie, Aberdeenshire, AB51 0ES **TEL** 01651-873450
WEBSITE www.morrisonbowmore.co.uk

THE RENEWAL OF ANY VINTAGE DISTILLERY is good news, but Glengarioch (one word for the premises; two for the whisky) has a special place for lovers of smoky Highlanders. The distillery, which traces its history to 1797, has its own floor maltings. Down one side of the maltings and distillery, a farm lane enters the Garioch Valley, rich in malting barley. The building's stonework, decorated with a clock that might grace a municipal building, faces on to the small town of Old Meldrum, on the road from Aberdeen to Banff.

In the days when the whisky was made primarily as a contributor to VAT 69, a peaty malt was not used, but that changed in 1970, when the distillery was acquired by its present owners. Their maltster, trained on Islay, was relatively heavy-handed with the peat. The result was a whisky with the "old-fashioned", smoky flavour that the Highland/Speyside region had largely forgotten. In 1995, quirky little Glengarioch temporarily lost the battle for attention with the higher-profile distilleries in the same company, and ceased production. Two years later, more enlightened sensibilities prevailed. The distillery (pronounced Glengeery) was refurbished and reopened, with a similar treatment planned for the maltings. Will the malt, and whisky, be as peaty in future? That currently being made for blending is more conventional in style. One good suggestion is that a well-peated edition will be made at least once a year.

HOUSE STYLE Lightly peaty, flowery, fragrant, spicy. Aperitif in younger ages. Digestif when older.

Most parts of the buildings date from the late 1800s. Veteran workers remember horse-drawn wagons bringing coal and taking away whisky.

GLEN GARIOCH 8-year-old, 40 vol

Colour Full gold.

Nose Autumn leaves, grass, hint of peat.

Body Medium, smooth.

Palate Malty start, buttery, but very clean. Then flapjack, nutty, lively flavours.

Finish Late surge of ginger, honey, and heather.

SCORE 76

An earlier ten-year-old, richer and slightly smokier, is no longer available. SCORE 77. Likewise a more flowery 1984. SCORE 76.

GLEN GARIOCH 12 year-old, 40 vol
This version is now hard to find.

Colour Bronze.

Nose Fragrant, leafy peatiness. Touch of dry oloroso?

Body Medium, firm.

Palate Interlocked heather-honey sweetness and peat-smoky dryness.

Finish Echoes of both elements. Quick and warming.

SCORE 77

GLEN GARIOCH 15-year-old, 43 vol

Colour Full gold.

Nose Good whiff of earthy peat, oily smoke. Very aromatic.

Body Medium, rich.

Palate Very gradual development from malty, licorice-like, rooty notes through heathery, flowery, perfumy smokiness. Full of character.

Finish Very long, spicy, warming.

SCORE 79

GLEN GARIOCH 21-year-old, 43 vol
The most recent bottlings have more peat, oak, and sherry than earlier versions at this age. A superb Highland malt.

Colour Burnished amber.

Nose Leathery, leafy, peaty, smoky, phenolic.

Body Medium to full.

Palate Sweet, juicy oak. Butter. Nutty, treacly, gingery cake.

Finish Big and very smoky, but smooth. Lots of lingering toffee and fruit. Currants. Flowering currant.

SCORE 81

GLEN GARIOCH 18-year-old, Selected Cask Vatting, 59.4 vol

Colour Deep, warm gold.

Nose Fresh, floral, fragrant, gentle. Peat-tinged.

Body Surprisingly rich.

Palate Rich, sweet, clean, syrupy maltiness.

Finish Very long. Treacle toffee. Gingery spiciness. Rooty dryness. Very warming. Extremely late echo of phenolic peat.

SCORE 80

GLEN GARIOCH 27-year-old, Selected Cask Vatting, 49.6 vol
This bottling is now hard to find.

Colour Bright amber.

Nose Softly peaty, still with a hint of phenol.

Body Medium.

Palate Interplay of malty sweetness and dryness.

Finish Spicy. Pepper and earthy saltiness.

SCORE 80

GLEN GARIOCH 29-year-old, Individual Cask Bottling, distilled April 1968, 56.6 vol, cask 626, Hogshead

Strictly for the lover of long-matured, oaky whiskies.

Colour Very dark orange to chestnut.

Nose Charred oak. Phenol. Earthy saltiness again.

Body Big, firm.

Palate Black-treacle toffee, developing late mint notes. Extra-strong peppermints. Very drying on the tongue.

Finish Extraordinarily long. Cough sweets.

SCORE 81

GLEN GARIOCH 200th Anniversary Limited Edition, 43 vol

Distilled in 1961, when Glen Garioch was scarcely peated, and when the stills were heated by coal rather than steam. Matured in first-fill American oak.

Colour Bright, deep gold.

Nose Astonishingly fresh for a whisky of such age. Remarkably minty.

Body Medium, firm, rounded.

Palate Freshly soft and clean. Almost menthol-like, developing to a leafier, garden-mint note. Some tasters have found flavours reminiscent of star-fruit. Dryish, against a lightly syrupy malt background.

Finish Long, minty, warming. Dryish hints of vanilla pod. Remarkably gentle.

SCORE 81

Other versions of Glen Garioch

A 1994 bottling of a 1971 Glen Garioch, from Oddbins, was notably peaty and phenolic, but with a deft balance or floweriness and nuttiness. SCORE 80. An earlier 17-year-old at 54.2 vol under the Caskieben label was sweet and leafy, with some vanilla, but lacked peat. SCORE 75.

GLENGLASSAUGH

PRODUCER Highland Distillers
REGION Highlands **DISTRICT** Speyside (Deveron)

ADDRESS Portsoy, Banffshire, AB45 2SQ

THE RECENT "FAMILY SILVER" BOTTLING from the owners, Highland Distillers, is welcome morsel from Glenglassaugh. This distillery, founded in 1875 and completely rebuilt in 1959–60, has been mothballed since 1986, and shows no sign of being reopened. The whisky has contributed to highly regarded blends such as The Famous Grouse, Cutty Sark, and Laing's, but its distinctiveness has always seemed a mixed blessing. "Sackcloth…hessian," proclaimed one taster, admiring the distinctive aroma of this malt. "Flax, perhaps?" says another admirer. Maybe it is the aroma of seaside sand dunes covered with rough grass and gorse. This is a coastal malt, produced near Portsoy, between the mouths of the rivers Spey and the Deveron.

HOUSE STYLE Grassy maltiness. Restorative or refresher.

GLENGLASSAUGH 1973 Vintage Reserve, 40 vol, The Family Silver
Colour Deep, old gold.
Nose Fresh, starched linen. Sea air.
Body Light to medium. Firm, smooth.
Palate Smooth, grassy. Slightly leathery and oily.
Finish Linseed. Soothing. Warming.

SCORE 78

Estd 1875

FINE HIGHLAND MALT

Glenglassaugh Distillery c 1875

GLENGLASSAUGH

SINGLE MALT SCOTCH WHISKY

BOTTLED IN SCOTLAND

75cl   DISTILLED AT
GLENGLASSAUGH DISTILLERY, PORTSOY, SCOTLAND   40% vol.

GLENGLASSAUGH, no age statement, 40 vol
This version, bottled by Highland Distillers, is labelled 12-year-old
in some markets. It is now hard to find.

Colour Gold.

Nose Fresh linen.

Body Light, but firm and smooth.

Palate Grassy, sweetish.

Finish Gentle, drying slightly.

SCORE 76

GLENGLASSAUGH 1986, 40 vol, MacPhail's Collection

Colour Bright lemony yellow.

Nose Light. Perfumy. Lemon. Gorse.

Body Light. Silky smooth.

Palate Clean. Oily. Hint of cedar. Very slight rooty licorice.

Finish Gentle, warming. Slight lemon zest.

SCORE 76

GLENGLASSAUGH 1974, 56.9 vol, Scott's Selection

Colour Deep old gold.

Nose Cream. Gorse. Oily. Salty.

Body Viscous.

Palate Dry, oily. Sherbety.

Finish Lemony. Hot lemon juice. Warming.

SCORE 77

GLENGOYNE

PRODUCER Lang Brothers
REGION Highlands   **DISTRICT** Highlands (Southwest)

ADDRESS Dumgoyne, Stirlingshire, G63 9LB   **TEL** 01360-550254 **VC**
WEBSITE www.glengoyne.com   **E-MAIL** shendry@edrington.co.uk

I NCREASING EMPHASIS IS BEING PLACED on the use exclusively of unpeated malt in this clean, nutty whisky, distilled just across the Highland line. It now describes itself as a Southern Highland malt. An outstanding Millennium edition (*see page 163*) is the latest among many special bottlings. These have included a deliciously creamy version made entirely with the Golden Promise variety of barley, from one farm in Northumberland; winter distillations benefitting from very cold weather; and even some made on December 25 in the days (until 1972) when the Scots worked at Christmas. Glengoyne is also unusual in its favoured style of sherry wood, palo cortado, though very limited bottlings have also been done from other styles, including fino and old amontillado. Coopers and bodegas in Jerez are commissioned to produce casks for the distillery.

Glengoyne is very attractive and eminently visitable, being only a dozen miles from the centre of Glasgow. The distillery and the hamlet of Dumgoyne take their name from the older Guin, a small river that eventually flows into Loch Lomond. Sheep graze on the hills behind, and burns flow into a well-tended glen, forming a waterfall. Glengoyne is said to have been established in 1833, and has been owned by Lang's since the 1870s. Since the mid 1960s, Lang's has been a subsidiary of Robertson and Baxter, owned by a holding company called The Edrington Group. The whisky contributes to the Lang's blends, Cutty Sark, and The Famous Grouse.

HOUSE STYLE Easily drinkable, but full of malty flavour. Restorative, with dessert, or after dinner.

Glengoyne's stills: the curve at the base of the neck swirls back some vapours for redistillation, making for a more refined spirit.

GLENGOYNE 10-year-old, 40 vol

Colour Yellowy gold.

Nose A fresh but very soft, warm fruitiness (Cox's apples?), with rich malty dryness, very light sherry, and a touch of juicy oak.

Body Light to medium, smooth, rounded.

Palate Clean, grassy, fruity, with more apple notes, tasty, very pleasant.

Finish Still sweet, but drying slightly. Clean, appetizing.

Score 74

GLENGOYNE 12-year-old, 43 vol
Now hard to find.
Very similar to the ten-year-old. A dash more of everything. Score 75.

GLENGOYNE 17-year-old, 43 vol

Colour Full gold, with an orange tinge.

Nose Warm, dry. Maltiness and fruitiness. Palo cortado sherry. Cedar and fresh oak.

Body Medium, very firm and smooth.

Palate Deep, rich flavours. Malt, clean fruitiness (hints of apple), nuttiness, cedar, more oak. Really hitting its stride as a mature, sophisticated whisky.

Finish Long and allusively sherryish.

Score 77

GLENGOYNE 21-year-old, 43 vol
A very well balanced edition.

Colour Full gold, with a darker orange tinge.

Nose Fragrant. Hints of apple, oak, and earth.

Body Firm, smooth.

Palate Very firm maltiness. Dry creaminess.
Clean fruit (hints of orange) and oak.

Finish Cream. Vanilla pods. Cinnamon.

SCORE 79

GLENGOYNE 30-year-old, 50 vol
An interestingly oaky interpretation.

Colour Deep, shining, gold to bronze.

Nose Polished oak.

Body Medium to full. Rounded.

Palate Soft, complex. Hints of apple and orange. Dryish spiciness.

Finish Firm dry. Hint of charred oak.

SCORE 79

GLENGOYNE MILLENNIUM, 50 vol
A delicious example of maltiness in a whisky. Comprises Glengoynes
of more than 30 years old.

Colour Very full gold, with orange tinge.

Nose Very aromatic, appetizing, and softly spicy.

Body Creamy.

Palate Very malty. Long and unfolding. Clean. Sweet start.
Creamy flavours, becoming cookie-like and nutty.

Finish Chewy, malty. Very soft, restrained, dessert apple.

SCORE 80

Some vintage-dated editions of Glengoyne

(Released each August, at about 25 years old and cask strength)

1972, 57.8 vol
Amber colour; arousing interplay of sherry, resiny, and grassy maltiness
in the aroma; rich, creamy, and nutty, with charred oak and earth
in the finish. SCORE 79.

1970, 48.5 vol
Full gold; fresh aroma, with hint of charred oak; light body, with
surprisingly fresh, creamy flavours. SCORE 78. An earlier release of a 1970,
identified as a Golden Promise varietal grown in Northumberland, was
fractionally richer, maltier, and less dry. SCORE 79.

1969 (bottled unfiltered, 47 vol)
Deep gold; polished oak aroma; firm, creamy, oily; more oiliness in the
creamy flavour, with a hint of fruity dryness in the finish. SCORE 77.

1968 (labelled as being from a single day's distillation,
matured only in sherry casks, 50.3 vol)
Gold with orange tinge; oak and sherry in the beautifully balanced aroma;
exceptionally smooth; chewy maltiness, sherry, ginger, and juicy oak.
SCORE 79.

Winter 1967 Christmas Day Reserve, 43 vol
Gold. Very fresh, fragrant aroma, with hint of honeysuckle and clean apple;
sweet, creamy, condensed milk in the palate; very sweet, fresh dessert
apple, tangerines, and nuts in the finish; beautifully rounded.
SCORE 80.

Some single-cask bottlings of Glengoyne

1972

Cask 583, at 55.9 vol: reddish, buttery notes of zesty lemon, orange and bitter chocolate. SCORE 78. Cask 1428, at 60.3 vol: paler, bronze, oily, very sweet, fruity, apples, cloves. SCORE 78.

1971

Cask 4855, at 56.2 vol: dark-orange colour, juicy oak, and sherry in the aroma; more sherry and creamy malt in the palate; oily. SCORE 78. Cask 4678, at 57 vol: dark copper, nutty oloroso, orangey fruit, then resiny dryness. SCORE 77.

1970

Cask 1186, at 51.5 vol: dark-walnut colour; oaky and nutty sherry in the aroma; very rich sherry flavours; late malty licorice and estery spiciness. SCORE 77. Cask 3854, at 53.4 vol; pale-walnut colour, polished-oak aroma; sweet apple and butter, almonds. SCORE 76. Cask 4606, at 54.7 vol: sunny gold; very fruity, apple-like aroma; sweet apple flavours; crisp finish. SCORE 76. Cask 4605, at 56 vol: golden, grassy, earthy (peaty?) aroma, apple-like, honeyish, very drying in the finish. SCORE 76.

1969

Cask 4464, at 54.4 vol: chestnut colour; sappy, resiny aroma; barley-sugar maltiness; brandy butter; oak finish. SCORE 77. Cask 3525, at 51.6 vol: reddish copper; oaky aroma; resiny, very sweet; wine gums; slight charred oak in the finish. SCORE 76.

1968

Cask 4617, at 52 vol: deep yellowy gold; clean, soft, perfumy maltiness; hints of apple and vanilla. SCORE 78.

Sherry variations of Glengoyne

The following very limited editions, bottled in the upper 50s by volume, offered a treat for lovers of very heavily sherried whiskies, but the weight of the wine seriously challenged the Glengoyne malt character.

A 1989 matured in a fino cask and bottled in 1998 had a dark walnut colour; a polished oak aroma; a big body; a fat, buttery palate; and a nutty dryness, developing some spiciness in the finish. SCORE 78.

A 1985 from palo cortado, bottled in 1997, was dark and reddish, also buttery, but more honeyish and medicinal (cough sweets). SCORE 77.

Another 1985, from old amontillado, had similar characteristics but was notably spicier, with ginger and especially cinnamon. SCORE 77.

GLEN GRANT

PRODUCER Chivas (Seagram)
REGION Highlands   **DISTRICT** Speyside (Rothes)

ADDRESS Rothes, Morayshire, AB38 7BS
TEL 01542-783318 **VC**

GLEN GRANT WAS THE LONE SINGLE MALT in many a bar from Glasgow to Guiana in the days when this form of whisky was scarcely known outside the Highlands. The distillery, founded in 1840 by John and James Grant, quickly gained a reputation for the quality of its whisky. James Grant, who was a prominent local politician, played a big part in bringing railways to the area, and they in turn distributed his product. The turreted and gabled offices in the "Scottish baronial" style, and the distillery, are set around a small courtyard. James Grant's son, a military major, brought plants from his travels in India and Africa, and created a garden in the glen behind the distillery. In 1995, the garden was restored and is open to visitors.

For the greater part of its history, and until the last couple of decades, Glen Grant has won its renown as a single malt in versions bottled by merchants. Older vintages can still be found bearing in small type the name of bottlers Gordon & MacPhail. Much the same classic label is now used under the name Glen Grant Distillery. Since 1977, the enterprise has been owned by Chivas. The whisky has long been a contributor to Chivas Regal, and is highly regarded by most blenders.

Glen Grant itself remains among the world's big-selling whiskies, but much of its volume is in the younger ages, especially in the important Italian market, where it has been marketed at five years. The version with no age statement, which is the principal Glen Grant in Britain, contains malt less than ten years old.

HOUSE STYLE Herbal, with notes of hazelnut. In younger ages, an aperitif; with sherry age, after dinner.

The Glen Grant distillery is tucked away at the end of the main street of Rothes, one of the whisky towns of the Spey Valley.

GLEN GRANT 5-year-old, 40 vol

Colour Very pale, white wine.

Nose Light, dry fruitiness, spirity.

Body Light, slightly sticky, almost resiny.

Palate Spirity. Pear brandy.

Finish Fruity, quick.

SCORE 65

GLEN GRANT, no age statement, 40 vol

Colour Gold.

Nose Fruity, flowery, nutty, faintly spirity.

Body Light but firm.

Palate Dry, slightly astringent at first, becoming soft and nutty.

Finish Herbal.

SCORE 74

GLEN GRANT 10-year-old, 43 vol
Glen Grant character without an obvious intervention of sherry.

Colour Full gold.

Nose Still dry, but much softer, with some sweetness.

Body Light to medium.

Palate Lightly sweet start, quickly becoming nutty and very dry.

Finish Very dry, with herbal notes.

SCORE 76

GLEN GRANT 15-year-old, 40 vol, Gordon & MacPhail

Colour Medium amber.

Nose Some sherry.

Body Light to medium.

Palate Sherryish, soft and nutty, dry.

Finish Mellow, warming.

SCORE 80

GLEN GRANT 13-year-old, 55.1 vol, Cadenhead
This version is now hard to find.

Colour Greeny-gold.

Nose Dry, flowery.

Body Light but firm, with some viscosity.

Palate Sweet, nutty.

Finish Dry, touches of vanilla, lingering herbal notes, with appetizing bitterness.

SCORE 76

GLEN GRANT 16-year-old, 46 vol, Cadenhead
This version is now hard to find.

Colour Fino sherry.

Nose Appetizingly fruity. Dessert apples? Hazelnut?

Body Light to medium, soft.

Palate Hazelnuts. Grassy. Bamboo shoots?

Finish Grassy, flowery.

SCORE 77

GLEN GRANT 21-year-old, 40 vol, Gordon & MacPhail
Take it slowly, and appreciate the subtlety and development.

Colour Full amber-red.

Nose Lots of sherry.

Body Medium, soft.

Palate Sherryish sweetness at first, then malt and grassy-peaty notes, finally the nutty Glen Grant dryness.

Finish Lingering, flowery.

SCORE 81

GLEN GRANT 23-year-old, 46 vol, Cadenhead
This version is now hard to find.

Colour As red as a ripe apple.

Nose Powerful sherry. Appetizing.

Body Medium, soft.

Palate Lots of sherry, but the nutty dryness of the whisky still fights through.

Finish Overwhelmingly dry. Woody. Astringent.

SCORE 69

GLEN GRANT 25-year-old, 40 vol, Gordon & MacPhail
Not so much chess as wrist-wrestling, with the sherry coming out on top.
A robust version.

Colour Dark.

Nose Lots of sherry.

Body Medium, firm.

Palate Dry oloroso character at first, then nutty dryness.
A lot of depth.

Finish Deep, flowery, peaty.

SCORE 81

GLEN GRANT 26-year-old, 46 vol, Cadenhead
This version is now hard to find.

Colour Ripe plum? Almost opaque.

Nose Powerful sherry.

Body Medium, soft.

Palate Overwhelmed by the sherry.

Finish Astringent.

SCORE 66

GLEN GRANT 29-year-old, 43 vol, Berry Brothers and Rudd
Labelled as Berry's Own Selection, with the words "1969 Speyside"
emphasized, and the distillery's name in small type. This is a
reminder of the days when wine merchants such as Berry's
customarily made their own bottlings of single malts.
While retaining Glen Grant as their own selection, Berry's
also market Glenrothes (see entry).

Colour Dark orange to oak.

Nose Creamy, nutty, juicy oak.

Body Creamy but light on tongue.

Palate Nutty, creamy, perfumy. Hints of raisins and char. Surprisingly
elegant and delicate for such a heavily sherried malt. Tightly
combined flavours.

Finish Treacle toffee. Medicinal. Dry warming. Very much an after-dinner
version, or a winter warmer.

SCORE 80

GLEN GRANT 1967, 51.8 vol, Signatory

Colour Full amber.

Nose Sherry, toffee, nuts.

Body Medium, creamy.

Palate Sherry, toffee, nuts, oak. Slight char.

Finish Burnt cake. Spicy.

SCORE 79

GLEN GRANT 1965, 40 vol, Gordon & MacPhail

Colour Very deep gold.

Nose Sherryish nuttiness, herbal notes.

Body Medium, smooth.

Palate Sherryish, lightly creamy, remarkable hazelnut character.

Finish Soothing, creamy, savoury.

SCORE 82

GLEN GRANT 1964, 46 vol, Signatory

Colour Amber-red.

Nose Sherry, nutty dryness.

Body Medium, smooth.

Palate Sherryish, nutty, with some sappy woodiness.

Finish Gently dry, with some sherryish, woody notes.

SCORE 79

GLEN GRANT 1960, 40 vol, Gordon & MacPhail
Less sherry, but a beautifully mellow, mature malt.

Colour Medium amber.

Nose Some sherry.

Body Medium.

Palate Sherryish and sweet, with mellow nuttiness.

Finish Very long and sweet, with gradual development of gentle dryness.

SCORE 81

GLEN KEITH

PRODUCER Chivas (Seagram)
REGION Highlands **DISTRICT** Speyside (Strathisla)

ADDRESS Station Road, Keith, Banffshire, AB55 3BS
TEL 01542-783044 **VC**

C HIVAS OWNS TWO DISTILLERIES next door to one another in the town of Keith, on the River Isla. One simply takes the name of the district, Strathisla, the other is Glen Keith, which was built on the site of a corn mill in 1957–60. It was one of the first of a new generation of malt distilleries at that time. Glen Keith had the first gas-fired still in Scotland, and pioneered the use of computers in the industry. Some 1960s' distillates were bottled by Gordon & MacPhail in the 1980s. A less chewy official bottling, initially with a 1983 vintage date, made its debut in 1993–94. The whisky is now simply identified as being ten years old. Like several malts from this district, it has a dry suggestion of fresh wood.

HOUSE STYLE Gingery, rooty, tart. Before dinner.

GLEN KEITH 10-year-old, 43 vol

Colour Solid gold.

Nose Flower petals. Lemon grass. Rooty. Ginger. Cedar. Oak.

Body Medium.

Palate Sweet, chewy, ginger cake. Not complex, but very approachable and pleasantly drinkable.

Finish Very late, fruity tartness.

SCORE 73

GLENKINCHIE

PRODUCER United Distillers
REGION Lowlands   DISTRICT Eastern Lowlands

ADDRESS Pencaitland, Tranent, East Lothian, EH34 5ET
TEL 01875-342004 **VC**

A CCORDING TO THE NEWISH SUB-TITLE on its label, "The Edinburgh Malt". About 15 miles from the capital, and near the village of Pencaitland, this is an eminently visitable distillery. It traces its origins to at least the 1820s and 1830s, to a farm in barley-growing country in the glen of the Kinchie. This burn flows from the green Lammermuir Hills, which provide medium-hard water, and flows toward the small coastal resorts where the Firth of Forth meets the sea. In the 1940s and 1950s, the distillery manager bred prize-winning cattle, feeding them on the spent grain. Delphiniums and roses grow outside the manager's office, and the distillery has its own bowling green. The buildings resemble those of a Borders woollen mill. For much of the distillery's history, the whisky was largely used in the Haig blends. In 1988–89, it was launched as a single in the Classic Malts range, and in 1997 an Amontillado finish was added. In the same year a new visitor centre was opened. Among the exhibits is a 75-year-old model of the distillery which was built by the firm of Basset-Lowke, better known for their miniature steam engines.

HOUSE STYLE Flowery start, complex flavours, and a dry finish.
A restorative, especially after a walk in the hills.

GLENKINCHIE 10-year-old, 43 vol

Colour Gold.

Nose Softly aromatic. Lemon grass. Sweet lemons. Melons.

Body Light but rounded.

Palate Soft, spicy. Cinnamon and demerara, then gingery dryness.
An extraordinary interplay.

Finish Fragrant, spicy, oaky dryness.

SCORE 76

GLENKINCHIE 1986, Distillers Edition, Double Matured, 43 vol
Finished in amontillado sherry.

Colour Full gold.

Nose Lightly floral aroma of polished oak. Sweet lemon. Spices.

Body Well-rounded.

Palate The amontillado seems to heighten the interplay between sweetness and dryness. First comes brown sugar and butter, then suddenly dry nuttiness and surprising saltiness.

Finish Sweet, astonishingly long, and soothing.

SCORE 79

JACKSON'S ROW, 40 vol
Described in its publicity as "an authentic Scotch…that breaks the rules". A "blond", all-malt whisky based on Glenkinchie, but also including the products of other distilleries. Old enough to be mellow, and heavily filtered for a "pure, smooth, unforgettably clean" (sic) "taste", to be served cold to compete with vodka in the youth market. This marketing-driven curiosity was briefly marketed in the mid 1990s.

Colour A very pale vinho verde.

Nose Faint grass, linseed, leather.

Body Light, thinnish.

Palate Clean, fresh. Grass. Dessert apples.

Finish Light. Dry. Slightly raw. Grassy. Leathery. Surprisingly, a very faint hint of peat.

SCORE 55

Other versions of Glenkinchie
A 21-year-old, at 46 vol, from Cadenhead, was notably grassy. SCORE 76. A 1974 Connoisseurs Choice, at 40 vol, was smokier, with a hint of hickory. SCORE 76.

THE GLENLIVET

PRODUCER Chivas (Seagram)
REGION Highlands DISTRICT Speyside (Livet)

ADDRESS Ballindalloch, Banffshire, AB37 9DB TEL 01542-783220 **VC**
WEBSITE www.theglenlivet.com

T HE MOST FAMOUS WHISKY-MAKING GLEN in Scotland is that of the small river Livet, which flows into the Spey. Among the distilling districts, it is the one most deeply set into the mountains. Its water rises from granite, and frequently flows underground for many miles. The mountain setting also provides for the weather that whisky makers like. When distilling is in progress, the condensers work most effectively if cooled by very cold water, and in a climate to match. The malt whiskies made in the area are on the lighter side, very clean, flowery, subtle, and elegant.

The Livet's fame also has historical origins, in the period when Highlanders were permitted to distil only on a domestic scale. The purported justification was a shortage of grain, but there was also a question of political vindictiveness. At that time, this relatively remote mountain glen was a famous nest of illicit distillation. After legalization in 1824, the legendary spirit "from Glenlivet" was greatly in demand among merchants in the cities to the south.

Distillers absurdly far from the glen have used the geographical allusion, as if it were a synonym for Speyside in general, but this practice is now in decline as the greater interest in single malts focuses attention on the issue of origin. The distillery highest in the glen is the one now known as Braeval. Until recently, it was known as Braes of Glenlivet, and it produces a honeyish, zesty whisky. Slightly lower is Tamnavulin, which has a notably light-bodied malt (though Tomintoul's, just across the hills in adjoining Avon valley, is lighter in palate). See entries for each.

Only one distillery in the area is permitted to call itself The Glenlivet. This is the distillery that was the first to become legal, and it now has an international reputation. The definite article is restricted even further in that it appears on only the official bottlings from the owning company of The Glenlivet distillery, Chivas. These carry the legend "Distilled by George & J. G. Smith" in small type at the bottom of the label, referring to the father and son who established the original business.

The Gaelic word "gobha", pronounced "gow" (as in typically Scottish names like McGowan) translates to Smith. It has been argued that the Gow family had supported Bonnie Prince Charlie and later found it politic to change their name to Smith, but this explanation is open to question.

When the legalization of distillers was proposed by the Duke of Gordon, one of his tenants, George Smith, already an illicit whisky maker, was the first to apply for a licence. His son, John Gordon

Smith, assisted and succeeded him. After distilling on two sites nearby, in 1858 the Smiths moved to the present location, Minmore, near the point where the Livet and Avon meet. The distillery stands at a point where the grassy valley is already beginning to steepen towards the mountains. In 1880, the exclusive designation "The Glenlivet" was granted in a test case. The company remained independent until 1953, when it came under the same ownership as Glen Grant. In the 1960s, considerable quantities of the whisky were acquired by Gordon and MacPhail, leading to subsequent bottlings by them. These very old and sometimes vintage-dated versions are identified as George and J. G. Smith's Glenlivet Whisky. The Glenlivet, Glen Grant, and Longmorn, and the blenders Chivas, were acquired by the North American and worldwide drinks group Seagram in 1977, since when the official bottlings have been energetically promoted. The Glenlivet has become the biggest-selling single malt in the large American market.

By virtue of its substantial sales, The Glenlivet might be deemed commonplace, but it is a whisky of structure and complexity. It is distilled from water with a dash of hardness, and the peating of the malt is on the light side. About a third of the casks used have at some stage held sherry, though the proportion of first-fill is considerably smaller than that. Glenlivet is believed to be planning a Cognac-finish edition.

HOUSE STYLE Flowery, fruity, peachy. Aperitif.

THE GLENLIVET 12-year-old, 40 vol

Colour	Pale gold.
Nose	Remarkably flowery, clean and soft.
Body	Light to medium, firm, smooth.
Palate	Flowery, peachy, notes of vanilla, delicate balance between sweetness and malty dryness.
Finish	Restrained, long, gently warming.

SCORE 85

THE GLENLIVET ARCHIVE, no age statement, 43 vol
From examples of The Glenlivet at least 15 years old that are felt
to show especially well for floral character and richness.

Colour Full gold.

Nose Light, fresh, peatiness. Appetizing.

Body Medium. Very firm. Smooth.

Palate Sweet, some syrupiness. Slightly lacking in middle. Nutty finish.
Rounded, gentle.

Finish Lightly dry, peaty, toasty. Warming.

SCORE 86

THE GLENLIVET 18-year-old, 43 vol

Colour Deep gold to amber.

Nose Elements beautifully combined. Depth of flowery aromas. Very light
touch of fresh peatiness. Some sweetness and a hint of sherryish oak.
Lightly appetizing.

Body Firm, smooth.

Palate Flowery and sweet at first, then developing peach-stone nuttiness.

Finish Dry, appetizing. Very long, with interplay of sweet and
bitter flavours.

SCORE 87

THE GLENLIVET 21-year-old, 43 vol

Colour Full amber.

Nose Emphatic sherry character.

Body Soft, medium.

Palate At first, very sherryish indeed, with an oloroso character. As the
palate develops, that flowery-spicy note becomes strongly evident.

Finish Again, lots of sherry.

SCORE 88

GLENLIVET 15-year-old, 57 vol, Gordon & MacPhail

Colour Deep yellowy gold.

Nose Clean, fresh peatiness. Touch of dry, nutty, sherry.

Body Medium, rounded, firm.

Palate Delicious malty sweetness. Barley sugar. Developing honeyish, flowery dryness. Remarkably fresh and complex.

Finish Intense, flowery, spicy, and long-lasting.

SCORE 87

An earlier 15-year-old at 40 vol was more gingery and sherryish. SCORE 86. A version at the same age with 46 vol was lighter but nuttier. SCORE 86.

GLENLIVET 21-year-old, 40 vol, Gordon & MacPhail

Colour Full gold.

Nose Earthy, sherryish (fino or amontillado?)

Body Soft.

Palate Sherryish, with a flowery-spicy balance eventually emerging. Dash of herbal, leafy, peaty smokiness.

Finish Smooth, long-lasting.

SCORE 87

Vintage editions of The Glenlivet, distillery bottlings

This first-ever "official" range of dated bottlings came from years with very limited stocks. The sequence has no 1971, because there was too little to make available. These are collectors' items, some in 20cl bottles.

THE GLENLIVET VINTAGE, 1972 (bottled 1998), 54.29 vol

Colour Bright gold.
Nose Peaty. Lightly phenolic.
Body Medium. Lots of texture.
Palate Sweet, syrupy. Lightly creamy. Developing light floweriness and sugared almonds.
Finish Peach-stone notes. Attenuated. Slightly woody. Dry. Powerful.

SCORE 84

THE GLENLIVET VINTAGE,1970 (bottled 1998), 56.58 vol

Colour Bright gold to full gold.
Nose Peaty.
Body Medium, syrupy, smooth.
Palate Sweet, syrupy. Raisins. Cinnamon. Oak. Complex.
Finish Firm. Some cream flavours. Raisins. Oak.

SCORE 84

THE GLENLIVET VINTAGE 1969 (bottled 1998), 52.2 vol

Colour Pale amber.

Nose Peaty, leafy, sappy, oaky.

Body Creamy.

Palate Nutty, toffeeish, creamy flavours. Big and assertive in the middle, but its development seems to have been attenuated by age.

Finish Rooty, dry, woody.

SCORE 84

THE GLENLIVET VINTAGE 1968 (bottled 1998), 52.75 vol

Colour Amber.

Nose Polished oak.

Body Smooth, slippery.

Palate Sugared almonds, spicy, flowery, fresh herbs. A dash of herbal, leafy, flowery peatiness.

Finish Sweet, flowery, long, smooth.

SCORE 88

THE GLENLIVET VINTAGE 1967 (bottled 1998), 53.32 vol

Colour Amber.

Nose Very aromatic. Hay. Grass. Peat.

Body Smooth, slippery.

Palate Lovely balance of sugared almonds, syrup, a hint of orange zest, grass, and peat. Lots of flavour development.

Finish Light, soft, warming. Deceptively long.

SCORE 89

GLENLIVET 1978, 60.2 vol, Gordon & MacPhail

An oddly uneven bottling.

Colour Pale yellowy gold.

Nose Flowery. Hint of peat.

Body Unusually light. Fluffy.

Palate Very sweet. Sugared almonds. Roses.

Finish Flowery, aniseedy, hot.

SCORE 86

GLENLIVET 1961, 40 vol, Gordon & MacPhail

Colour Very full gold.

Nose Well balanced, fragrant, complex, with some smokiness.

Body Soft.

Palate Sherryish, with long flavour development and
some smokiness.

Finish Big, long, warming.

SCORE 88

GLENLIVET 1973, 57.2 vol, Signatory Cask Strength Series

Colour Deep orange.

Nose Grassy, peaty, sappy.

Body Medium, smooth, almost buttery.

Palate Barley sugar. Nuts. Flowery.

Finish Suddenly lemony. Fruity at first, then lemon-pith bitterness.
Extraordinary.

SCORE 85

GLENLOCHY

PRODUCER DCL/UDV (Diageo)
REGION Highlands   DISTRICT Western Highlands

ADDRESS North Road, Fort William, Inverness-shire, PH33 6TQ

THE LOCHY IS A RIVER that flows through the town of Fort William, at the foot of the mountain Ben Nevis. In addition to the Ben Nevis malt distillery, which is still very much in operation, Fort William for many years had another, called Glenlochy. This was built in 1898–1900, and changed little over the decades. It passed to DCL in 1953, lost its railway spur in the 1970s, and was closed in 1983. Although the pagoda still stands, the equipment has gone, and the premises are now used as offices by unrelated businesses. One sophisticated and geographically precise taster was reminded of Lebanese hashish by a Scotch Malt Whisky Society bottling of Glenlochy in the mid 1990s. The smokiness is less obvious in some recent bottlings, in which the wood seems tired but more oxidation and ester notes emerge. In 1995, United Distillers released a Rare Malts edition, with a similar bottling the following year.

HOUSE STYLE Peaty, fruity, creamy. With dessert or a book
at bedtime.

GLENLOCHY 25-year-old (distilled 1969, bottled 1995), 62.2 vol,
Rare Malts

Colour Old gold.
Nose Charred oak and roasted chestnuts.
Body Firm, smooth, oily.
Palate Marron glacé and clotted cream.
Finish Dry, big. Lemon zest and pepper.

SCORE 71

GLENLOCHY 1977, 40 vol, Connoiseurs Choice

Colour	Full gold to peach.
Nose	Vanilla-flavoured tobacco.
Body	Light, firm, smooth, oily.
Palate	Vanilla, coconut, white chocolate.
Finish	Light lemon zest. Cedar.

SCORE 70

An earlier bottling, from 1974, seemed peatier and smokier. SCORE 70.

GLENLOCHY 20-year-old (distilled 1977, bottled 1998), 55.8 vol, individual cask, Cadenhead

Colour	Full gold.
Nose	Attractive, perfumy sweetness. Malty. Slight sweet smoke.
Body	Much fuller. Soft.
Palate	Marshmallowy maltiness, but falls away in middle.
Finish	Lemony, grassy, peaty. Long, soothing peatiness.

SCORE 70

This was more dimensional, and longer, than an earlier 27-year-old. SCORE 69.

GLENLOCHY 32-year-old (distilled 1965, bottled 1997), Signatory "Silent Stills" Series

Colour	Warm, full gold.
Nose	Light grass and vanilla.
Body	Light but creamy.
Palate	Oily, coconut, citrus.
Finish	Oily. Citrus zest, grass. Very attractive peat. Long.

SCORE 69

An earlier bottling, from 1963, was more sherryish and oaky. SCORE 69.

GLENLOSSIE

PRODUCER UDV (Diageo)
REGION Highlands   **DISTRICT** Speyside (Lossie)

ADDRESS By Elgin, Morayshire, IV30 8FF
TEL 01343-547891

R ESPECTED IN THE INDUSTRY (its whisky was once an important element in Haig blends), this distillery has a much lower profile among lovers of malts. A Flora and Fauna edition introduced in the early 1990s has made more connoisseurs aware of it, and there have since been bottlings from Signatory and Hart. The distillery, in the valley of the Lossie, south of Elgin, was built in 1876, reconstructed 20 years later, and extended in 1962. Next door is the Mannochmore distillery, built in 1971.

HOUSE STYLE Flowery, clean, grassy, malty. Aperitif.

GLENLOSSIE 10-year-old, 43 vol, Flora and Fauna

Colour Fino sherry.

Nose Fresh. Grass, heather, sandalwood.

Body Light to medium. Soft, smooth.

Palate Malty, dryish at first, then a range of sweeter, perfumy, spicy notes.

Finish Spicy.

SCORE 76

GLENLOSSIE Vintage 1981, Sherry Cask edition (butt 1680, bottle 588 of 595, 1998), 43 vol, Signatory

Colour Gold.

Nose Very light sherry. Sweet maltiness. Cereal grains. Grass. Sandalwood.

Body Lightly creamy. Smooth.

Palate Notably clean maltiness, again with an interplay of dryness and sweetness. Some honeyish, creamy, buttery notes.

Finish Fudge, then very late, gentle touch of grass, peat, and sandalwood.

SCORE 77

GLENLOSSIE 16-year-old (distilled 1981), 43 vol, Hart Brothers

Colour Gold.

Nose Malt. Cereal grains. Hint of peat.

Body Slightly lighter and firmer.

Palate Nutty sweetness, with a hint of sherry and some butteriness.

Finish Fresh, grassy peatiness.

SCORE 77

GLENLOSSIE 1974, 40 vol, Connoisseurs Choice

Colour Full gold to amber.

Nose Very attractive interplay of sherry, malt, and floweriness.

Body Firm, smooth, rounded.

Palate Fresh. Dryish sherry. Clean maltiness and light touch of butter.

Finish Nutty sherry and a hint of fresh peatiness.

SCORE 77

Earlier bottlings of Glenlossie

A Gordon & MacPhail 1971 at 40 vol was sherryish, but still with plenty of distillery character. SCORE 76. A Scotch Malt Whisky Society 1981 at 55.3 vol was somewhere between the two. SCORE 76.

GLEN MHOR

PRODUCER DCL
REGION Highlands   DISTRICT Speyside (Inverness)

ADDRESS Telford Street, Inverness, Inverness-shire, IV3 5LU

P URISTS PRONOUNCE IT THE GAELIC WAY, "Glen Vawr". The distillery, built in 1892 in Inverness and demolished in 1986, was one of several at which the poet, novelist, and pioneering whisky-writer Neil Gunn worked as an exciseman. In his book *Scotch Missed*, Brian Townsend writes that Gunn was inspired by Glen Mhor to let slip his observation that "until a man has had the luck to chance upon a perfectly matured malt, he does not really know what whisky is". Even in Gunn's day, Glen Mhor could be found as a single malt, and casks still find their way into independent bottlings.

HOUSE STYLE Aromatic, treacly. Quite sweet. With dessert or after dinner.

GLEN MHOR 1979, 66.7 vol, Gordon & MacPhail "Cask" Series

Colour	Deep gold to peach.
Nose	Licorice. Rooty. Grassy.
Body	Rich.
Palate	Licorice, treacle toffee, Madeira.
Finish	Winey acidity. Hessian. Light oak. Toast. Spicy warmth. Wins points for its voluptuousness.

SCORE 77

GLEN MHOR Vintage 1977, 43 vol, Signatory (cask 1546)

Colour Greeny-gold.

Nose Soft licorice. Waxy.

Body Light but smooth, and oily.

Palate Licorice. Fruit gums. Lemon jelly. Quite sweet.

Finish Limes. Chilli.

SCORE 72

GLEN MHOR 20-year-old (distilled 1976, bottled), 57.9 vol, Cadenhead

Colour Primrose.

Nose Light lipstick.

Body Light to medium. Syrupy.

Palate Sugary. Lemony. Flowery, perfumy, lemon character.

Finish Sherbety. Spicy, becoming drier. Warming.
Wins points for balance, especially in that late dryness.

SCORE 74

GLEN MHOR 21-year-old (distilled 1976), 43 vol, Hart Brothers.

Colour Pale greeny-gold.

Nose Fruit gums. Lemon. Lime. Developing to lemon grass.

Body Syrupy but gritty (like a golden, sweet molasses).

Palate Sugary. Lemony. Then a lemon-pith dryness.

Finish Sugar. Strong peppermint sweets. Mint imperials. Warming.
Long. Digestif.

SCORE 73

GLENMORANGIE

PRODUCER Glenmorangie plc
REGION Highlands   DISTRICT Northern Highlands

ADDRESS Tain, Ross-shire, IV19 1PZ   TEL 01862-892477 **VC**
WEBSITE www.glenmorangie.com   E-MAIL visitors@glenmorangieplc.co.uk

THE BIGGEST-SELLING MALT IN SCOTLAND has become available in a far larger range of versions in the past ten years. Glenmorangie briefly led the field in "official" cask-strength bottlings, then pioneered "wood finishes", from sherry variations such as fino to port and French wines. More recently, it has launched several "first-fill" versions based on Bourbon barrels, the wood used to mature its principal product. The company selects its own trees in the Ozark mountains of Missouri, has its wood seasoned by air-drying (rather than kilning), and loans its casks for four years to the Heaven Hill Bourbon distillery in Kentucky.

All this from one of the smaller companies in the industry. The distillery is at the pretty, sandstone town of Tain (pop. 4,000). The town and distillery are on the coast about 40 miles north of Inverness. From the A9 road, the short, private drive passes between an assortment of trees and a dam shaped like a millpond. Beyond can be seen the waters of the Dornoch Firth. The distillery comprises solid-looking stone buildings with rather utilitarian pagodas and a water wheel.

The distilling water flows from springs, on sandstone hills, and flows over heather and clover, the geology contributing to the whisky's firmness of body, the flowers to its famously scenty character. (A French perfume house identified 26 aromas, from almond, bergamot, and cinnamon to verbena, vanilla, and wild mint. More recently, a New York fragrance company managed only 22). Some of the fruitiness may be derived from the house yeast. The spirit's delicacy is owed also to the tallest stills in Scotland, at 5.13 metres (16ft 10¼ in). Finally, the sea adds a breezy touch of saltiness. There is even a very faint hint of seaweed.

Records show illicit brewing and distilling in the region in the 1600s, and at the Morangie farm in the early 1700s. There was a Morangie brewery on the present site, and this was converted into a legal distillery in 1843. The present buildings date mainly from 1887, and the company from 1918. Two years later, the company bought the Glen Moray distillery, on Speyside. Much more recently, in 1997, it acquired and restored Ardbeg, on Islay.

The company was called Macdonald and Muir until 1996. Although the fourth generation of the original family is still involved, the name was changed to that of the flagship distillery (pronounced to rhyme with "orangey"). It means "Glen of Tranquillity".

HOUSE STYLE Delicately spicy. In younger ages, an aperitif; in older ages, after dinner.

GLENMORANGIE 10-year-old, 40 vol
The principal version.

Colour Pale gold.

Nose Spicy (cinnamon, walnut, sandalwood?), with some flowery sweetness, fresh, a whiff of the sea, enticing.

Body On the light side of medium, but with some viscosity.

Palate Spicy, flowery, and malty-sweet tones that are creamy, almost buttery.

Finish Long and rounded.

SCORE 80

The Native Ross-shire Glenmorangie 10-year-old, 57.6 vol
This version is now hard to find.

Colour Bright, pale gold.

Nose Fragrant, salty.

Body Medium, smooth.

Palate Malty-sweet start, then butterscotch, walnut, sandalwood, sandy-salty notes.

Finish Robust, spicy.

SCORE 80

GLENMORANGIE 18-year-old, 43 vol

Colour Full reddish-amber.

Nose Sherry, mint, walnuts, sappy, oaky.

Body Medium, smooth, fleshier.

Palate Sherryish and sweet at first, more walnuts, then the whole pot-pourri of spiciness.

Finish Aromatic, nutty, lightly oaky.

SCORE 80

Some special editions of Glenmorangie

GLENMORANGIE Cellar 13, 43 vol
Among the distillery's 14 cellars, this one is nearest to the sea.
The whiskies in this bottling are in the range of ten to 12 years and more,
all matured in first-fill Bourbon barrels.

Colour Primrose.

Nose Soft, with fresh sandalwood, vanilla, and wild mint.

Body Light to medium. Very smooth.

Palate Notably soft and malty-sweet, with butterscotch, vanilla, and honey.

Finish Buttercups. Juicy, then late, emphatic saltiness. Very long indeed.

SCORE 81

GLENMORANGIE Millennium Malt, 12-year-old, 40 vol
The earlier of two millennium bottlings, from first-fill Bourbon barrels.

Colour Full gold.

Nose Lightly oaky. Hint of brown sugar.

Body Slightly syrupy.

Palate Similar to the Cellar 13, but perhaps more buttery.

Finish Light, refreshing. An almost spritzy, crunchy, toasty dryness.

SCORE 80

GLENMORANGIE Traditional, 100 Proof, 57.2 vol
In the same style as the two above, but without chill-filtering and
at cask strength (in the British version of the old proof system,
100 equalled 56.6–57.1 vol).

Colour Primrose, slightly oily.

Nose Very aromatic and spicy.

Body Smooth, firm, slightly gritty.

Palate Richer, more substantial. Fuller flavours. Sandy-salty notes.

Finish. Robust. Intensely salty. Very long. Soothing.

SCORE 83

GLENMORANGIE Elegance, 21-year-old 43 vol
Presented in a Caithness Glass decanter in the shape of Glenmorangie's stills.

Colour Greeny-gold.
Nose Soft. Earthy. Lightly oaky. A hint of peat.
Body Soft. Very oily.
Palate More oak and vanilla. Sweet, juicy, and oily, then a surprisingly fresh surge of peatiness.
Finish Peaty, grassy, salty, warming. Very soothing.

SCORE 82

GLENMORANGIE 21-year-old, 43 vol, Sesquicentennial Bottling
Issued in 1993 to mark the company's 150th anniversary. This version, in a stoneware "lemonade" bottle, is now hard to find.

Colour Deep gold, oily, almost mustardy.
Nose Intensely spicy.
Body Medium, fleshy.
Palate Toffeeish, very satisfying, with walnut, then big development of spices. Lemon grass and pronounced peat.
Finish Juicy oakiness.

SCORE 85

GLENMORANGIE ORIGINAL, 24-year-old, 43 vol
An "extra special" millennium edition, dating from the time when the distillery operated its own maltings.

Colour Walnut.
Nose Very distinctive, clean, oaky peatiness. This character is in the bakcground throughout.
Body Medium. Very firm. Rounded.
Palate Flowery. Fudgy. Toffeeish. Nutty. Very soft, restrained, spiciness. Then toasty and peaty.
Finish Firm, clean (almost crisp), peatiness. Then long, very soft, spicy and remarkably warming.

SCORE 86

Some vintage-dated limited bottlings

GLENMORANGIE 1979 (bottled 1995), 40 vol

Colour Lemony gold.

Nose Light, fragrant, hint of peat. Faint smoke. Very appetizing.

Body Surprisingly rich.

Palate Beautifully balanced. Malty, with some butteriness, moving to spice and salt. Very lively flavours.

Finish Gentle, soothing.

SCORE 84

GLENMORANGIE 1977 (21-year-old), 43 vol

Colour Bright, greeny-gold.

Nose A hit of oaky vanilla and spice, then grassy peat, and finally a surprisingly emphatic whiff of sea air.

Body Light but smooth and firm. Slightly oily.

Palate Sweet and juicy. The fresh oak character combines with the typical walnut, but somewhat overpowers the usual spiciness.

Finish That very slight peat again, its quick, smoky, fragrant dryness adding an appetizing full-point.

SCORE 84

GLENMORANGIE 1972 (cask 1740, bottle 066, 1993), 46 vol

Colour Very full gold.

Nose Lightly peaty, flowery, then very spicy. Lots of cinnamon.

Body Light to medium but smooth and textured.

Palate Very nutty. Grassy. Dry. Full of fresh flavours.

Finish Peaty. Grassy. Garden mint. Salty. Slightly sandy or stony. Lightly dry. Crisp, cracker-like.

SCORE 85

GLENMORANGIE 1971, 43 vol

Colour Amber.

Nose Soft, complex, citrus, and spices.

Body Rich.

Palate Soft. Treacly malt. Licorice. Aniseed. Spices.

Finish Rooty. Lemony. Salty. Warming. Soothing.

SCORE 86

Wood finishes regularly available

GLENMORANGIE Port Wood Finish, 43 vol

No age statement, but typically ten to 12 years in Bourbon wood and up to two in port pipes. Similar regimes for the other wood finishes.

Colour Orange, with pinkish blush.

Nose Pronouncedly fruity and winey.

Body Very soft indeed, and smooth.

Palate The port seems to bring out the toffeeish notes. It also adds sweeter, winey notes, and melds beautifully with the spiciness of Glenmorangie.

Finish Soothing, soporific, relaxing.

SCORE 87

GLENMORANGIE Madeira Wood Finish, 43 vol

Colour Deep lemony gold.

Nose Sweet. Very spicy. Cakey.

Body Soft, but becoming almost grainy as it dries on the tongue.

Palate Unusually buttery. Barley-sugar sweetness at first: toffeeish, chewy, cakey. Then nutty and seed-like as it dries. Cinnamon and spices. A teasing interplay of the Madeira and the distillery character.

Finish Short and sweet. Some rummy warmth.

SCORE 86

GLENMORANGIE Sherry Wood Finish, 43 vol

The sherry is dry oloroso.

Colour Darkish gold.

Nose Nutty. Dry. Faint peat. Sea air.

Body Soft and curvaceous.

Palate Voluptuous. Long, sustained development of barley-sugar sweetness, almost overpowers the distillery character.

Finish Licorice. Rooty. Late, restrained saltiness.

SCORE 85

Limited-edition wood finishes

GLENMORANGIE Fino Sherry Finish, 43 vol

Colour Pale, refractive, greeny-gold.

Nose Gentle sea fragrance. Very appetizing.

Body Light, firm, smooth.

Palate Very delicate and teasing. Lightly toasty. Cinnamon toast. Faintly rhubarby fruitiness and wineyness. Tinge of sourish acidity.

Finish The coastal whisky and near-coastal sherry combine in a clinching hug of saltiness and oakiness. A wonderfully stylish whisky.

SCORE 89

GLENMORANGIE Tain L'Hermitage (Rhône wine), 43 vol

Colour Distinctively elegant orange.

Nose Very fruity and sweet.

Body Creamy.

Palate Very clean toffee and vanilla, developing to nuttiness and remarkably dry fruitiness. Great length.

Finish Astonishingly lean and winey. Full of fruity, winey, spicy flavours. Very lively.

SCORE 88

GLENMORANGIE Claret Wood Finish, 43 vol

Colour Orangey amber.

Nose Fruity, fragrant, cedary.

Body Firm, drying on the tongue.

Palate Dry, cedary start. Becoming slightly raisiny. Long development of more spicy notes.

Finish Dry, with a slightly cookie-like sweetness and fruity perfuminess.

SCORE 87

GLEN MORAY

PRODUCER Glenmorangie plc
REGION Highlands   DISTRICT Speyside (Lossie)

ADDRESS Bruceland Road, Elgin, Morayshire, IV30 1YE   TEL 01343-542577
WEBSITE www.glenmoray.com   E-MAIL visitors@glenmorangieplc.co.uk

CHARDONNAY AND CHENIN BLANC finishing (for six to 12 months) gives a new flourish, seemingly intended to be feminine, to a range of three Glen Moray malts launched in 1999. The wine character is most obvious in the youngest of the three. The use of whites is an innovation in the industry. Glen Moray shares owners with the more northerly Glenmorangie distillery, which pioneered the notion of "wine" finishes but with reds, port, and Madeira. The two distilleries' similar names pre-date their common ownership. It is a second coincidence that both were formerly breweries. Glen Moray was converted into a distillery in 1897, acquired by its present owners in the 1920s, and extended in 1958. Its whiskies are admired, but have never enjoyed great glamour. Now they sport a change of orientation: skirts instead of kilts; the distillery previously favoured gift tins decorated with the liveries of Highland regiments.

HOUSE STYLE Grassy, with barley notes. Aperitif.

GLEN MORAY 8-year-old, 43 vol
Mainly available in Italy.

Colour Very pale, satiny gold.

Nose Fresh but soft. Sweet, with a late, oily hint of peat.

Body Very light, but smooth and oily.

Palate Very light indeed. Oily. Gin-like.

Finish Light touch of cereal-grain firmness. Late, very light, smoky warmth.

SCORE 71

GLEN MORAY Single Speyside Malt, no age statement, 40 vol
Six to ten years in Bourbon casks, then "mellowed" in Chardonnay.

Colour Very pale gold.

Nose Fresh, scented, fruity. Like an unpeeled dessert grape. Perhaps a suggestion of banana. Very light hint of the sea.

Body Very soft, textured.

Palate Water melon. Banana. White chocolate. Lightly creamy. Shortbread.

Finish Grape skins. Apple cores. Hay. Cereal grains.
Lighty dry and very crisp.

SCORE 78

GLEN MORAY 12-year-old, 40 vol
This version, without the wine finish, is now hard to find.

Colour Pale gold.

Nose Big, rounded, fresh, grassy, new-mown hay, barley notes.

Body Light, but smooth and firm.

Palate Ripe, fat barley.

Finish Fresh, leafy, oatmeal dryness.

SCORE 75

GLEN MORAY 12-year-old, "mellowed" in Chenin Blanc, 40 vol

Colour Softer, more yellowy.

Nose Pears. Walnuts. Fresh oak.

Body Smooth, oily. Beeswax. Honeyed.

Palate Pears in cream. Late, lively, peachy fruitiness. Garden mint.

Finish Raisiny. Also resiny. Fresh oak. Soothing warmth.
The wine adds an element, but many loyalists will miss the previous version.

SCORE 76

GLEN MORAY 15-year-old, 43 vol
Another version without a wine finish. Now hard to find.

Colour Gold.

Nose Clean, dry, perfumy fruitiness.

Body Smooth and firm.

Palate Very clean, sweetish malty notes, moving to a slightly oily, barleyish dryness.

Finish A complex of leafy, perfumy notes, and an oatmeal or barley dryness.

SCORE 76

GLEN MORAY 16-year-old, "mellowed" in Chenin Blanc, 40 vol

Colour Old gold.

Nose Very aromatic. Hint of cloves. Apples. Tannin.

Body Smooth and very firm.

Palate More assertive. Toffee, apple, oak.

Finish Long. Hints of peat. Grassy. Leafy. Resiny. Peppery.

SCORE 76

GLEN MORAY 17-year-old, 43 vol.
Now hard to find.

Colour Gold.

Nose Perfumy, fruity, very appetizing.

Body Smooth, rounding somewhat.

Palate Remarkably clean, fresh sweetness, moving again towards barleyish dryness.

Finish Slight peat. Lots of development. Long, warming.

SCORE 77

Some vintage editions of Glen Moray

GLEN MORAY 1974, Port Wood Aged. Limited edition, bottled in 1997

Colour Full gold.

Nose Lovely, perfumy complexity.

Body Far richer than other versions.

Palate Oily cereal grain. Honey-roast nuts.

Finish Perfumy again. Sugared almonds. An after-dinner malt of extraordinary delicacy. Beautiful balance of distillery character and port.

SCORE 80

GLEN MORAY 1973, 43 vol

Colour Pale gold, with a tinge of green.

Nose Very sweet, but still extremely clean.

Body Very smooth indeed.

Palate Very complex, with lots of development of sweet (barley, malt and chocolate), delicately spicy notes.

Finish Light sweetness and light peatiness. Long and lingering, with surges of flavour.

SCORE 78

GLEN MORAY 1966, 43 vol

Colour Solid amber.

Nose Nutty, juicy, oaky but fresh.

Body Smooth, soft.

Palate Nutty dryness, malty sweetness, and a hint of grassy peatiness, beautifully balanced and rounded. A confident, elegant malt.

Finish Sweetness and dryness, with the latter eventually winning. Touches of sappy oakiness. A curiously spicy lift at the very end.

SCORE 80

GLEN MORAY 1959 (bottled 1999), 48.4 vol

Colour Full amber.

Nose Rich fruit cake steeped in sherry.

Body Very creamy indeed.

Palate Rich. Fruit cake. The dryness of burnt currants. Intensely nutty, almondy, marzipan development.

Finish Light, nutty dryness. Chewy. Long. Developing a touch of charred oak.

SCORE 79

GLEN ORD

PRODUCER UDV (Diageo)
REGION Highlands **DISTRICT** Northern Highlands

ADDRESS Muir of Ord, Ross-shire, IV6 7UJ   **TEL** 01463-872008 **VC**
WEBSITE www.glenord.com

A YOUNG WOMAN, ALISON CURRIE, runs the modern maltings at Glen Ord, and in doing so she maintains a tradition. In more labour-intensive days, the maltings was staffed by five women. One formidable maltster, Betty McIntosh, also sold her homemade fudge at the distillery's shop. Today, Glen Ord's "brand ambassador" is a woman, too, the energetic Barbara Ogilvie.

This is the barley-growing district called the Black Isle, actually a peninsula jutting into the Moray Firth. The Glen Ord distillery was established in 1838 and modernized in 1966. It is at a village called Muir of Ord ("the Moor by the Hill"). Not far away, just south of Inverness, Drumossie Moor provides some of the peat visible in open-sided barns at Glen Ord. The water comes from the "Loch of Smoke", linked by a waterfall to the "Loch of Birds", then by the White Burn six miles from the distillery. The whisky has traditionally been an important contributor to the Dewar's blends, but in recent years has been more widely marketed as a single malt. In distillery bottlings, the selections have a distinct oloroso-sherry character. Confusingly, some older bottlings are labelled variously as Glenordie, Ordie, or simply Ord.

HOUSE STYLE Flavoursome, rose-like, spicy, and malty, with a dry finish. After dinner.

GLEN ORD 12-year-old, 40 vol

Colour Amber.

Nose Rounded, with sherry, sweet and dry malt notes, and a whiff of peat.

Body Medium to full, soft.

Palate Light touch of sherry. Malty and very clean. Begins simply with the malt, then comes a dash of barley-sugar sweetness, and a spicy, gingery note, followed by a restrained, malty dryness and a crisp hit of peat.

Finish Dry, gingery, spicy, citric, smooth.

SCORE 76

RARE MALTS
SELECTION

Each individual vintage has been specially selected from Scotland's finest single malt stocks of rare or now silent distilleries. The limited bottlings of these scarce and unique whiskies are at natural cask strength for the enjoyment of the true connoisseur.

NATURAL
CASK STRENGTH
SINGLE MALT
SCOTCH WHISKY

AGED **23** YEARS

DISTILLED 1974

GLEN ORD
DISTILLERY
ESTABLISHED 1838
MUIR OF ORD, ROSS-SHIRE

60.80%vol 70cle

PRODUCED AND BOTTLED
IN SCOTLAND

LIMITED EDITION
BOTTLE
OCTOBER 1998 N° 6018

GLEN ORD 1974, 23-year-old, 60.80 vol, Rare Malts

Colour Very pale primrose.

Nose Very fresh, assertive. Leafy, lightly peaty. Fragrant smoke.

Body Big, soft, slightly syrupy.

Palate Nutty malt, raisins, ginger, lemon peels, roses.

Finish Spicy, flowery, peaty.

SCORE 78

GLENORDIE 12-year-old, 40 vol

Colour Full, gold.

Nose Profound, with sweet and dry malt notes and a hint of peatiness.

Body Medium to full, very smooth.

Palate Malty, very clean, accented towards sweetness, but with a balancing dryness. So easy to drink, yet full of taste.

Finish Dry, gingery, spicy, smooth.

SCORE 75

Earlier versions of Glen Ord
A 24-year-old, 46 vol, from Cadenhead.

Colour Bronze.

Nose Deep and dry, with a hint of peat.

Body Medium to full, very smooth.

Palate Malty, with a peaty dryness quickly emerging.

Finish Peaty, very long, some sherry notes.

SCORE 77

GLENROTHES

PRODUCER Highland Distillers
REGION Highlands   **DISTRICT** Speyside (Rothes)

ADDRESS Burnside Street, Rothes, Aberlour, AB38 7AA

THE MOST ARISTOCRATIC of wine and spirit merchants, Berry Brothers and Rudd have over the past five to ten years showcased Glenrothes as their house malt (rendered variously as one or two words). At first sight, it seems a paradox that a company synonymous with wine should give new life to a single malt, but that simply reflects the new appreciation of Scotland's finest whiskies. It also represents a return to tradition. Once, many respected wine merchants in England as well as Scotland offered their own bottlings of single malts, as well as combining them in house blends. Glenrothes' quietly noble whisky has traditionally been a component of Berry's internationally known Cutty Sark, and a favourite among blenders. The distillery, established in 1878, is one of five in the small town of Rothes.

The firm of Berry's began in the 1690s, selling tea, groceries, and wine. Cutty Sark was launched in the 1920s. It is named after the famously fast tea clipper Cutty Sark, which was built in Scotland. Both Glenrothes and Cutty Sark are sold not only in Berry's 1730s' premises in stately St James's, London, but also in the company's stores at London's Heathrow airport (terminals 3 and 4).

HOUSE STYLE Perfumy, sweet, spicy-fruity, complex. After dinner.

GLENROTHES 1987 (bottled 1999), 43 vol

Colour	Gold, with tinge of bronze.

Nose Dry spiciness. Depth of tightly combined aromas. Extremely delicate hint of peat.

Body Silky, developing slight viscosity.

Palate Licorice. Layers of toffeeish malt, at first chewy, momentarily crunchy, then syrupy.

Finish Soft, spiciness. Dusty. Hints of icing sugar, but ultimately a smooth dryness.

SCORE 81

GLENROTHES 1985 (bottled 1997), 43 vol

Colour Perhaps fractionally brighter gold.

Colour Perhaps fractionally brighter gold.

Nose Drier, rootier. More oily and aromatic.

Body Lightly silky.

Palate Drier, spicier.

Finish Firm hit of creamy malt, then very late surge of lemon grass and peaty warmth.

SCORE 81

GLENROTHES 1984 (bottled 1996), 43 vol

Colour Full gold.

Nose Notably flowery, then fruity and nutty (a touch of sherry). Both sweetness and dryness.

Body Silky, very smooth.

Palate Sweet maltiness. Almost malted milk. Creamy. Orange skins. Peaches. Fleshy. Sherry trifle. Good depth.

Finish Grassy. Lightly peaty. Dry.

SCORE 81

GLENROTHES 1982 (bottled 1997), 43 vol

Colour Bright gold.

Nose Decidedly peatier.

Body Slightly firmer and bigger.

Palate Vanilla and buttery maltiness. Ripe, sherryish fruitiness. Then a robust, spicy complexity.

Finish Astonishingly dusty-spicy character. Late warmth.

SCORE 82

GLENROTHES 1979 (bottled in 1994), 43 vol
This bottling is now hard to find.

Colour Solid gold.

Nose Delicate peat, as promised on the label.

Body Still silky-smooth, but lighter.

Palate Licorice. Lots of flavour development. Lots of spiciness.
Touches of dried fruit and peat.

Finish Spicy, long, dry.

SCORE 83

GLENROTHES 1972 (bottled 1996), 43 vol

Colour Pale to medium amber.

Nose Sherry. Polished oak. Polished leather.

Body Buttery but firm, even lean.

Palate Luxurious, sophisticated, elegant, its flavours sweet and rum-buttery but restrained and tightly combined. Underpinned almost imperceptibly by smoky peat. Like sitting in a leather armchair and eating cherryish nougat in front of a log fire.

Finish Light, with a hint of fresh oak.

SCORE 85

Other versions of Glenrothes
A MacPhail Collection bottling, at a remarkably mature eight years old and 40 vol, has a full, burnished gold colour; a big, flowery-fruity (dried apricots?) aroma; a light but silky body; wonderfully soft spiciness in the palate; and a clean, crisp, gingery finish. SCORE 80. An earlier version from the same bottler (1956 at 40 vol), under the full name Gordon & MacPhail, was slightly darker and more sherryish in palate, with some nutty dryness. SCORE 80. A Berry Brothers bottling at 12 years old and 43 vol, now hard to find, is perfumy and very complex. SCORE 81.

GLEN SCOTIA

PRODUCER Loch Lomond Distillery Co
REGION Campbeltown

ADDRESS 12 High Street, Campbeltown, Argyll, PA28 6DS
TEL 01586-552288 **VC** By appointment only

THE FIRST DISTILLING SEASON of the new millennium should see production well under way once more at Glen Scotia. In the second half of the 1990s, the distillery was refitted, after being acquired by the Loch Lomond company. Production had been very sporadic for more than a decade. Glen Scotia is known for more than one manifestation of spirit: it is said to be haunted by the ghost of a former proprietor who drowned himself in Campbeltown Loch.

Glen Scotia, founded around 1832, should be cherished as one of the only two survivors in the once-great distilling centre of Campeltown. The other, Springbank, is better known and deservedly esteemed, but Glen Scotia's whisky is a splendidly briny example of the town's coastal style.

HOUSE STYLE Fresh, salty. Aperitif, or with salty foods.

GLEN SCOTIA 14-year-old, 40 vol

Colour Full, refractive gold.
Nose Aromatic, oily, briny, big.
Body Seems light on the tongue, then quickly becomes oily and smooth.
Palate Dry maltiness, oiliness, saltiness. Very appetite-arousing.
Finish Remarkably long and powerful.

SCORE 87

Independent bottlings of Glen Scotia

A 1977 (13-year-old), at 58.6 vol from Cadenhead, has an olivey-gold colour; a salty, woody, oily aroma, with a late suggestion of peatiness; a quite rich, oily body; salty, sandy, earthy, faintly peaty flavours; and a grassy sweetness in the finish. SCORE 88. An earlier 16-year-old at 57.6 vol from the same bottler was softer, fuller in flavour, saltier, and longer. SCORE 88. A 12-year-old at 55.8 vol from James MacArthur was smooth and rounded, with a good salty finish. SCORE 86.

GLEN SPEY

PRODUCER UDV (Diageo)
REGION Highlands **DISTRICT** Speyside (Rothes)

ADDRESS Rothes, Morayshire, AB38 7AU
TEL 01340-832000

A CONTRIBUTOR TO THE WELL-KNOWN WHISKY J&B. That blend is named after the wine merchants Justerini and Brooks, which was established in 1749, and still operates in St James's London. Glen Spey, founded in the 1880s, was rebuilt in 1970.

HOUSE STYLE Light, grassy, nutty. Aperitif.

GLEN SPEY 8-year-old, 40 vol
This bottling is hard to find.

Colour Gold.

Nose Light, fragrant.

Body On the light side of medium.

Palate Aromatic, faint hints of peat, grassiness, and nuttiness.

Finish Light, dryish.

SCORE 73

GLEN SPEY, 12-year-old, 43 vol, Master of Malt

Colour Bright gold.

Nose Light, dry. Fragrant, faint peat.

Body Soft, marshmallow-like.

Palate Malty. Very sweet. Slightly oily. Nutty.

Finish Delicate peat. Rather quick.

SCORE 71

GLENTAUCHERS

PRODUCER Allied Distillers
REGION Highlands   DISTRICT Speyside

ADDRESS Mulben, Keith, Banffshire, AB5 2YL

ORIGINALLY A CONTRIBUTOR TO THE BUCHANAN "Black and White" blends, this distillery was founded in 1898 and rebuilt in 1965. It has been owned by Allied since 1989. Glentauchers is an attractive enough distillery, but with no visitor centre or official bottlings, has not had the attention it merits. With Auchroisk ("The Singleton") as a neighbour, it is in the countryside near the village of Mulben, between the distilling towns of Rothes and Keith.

HOUSE STYLE Clovey dryness and malty sweetness.
A soothing malt.

Vintage 1975
Single Highland Malt Scotch Whisky
Matured in oak casks for 21 years
Distilled at Glentauchers Distillery
on 26.11.75   Bottled 12.9.97
Cask No. 8888   Bottle No.   of 806
This whisky has been selected, produced and bottled in Scotland for and under the sole responsibility of Signatory Vintage Scotch Whisky Co. Ltd.
70cl   *Edinburgh EH6 6RY Scotland*   55.6%vol

GLENTAUCHERS 1975 (bottled 1997), 55.6 vol, Signatory
This is less dry and overtly medicinal than earlier bottlings.

Colour Very full gold.
Nose Earthy, peaty, fragrant.
Body Rich.
Palate Richly malty. Emphatically fruity (apples, raisins?). Sweet. Beautifully balanced.
Finish Powerful. Clean, clovey spiciness, with an interplay of sweetness and dryness. Long. Warming. Late peat smoke.

SCORE 74

Earlier bottlings of Glentauchers

Gordon & MacPhail has offered some sherryish versions (less rich and more nuttily dry), such as a 1979 at 40 vol that was distinctly clovey. SCORE 72. A Cadenhead 17-year-old, at 46 vol, was peatier and more phenolic. SCORE 71.

GLENTURRET

PRODUCER Highland Distillers
REGION Highlands   DISTRICT Midlands
ADDRESS Crieff, Perthshire, PH7 4HA   TEL 01764-656565 VC
WEBSITE www.glenturret.com

THE MOST VISITABLE OF ALL MALT WHISKY DISTILLERIES: one of the smallest, and a claimant to being Scotland's oldest, tucked in a pretty glen just an hour by road from Edinburgh or Glasgow. The distillery works for 11 months of the year (the traditional "silent season" is very short: just the month of January), but is very much oriented toward visitors. Being small and traditional in style, it offers a good view of whisky production. At their best, its malts are very complex, with beautifully dovetailed flavours. There is also a surprisingly nutty, flowery, subtle liqueur based on the whisky.

The malt is bottled in a wide range of versions, several offered for tasting at the distillery. Glenturret also has a restaurant providing Scottish dishes (no reservations necessary for lunch; dinner for groups only). Although its world-famous cat Towser is now hunting mice in the heavens, he is remembered in a statue. There is no monument to his alleged 28,899 victims (who documented them so precisely on behalf of the *Guinness Book of Records*?). Given the amount of mouse-tempting grain on the premises, most distilleries employ a cat. Towser's successor is called Amber.

The distillery is on the banks of the River Turret, near Crieff, in Perthshire. There are records of whisky making in the neighbourhood at least as early as 1717, and some of the buildings on the present site date from 1775. The distillery itself was dismantled in the 1920s, then revived in 1959 by a noted whisky enthusiast, James Fairlie. It was acquired in 1981 by Cointreau, the French liqueur company, and became part of Highland Distillers in 1990.

HOUSE STYLE Dry, nutty, fresh, flowery. Young as an aperitif; older after dinner.

This classic farmhouse distillery hosts events from ceilidhs to conferences.

GLENTURRET 8-year-old, 40 vol
Now hard to find.

Colour Pale, fino sherry.

Nose Sweet, malty, fresh.

Body Light and smooth.

Palate Malty, creamy.

Finish Surprisingly long, and very lively.

SCORE 76

GLENTURRET 10-year-old, 57.1 vol ("100° proof")
Now hard to find.

Colour Bright, white wine.

Nose Very appetizing, toffeeish maltiness.

Body Big, soft.

Palate Toffee, roasty notes, very powerful.

Finish Nutty, almost juicy.

SCORE 77

GLENTURRET 12-year-old, 40 vol

Colour Gold.

Nose Flowery, nutty.

Body Light to medium. Smooth.

Palate Nutty. Cereal-grain maltiness and vanilla pod. Becoming drier, with a hint of apple.

Finish Crisp, dry. Appetizing. Refreshing.

SCORE 75

GLENTURRET 5,000 days old, 40 vol
A neater way of saying between 13 and 14 years old.

Colour Full gold.

Nose Sweet, with a little more depth.

Body Light to medium, smooth.

Palate Very tasty. Some raisiny notes, and a good,
creamy maltiness.

Finish Long.

SCORE 75

GLENTURRET 15-year-old, 40 vol
A lovely balance of the components in this luscious malt.

Colour Full gold.

Nose Profound, with malty and oaky notes.

Body Medium, chewy.

Palate Malty, roasty, perfumy.

Finish Creamy, smooth, glowing.

SCORE 81

GLENTURRET 15-year-old, 50 vol

Colour Full gold.

Nose Very flowery, with touches of peat and oak.

Body Medium, smooth, becoming chewy.

Palate Malty, toasty, nutty, flowery, very perfumy. Some tasters have found elderflower.

Finish Smooth, glowing. Very long, with lots of development.

SCORE 82

GLENTURRET 18-year-old, 40 vol

Colour Full gold.

Nose Hint of peat and lemon grass. Honeyed dessert apple.

Body Full, creamy.

Palate Sweet, clean maltiness. Vanilla pod. Perfumy.

Finish Dry, fragrant, hint of peat. Long, glowing.

SCORE 83

GLENTURRET 21-year-old, 40 vol
Packaged in a "copper" flagon (actually ceramic).

Colour Deep gold to amber.

Nose Pronounced sherry. Nutty maltiness. Hint of warm smoke.
Very attractive.

Body Firm. Slightly oily.

Palate Nutty. Lovely balance of floweriness, maltiness, and sherry.

Finish Nutty. Hint of aniseed. Perfumy.

SCORE 86

GLENTURRET 25-year-old, 43 vol
Packaged in a ceramic globe. A world of whisky?

Colour Bright gold to amber.

Nose Sherry and nutty malt, but also a hint of oily peatiness.

Body Big, smooth.

Palate Assertive and characterful, but in a peatier, much oakier style.

Finish Oaky, sappy, dry.

SCORE 86

GLENTURRET 1972, 43 vol

Colour Full gold, with some depth.

Nose Profound, with malt, nuttiness, and some sherry.

Body Medium, rounded.

Palate Very complex, with all the components
beautifully dovetailed.

Finish Nutty, rich, powerful.

SCORE 90

GLENTURRET 1967, 50 vol

This huge malt is a delight for lovers of heavily sherried whiskies. Given its vintage in combination with its proof, it may well have more intensity of sherry character than any other malt.

Colour Deep amber-red.

Nose Rich sherry aroma.

Body Full, slightly liqueurish, but by no means overbearing.

Palate Very sherry-accented.

Finish Soft, rich, warming, long.

SCORE 86

GLENTURRET 1966 (bottled 1993), 45.7 vol, Natural Cask Strength

Colour Deep orange.

Nose Polished oak. Beeswax. Earthy, hay, hint of grassy saltiness.

Body Medium to full. Rich. Again, slightly liqueurish.

Palate Great depth of clean malty-nutty and sherry flavours.
Hints of butter.

Finish Earthy, nutty, flapjack. Developing great warmth and length,
with a faint saltiness.

SCORE 89

GLENTURRET 1966, 40 vol

Colour Full gold, with a touch of russet.
Nose Juicy oak, peat, and flowery notes.
Body Full, firm, smooth.
Palate Very nutty, firm, becoming chewy, but staying just on the sweet side.
Finish Dry, oaky, peaty, with late floweriness.

SCORE 91

GLENTURRET Neil's Dram, 48.4 vol

A marriage of vintages. The matchmaker is distillery manager Neil Cameron. The idea is to balance the differing characteristics of Glenturret at various ages. Available only in a 200ml sample bottle.

Colour Deep yellowy gold.
Nose Gentle, fresh, sherry.
Body Firm, smooth, slightly syrupy.
Palate Very appetizing, dryish sherry. Big, nutty maltiness. Sweet heather and honey.
Finish Long and complex. Both sweet and dry, slightly acidic sherry notes. Floweriness. Spiciness. That typically long glow.

SCORE 87

Some independent bottlings

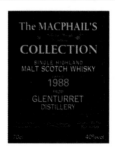

The MACPHAIL'S
COLLECTION
SINGLE HIGHLAND
MALT SCOTCH WHISKY
1988
FROM
GLENTURRET
DISTILLERY

70cl   40%vol

GLENTURRET 1988, 40 vol, The MacPhail's Collection

Colour Bright gold.
Nose Very flowery. Lemon peels. Passion fruit. Slightly vegetal.
Body Light. Firm.
Palate Lemon sherbet. Zest of lemon. Slightly oily.
Finish Very light. Faint lemon grass and peat.

SCORE 70

GLENTURRET 1980 (re-fill sherry cask, bottled 1997), 46 vol, Murray McDavid

Colour Bright pale yellow.

Nose Delicately flowery. Very faint, dry peatiness.

Body Soft.

Palate Much peatier and smokier than any other version.

Finish Smoky, oily, grainy. Late lemon juice and pepper.
This version is atypical and unbalanced, but full of character.

SCORE 77

GLENTURRET Aged 13 years (distilled 1979), 43 vol, The Castle Collection

Colour Bright primrose.

Nose Softly lemony. Hint of lemon grass and peat.

Body Lightly syrupy.

Palate Very sweet start. Then lemony. Then lemon grass and peat.

Finish Peppery.

SCORE 73

GLENTURRET 1978, 51.5 vol, Signatory

Colour Pale greeny-gold.

Nose Very light. Lemony.

Body Lightly syrupy.

Palate Lemon peels. Dried buttercups. Pepper.

Finish Sharp lemon and pepper.

SCORE 72

GLENUGIE

PRODUCER Long John (Whitbread)
REGION Highlands   DISTRICT Eastern Highlands

ADDRESS Peterhead, Aberdeenshire, AB42 0XY

T HERE ARE MORE VERSIONS OF THIS MALT available than ever, yet the distillery has long closed. Such contradictions are not altogether unusual. Blenders presumably phased out its use, and residual stocks were acquired by independent bottlers.

The distillery site is close to the remnants of a fishing village near Peterhead, where the river Ugie reaches the sea. The site incorporates the stump of a windmill. There had been distilling there since the 1830s, and the surviving buildings date from the 1870s.

The Whitbread brewing company, owners since the 1970s, gradually withdrew from the production of spirits during the 1980s, when the whisky industry was suffering one of its cyclical downturns. Industrial premises in Aberdeenshire were being snapped up by small engineering firms servicing the oil boom, and that was Glenugie's fate in 1982–83. Its whisky-making equipment was removed.

HOUSE STYLE Sweet, butterscotch-like. With some flowery, resiny notes. Can be medicinal. Book-at-bedtime.

GLENUGIE 1980 (12-year-old), 59.7 vol, Cadenhead
Interesting for its very heavy sherry.

Colour Dark chestnut.

Nose Powerful. Sweet sherry, then fino-like acidity. Sappy. Woody. Shellac-like. Medicinal.

Body Creamy.

Palate Malty. Sherry. Raisiny. Sweet smokiness. Earthy.

Finish Assertive. Rooty, gingery, warming, long.

SCORE 71

GLENUGIE 1967, 40 vol, Connoisseurs Choice

Colour Full gold.

Nose Flowery. Faintly medicinal. Resiny. Faint wood.

Body Firmly smooth. Almost slippery.

Palate Dry at first. Firm and clean, but curiously lacking in flavour. Faint leafy resin. Then develops hard-toffee and butterscotch notes, the latter lingering.

Finish Very light. Slight bite into butterscotch. Faint ginger.

SCORE 68

SINGLE
HIGHLAND MALT
SCOTCH
WHISKY

31 YEARS OLD
Distilled at
GLENUGIE DISTILLERY
Distilled 31.12.66   Bottled 5.6.98
Cask No. 5082   Bottle No.   of 206
70cl   **53.9%vol**
Bottled in Scotland by
Signatory Vintage Scotch Whisky Co. Ltd. Edinburgh EH6 5PY

GLENUGIE 1966, 53.9 vol, Signatory "Silent Stills" Series

Colour Bright greeny-gold.

Nose Flowery. Dry.

Body Soft, syrupy.

Palate Sweet, again falling away.

Finish Lightly spicy, gingery.

SCORE 67

GLENUGIE 1996 (30-year-old, cask 852), 61.8 vol, The Bottlers

Colour Bronze to amber.

Nose Nutty sherry. Hint of resin.

Body Medium, soft.

Palate Starts light, moving to butterscotch syrupiness, rich enough to pour on ice cream.

Finish Dries slightly. Freshly milled ginger.

SCORE 71

GLENUGIE 1965 (23-year-old), 43 vol, Hart Brothers

Colour Greeny-gold.

Nose Very flowery, resiny, medicinal.

Body Light but firm. Slippery.

Palate Quick hint of old books and pressed leaves or flowers. Then buttercups, butterscotch, and sugar-sweet.

Finish Very light, quick, ginger.

SCORE 67

GLENURY ROYAL

PRODUCER DCL
REGION Highlands   DISTRICT Eastern Highlands

ADDRESS Stonehaven, Kincardineshire, AB3 2PY

G LENURY ROYAL WAS ON THE EAST COAST, south of Aberdeen, and close to the fishing port of Stonehaven. The distillery's name derived from the glen that runs through the Ury district. The water for the whisky came from the Cowie, a river known for salmon and trout. The distillery was founded in 1825, partly to provide a market for barley in a period of agricultural depression. Founder Captain Robert Barclay was an athlete, known for an odd achievement: he was the first man to walk 1,000 miles in as many hours without a break. He was also a local Member of Parliament. Barclay had a friend at court to whom he referred coyly as "Mrs Windsor", and through whose influence he was given permission by King William IV to call his whisky "Royal". It was latterly a component of blends such as King William IV and Auld Toun, made by the small company John Gillon, a subsidiary of DCL. The distillery was mothballed in 1985, and the site was later sold for a housing development.

HOUSE STYLE Aromatic, herbal, oily. Book-at-bedtime.

GLENURY ROYAL 12-year-old, 40 vol
A John Gillon bottling that is now hard to find.

Colour Bronze.
Nose Aromatic, dry, smoky.
Body Light to medium, firm.
Palate Toasty, dry maltiness, developing towards smokiness.
Finish Smoky, with a hint of buttery, honeyish sweetness. Very long.

SCORE 76

GLENURY ROYAL 23-year-old (distilled 1971), 61.3 vol, Rare Malts

Colour Deep reddish amber.

Nose Peat, sherry, and polished oak.

Body Medium, firm, smooth.

Palate Smooth, tightly combined flavours, beautifully rounded.
Treacle toffee, nuts, cedary notes.

Finish Very long. Starts oaky, then an explosion of long, warming
smokiness. A superb example of a Highland malt, hitting as
an oak-fisted heavyweight.

SCORE 80

GLENURY ROYAL 28-year-old (distilled 1970), 58.4 vol, Rare Malts

Colour Shining gold.

Nose Nutty, almondy, oloroso sherry.

Body Very firm, rounded. Less sherryish muscle, more of an
elegant middleweight.

Palate Honey, lemons, pistachio nuts, angelica, garden mint.

Finish Like biting into a green leaf. Tree-bark woodiness.
Cinnamon. Fragrant. Long.

SCORE 79

Other versions of Glenury Royal

A 1971 Rare Malts, at cask strength, tasted as a work in progress, was very
similar in character to the 23-year-old. A 1976, at 40 vol, from Gordon &
MacPhail, has a deep gold colour and a lovely interplay of sherry, honey,
and smoke. A 1973, at 53.7 vol, in Signatory's "Silent Stills" series, is bright
gold, with more cereal grain and flowery honey. An earlier 14-year-old,
from Master of Malt, at 43 vol, was very pale, toasty, honeyish, and spicy.
SCORE 72. A 13-year-old, at 46 vol, from Cadenhead, was also toasty, with
hints of fino sherry. SCORE 75. A 22-year-old at the same strength, from
this bottler, had a distinct oloroso character. SCORE 77.

HIGHLAND PARK

PRODUCER Highland Distillers
REGION Highlands **ISLAND** Orkney

ADDRESS Kirkwall, Orkney, KW15 1SU **TEL** 01856-874619 **VC**
WEBSITE www.highlandpark.co.uk

THE GREATEST ALL-ROUNDER in the world of malt whisky. Definitely in an island style, but combining all the elements of a classic single malt: smokiness (with its own heather-honey accent); maltiness; smoothness; roundness and fullness of flavour; and length of finish – lovely any time. As a single malt, Highland Park develops to great ages. The distillery is now beginning to make available some older examples, which have considerable depth and richness.

Highland Park, the northernmost of Scotland's distilleries, dates from at least 1798. Most of today's buildings, in local Walliwall stone (flecked with yellow and red), and its gilded-iron gateway, have an 1890s' look that is slightly incongruous in rural Orkney. The distillery is on the edge of Kirkwall, the islands' capital. Some experts believe that Highland Park's water falls as rain on the Scottish mainland, and seeps under the sea. It rises from Walliwall stone. Highland Park has its own floor maltings, using peat dug locally, from shallow beds that provide a "young", rooty, heathery character.

HOUSE STYLE Smoky and full-flavoured. At 18 or 25 years old, with dessert or a cigar. The yet older vintages with a book at bedtime.

The Dark Island, reaching towards the Midnight Sun, is one of the most striking locations of whisky production.

HIGHLAND PARK 12-year-old, 40 vol

Colour Amber.

Nose Smoky, "garden bonfire" sweetness, heathery, malty, hint of sherry.

Body Medium, exceptionally smooth.

Palate Succulent, with smoky dryness, heather-honey sweetness, and maltiness.

Finish Teasing, heathery, delicious.

SCORE 90

HIGHLAND PARK 18-year-old, 43 vol

Colour Refractive, pale gold.

Nose Warm, notably flowery. Heather honey, fresh oak, sap, peat, smoky fragrance. Very aromatic and appetizing.

Body Remarkably smooth, firm, rounded.

Palate Lightly salty. Leafy (vine leaves?), pine nuts. Lots of flavour development: nuts, honey, cinnamon, dryish ginger.

Finish Spicy, very dry, oaky, smoky, hot.

SCORE 92

HIGHLAND PARK 24-year-old (1967), 43 vol
Now very hard to find.

Colour Amber.

Nose Honey, with smooth background smokiness.

Body Full.

Palate Starts with smooth honey, becoming deeper in flavour,
developing to a smooth, perfumy smokiness.

Finish Smooth, honeyish, with light fruitiness. Soothing.

SCORE 93

HIGHLAND PARK 25-year-old, 53.5 vol

Colour Apricot.

Nose Full, rounded. Fudge, white chocolate, oloroso sherry,
honey, melon, lemon. Fruity.

Body Firm, rounded.

Palate More honey, slightly chewy. Nutty toffee. Nougat. Pistachio nuts.
Turkish delight. Cedar.

Finish Lemon, honey, roses. Fragrant, smooth. Balancing dryness.

SCORE 93

JAMES GRANT & CO. (HIGHLAND PARK DISTILLERY) KIRKWALL, ORKNEY ISLANDS, SCOTLAND

BICENTENARY

VINTAGE 1977 RESERVE

ORKNEY ✦ ISLANDS

SINGLE MALT SCOTCH WHISKY

750ml 43% alc./vol.

DISTILLED AND BOTTLED IN SCOTLAND, PRODUCT OF SCOTLAND

HIGHLAND PARK 1977 Bicentenary Vintage Reserve

Colour Pale walnut.

Nose Polished oak. Leather upholstery.

Body Firm satin richness.

Palate Minty. Creamy. Freshly peeled satsumas. Orange peels. Dark cherry flavours. Very bitter black chocolate. Astonishing complexity and length. Great power. Long development of drier flavours.

Finish Violets. Lingering flowery, scented flavours.

SCORE 94

DISTILLED AND BOTTLED IN SCOTLAND, PRODUCT OF SCOTLAND

HIGHLAND PARK

ORKNEY ✦ ISLANDS

ONLINE TASTING

SINGLE MALT SCOTCH WHISKY

700 ml 52.6% vol.

Cask Strength

Character Burnished copper; hints of pepper, dough, rich, lingering peat.

BOTTLE Nº 231 | Nº PRODUCED 228

LIMITED **1974** EDITION

Checked *James Labott* Date 7 Aug. 98

JAMES GRANT & CO. HIGHLAND PARK DISTILLERY) KIRKWALL, ORKNEY ISLANDS, SCOTLAND

HIGHLAND PARK Online Tasting, 1974 (bottled 1988), 52.6 vol
(A limited edition created on the basis of a sampling conducted on Highland Park's website.)

Colour Reddish oak.

Nose Winey, perfumy, fragrantly smoky.

Body Big, smooth.

Palate Smooth, tightly combined flavours. Dried fruits. Soft licorice. Cigar-like tobacco. Smoky, sappy, oak. Scores points for robustness.

Finish Huge sweet smokiness.

SCORE 93

HIGHLAND PARK 35-year-old cask strength, 44 vol
Tasted as a work in progress.

Colour Deep reddish orange.

Nose Polished oak. Then toasted almonds. Toasty, smoky.

Body Big. Astonishingly smooth and slippery.

Palate Nutty, fudgy, surprisingly sweet maltiness. Distinctly malty.

Finish Sudden surge of nutty dryness; burnt toast; smoky sappiness; cigar smoke; log fires, with a hint of soot; very late peat. Very long and complex.

HIGHLAND PARK 1958, 44 vol

Colour Deep orange.

Nose Sweet tobacco. Scenty. Sandalwood. Walnuts.

Body Lean. Astonishingly smooth.

Palate Sultanas, lemons, vanilla, butterscotch, toasted almonds. Very restrained sweetness. Scores points for elegance and subtlety.

Finish Long and soothing. Late hint of spicy, heathery smoke.

SCORE 93

Some independent bottlings of Highland Park

HIGHLAND PARK 8-year-old, 40 vol, The MacPhail's Collection

Colour Bright full gold.

Nose Very flowery, honeyish, lemony.

Body Medium.

Palate Very honeyish, with a grassy, balancing dryness.

Finish Buttery, vanilla, fresh-oak crispness.

SCORE 81

From the same bottler, a 1987, at 63.7 vol, was paler, with the aroma of heathery, windswept hillsides; a hint of smoky fragrance; and a warming, lemon-honey finish. SCORE 86.

HIGHLAND PARK 10-year-old (distilled 1988, bottled 1998), 59.8 vol, Adelphi (cask 1922)

Colour Deep gold.

Nose Distinctly honeyish.

Body Lightly syrupy.

Palate Very honeyish. Some sherry and oak.

Finish Creamy flavours. Honey. Hint of ginger. Touch of crisp oak.

SCORE 86

HIGHLAND PARK 1978 (bottled 1997), 46 vol, Murray McDavid

Colour Pale, lemony.

Nose Fragrantly peaty.

Body Silky.

Palate Good flavour development, beautifully balanced as it unfolds. Fragrantly smoky, then nutty, becoming flowery, and finally honeyish. Very good indeed as a lightish, delicate interpretation of Highland Park.

Finish Late, clean, appetizing smokiness.

SCORE 89

Other versions of Highland Park

Three bottlings from Signatory: a 1977, at 43 vol, is very pale indeed, peaty and earthy in nose and finish, with an oily middle. SCORE 81.
A 1975, at 52 vol, is bright gold, with a superbly peaty aroma and beautiful balance of grass, heather honey, and oak. SCORE 89. A 1972, at 55.7 vol, has a fuller gold colour, with a hint of the sea, and a peaty, oaky dryness and hotness. SCORE 87.

IMPERIAL

PRODUCER Allied Distillers
REGION Highlands   DISTRICT Speyside

ADDRESS Carron, Morayshire, AB34 7QP

AN UNDER-RATED SPEYSIDER that can be found only in independent bottlings. The Imperial distillery is in Carron, just across the river from Dailuaine, with which it was historically linked. It was founded in 1897 and extended in 1965. It closed in 1985, but was reopened by Allied in 1989, then mothballed in 1998. Imperial's unusually large stills make it hard to use flexibly. "You either make a lot of Imperial or none at all," commented one observer. The whisky contributes to many blends.

HOUSE STYLE Big and (often sweetly) smoky. After dinner
or at bedtime.

Imperial 1979, 40 vol, Gordon & MacPhail

Colour Full gold, with an amber tinge.

Nose Some peaty oiliness.

Body Medium to full, soft.

Palate Sherry, juicy oak, and vanilla at first, developing to an intense, spicy sweetness and malty, cereal-grain notes. A complex of lively, distinct flavours.

Finish Sweet, lively, intense.

SCORE 76

Other versions of Imperial

A 1976, at 43 vol, from Signatory, is very pale, with a lightly peaty, medicinal aroma; a medium, soft body; a malty middle; and a deliciously smoky finish. SCORE 76. An earlier 15-year-old, at 43 vol, from James MacArthur, had a full gold colour; a faintly flowery aroma; a nutty maltiness; and a smoky dryness. SCORE 77. A 14-year-old, at 64.9 vol, from Cadenhead, was very sweet in its maltiness, with a touch of heather. SCORE 76.

INCHGOWER

PRODUCER UDV (Diageo)
REGION Highlands   **DISTRICT** Speyside

ADDRESS Buckie, Banffshire, AB56 5AB

TASTES MORE LIKE A COASTAL MALT than a Speysider. It is both, the distillery being on the coast near the fishing town of Buckie, but not far from the mouth of the river Spey. To the palate expecting a more flowery, elegant Speyside style, this can seem assertive, or even astringent, in its saltiness. With familiarity, that can become addictive. The Inchgower distillery was built in 1871, and expanded in 1966. Its whisky is an important element in the Bell's blend.

HOUSE STYLE Dry, salty. Restorative or aperitif.

INCHGOWER 14-year-old, 43 vol, Flora and Fauna

Colour Pale gold.

Nose An almost chocolatey spiciness, then sweet notes like edible seaweed, and finally, a whiff of saltier sea character. Overall, dry and complex.

Body Light to medium. Smooth.

Palate Starts sweet and malty, with lots of flavour developing, eventually becoming drier and salty.

Finish Very salty, lingering appetizingly on the tongue.

SCORE 76

Other versions of Inchgower

A Rare Malts 1974, at cask strength, had fresh sea air in the nose; salted nut, cashew, and edible-seaweed flavours; and a long, appetizing finish. SCORE 79. A much earlier bottling, at 12 years old and 40 vol from Bell's, was sweeter, with a touch of sherry, more chocolate, and perfume. SCORE 76. An Oddbins bottling at the same age was very similar, possibly slightly more intense. SCORE 77.

INVERLEVEN

PRODUCER Allied Distillers
REGION Lowlands   **DISTRICT** Western Lowlands
ADDRESS 2 Glasgow Road, Dumbarton, Dunbartonshire, G82 1ND

A VERY RARE MALT, produced in the imposing 1930s' distillery complex by the river Leven at Ballantine's home-base in Dumbarton. For many years, this complex operated not only a column-still making grain whisky, but also two pot-still houses to produce malt whisky for the Ballantine blends. One of the malt distilleries, called Inverleven, had conventional stills. The other produced a heavier, Lomond-still whisky. The malt stills have not operated since 1991–92, and the equipment is no longer complete. Although this part of the complex is regarded as being mothballed, it is unlikely to produce again. Neither malt has ever been officially released as a single, but Inverleven can be found in independent bottlings. In addition to these whiskies, a very wide range of other malts go into the soft but complex Ballantine blends.

HOUSE STYLE Perfumy, fruity, oily. With a summer salad when young; with nuts at Christmas when older.

The home of some famous blends and a hard-to-find malt: the edifice of the Ballantine's cluster of distilleries towers above the River Leven.

INVERLEVEN 1985, 40 vol, Gordon & MacPhail

Colour White wine.

Nose Freshly cut, ripe, sweet pears. Scented, summery.

Body Lightly creamy.

Palate Cream flavour. Nectarine, melon, pear.
Soft, stalky, woodiness.

Finish Refreshing.

SCORE 71

A 1979 edition from the same bottler was slightly less fruity
and drier. SCORE 71.

DUMBARTON (Inverleven stills), 1969, 27-year-old, 51.4 vol, Cadenhead

Colour Bright orangey amber.

Nose Distinctly clean, peaty smokiness, with surprisingly fresh,
orangey notes.

Body Firmly creamy.

Palate Juicy, fruity. Orange cream. Nutty, stalky, dryness. Slightly woody,
but an unusual and very pleasant malt.

Finish Grassy. Fragrant, smoky dryness.

SCORE 71

A 1966 (bottled 1984) from Cadenhead was similar but more cedary and
spicy. Score 67. A 21-year-old from the same bottler was very gingery and
orangey. Score 69.

JURA

PRODUCER JBB
REGION Highlands   ISLAND Jura

ADDRESS Craighouse, Jura, Argyll, PA60 7XT
TEL 01496-820240

IN THE INNER HEBRIDES, close to Islay, lies the isle of Jura. Its name derives from the Norse word for deer. These outnumber people, on an island 34 miles by seven. Jura has about 225 human inhabitants, among whom its most famous was George Orwell. He went there to find a healthy, peaceful place in which to write the novel *1984*. The island is also noted for two mountain peaks known as the Paps (breasts) of Jura, and one malt distillery.

The latter seems to have been founded around 1810, and was rebuilt in 1876. Although a couple of buildings dating back to its early days are still in use, the present distillery was built during the late 1950s and early 1960s, and enlarged in the 1970s. It was owned by Scottish and Newcastle Breweries when they produced the Mackinlay blended Scotches, in which it is an important component.

The very soft water flows primarily over rock, even passing through a cave. The densely wooded hillsides are in places carpeted with bluebells, pimpernels, and wild garlic. Lightly peated malt, mainly from Port Ellen, is used at the distillery, and the stills have very high necks. As these produce a light spirit, first-fill Bourbon or sherry casks could mask the natural flavours of the whisky. There is a very small proportion (less than ten per cent) of second-fill sherry.

HOUSE STYLE Piny, lightly oily, soft, salty. Aperitif.

The allegedly breast-shaped mountains, the Paps of Jura, seen from across the Sound of Islay. The local fishermen bring in lobster and scallops.

ISLE OF JURA 10-year-old, 40 vol

Colour Bright gold.

Nose Oily, lightly piny, earthy, salty, dry.

Body Light, slightly oily, soft.

Palate Sweetish, malty, oily, slowly developing a slight island dryness and saltiness.

Finish A little malty sweetness and some saltiness.

SCORE 72

ISLE OF JURA 20-year-old, 54 vol, cask strength
Limited edition released in the mid 1990s.

Colour Golden.

Nose Creamy, oily, dryish.

Body More round.

Palate Flavours more tightly combined, but slowly revealing themselves. Flowery, sweet, piny, earthy.

Finish Intensely salty and satisfying.

SCORE 78

ISLE OF JURA 26-year-old, 45 vol, Stillman's Dram

Colour A good, medium amber.

Nose Sherry, oak, salt, malt, faint peatiness.

Body Smooth.

Palate Sherryish and pronounced sweetness to start, then rhubarb and sweet lemons, oily flavours, becoming salty. An unusually sherried version.

Finish Lightly peaty.

SCORE 78

Independent bottlings of Jura

ISLE OF JURA 1975, 43 vol, Signatory
Similar in style to the 20-year-old reviewed on the previous page.

Colour Bright pale gold.

Nose Surprisingly fresh. Flowery and salty. Very appetizing.

Body Light and soft. Very slightly syrupy.

Palate Fresh, salty. Cracker-like, crunchy maltiness.

Finish Salty. Very gently piny. Warming. Long. Soothing.

SCORE 78

ISLE OF JURA 1966 (32-year-old), 56.6 vol
Released for the tenth anniversary of Signatory.

Colour Bright gold.

Nose Piny. Unusually peaty. Would appear to have been made from a more heavily peated malt than is used today.

Body Slightly fuller and creamier than is typical for Jura.

Palate Malty. Cracker-like. Late salt and peat.

Finish Lightly toasty. Considerable, long saltiness. Appetizing.

SCORE 79

Earlier bottlings of Jura
A 10-year-old, at 63.9 vol, from Cadenhead, was notably flowery. SCORE 71.
A 20-year-old, at 46 vol, from the same bottler (with its earlier, black-and-white label), showed a much more pronounced island character, despite a medium-to-full sherry overlay. SCORE 76.

KINCLAITH

PRODUCER Whitbread/Long John
REGION Lowlands   DISTRICT Western Lowlands

ADDRESS Moffat Street, Glasgow, G5 0ND

THERE WAS ONCE QUITE A SCATTER of malt distilleries in Glasgow, and there have been about half a dozen this century. Kinclaith was the last. It was built in 1957, as part of the complex already housing the Strathclyde grain distillery. The original owner was the American company Schenley, through its subsidiaries Seager Evans and Long John. During the 1960s, when the bulk of Kinclaith production was presumably going into the Long John blends, some trickled out to independent bottlers. Long John was sold to Whitbread in 1975, and Kinclaith was dismantled. In the 1980s, the bottlers Cadenhead released a typically gingery but quite smoky 20-year-old. In the past two decades, Gordon & MacPhail has bottled at least a couple of versions from successive years. The first was gingery and melony; the more recent, with a greater sherry note, is reviewed below. This may linger still on the shelf of some bars or shops. It could be the last of Kinclaith, or perhaps the odd cask will turn up in some broker's warehouse.

HOUSE STYLE Light, melony. Aperitif.

KINCLAITH 1967, 40 vol, Connoisseurs Choice

Colour Amber.
Nose Smoky, some sherry, faintly sulphury.
Body Light, delicate.
Palate Light, soft, restrained fruitiness. Melon?
Finish Soothing, tasty. Melon. Sherry.

SCORE 68

KNOCKANDO

PRODUCER UDV (Diageo)
REGION Highlands DISTRICT Speyside

ADDRESS Aberlour, Morayshire, AB38 7RT

T HE NAME, PRONOUNCED KNOCK-AN-DO (or 'du) sounds allusively comical to English speakers, but the whisky is a single of some elegance. Knockando is the keynote among several malts that are especially influential in the Justerini and Brooks J&B blends (see Glen Spey, The Singleton/Auchroisk, and Strathmill). The sophistication of Knockando's malt whisky seems to match that of the company. Giacomo Justerini was an Italian, from Bologna. He emigrated to Britain in pursuit of an opera singer, Margherita Bellion, in 1749. The romance does not seem to have come to fruition, but Justerini meanwhile worked in Britain as a maker of liqueurs. By 1779, he was already selling Scotch whisky. Brooks was a later partner in the firm.

In the US, where some people believe the guarantee "12-year-old" essential to identify a premium malt, this phrase is used, along with the year of distillation, on the label of the principal version. In Britain, the malt is marketed under its season of distillation, with the year of bottling also on the label. The notion is that the malt is bottled when it is mature, rather than at a specific age. In both cases, some of the whisky in the bottle will be up to 15 years old. (In all whiskies, the age shown on the label represents the youngest component, and most contain some older distillates.) In this version, one vintage does not differ dramatically from another, though there are very subtle differences. At older ages, the whisky gains greatly in complexity and sherry character.

The water with which the whisky is made rises from granite and flows over peat. The distillery's name translates as "a little black hill". Knockando is hidden in a fold in the hills overlooking the river Spey at a fine spot for salmon fishing. The distillery was established in 1898.

HOUSE STYLE Elegant, with suggestions of berry fruits. Aperitif.

KNOCKANDO 12-year-old, 1986 (bottled 1999), 43 vol

Colour Pale gold.

Nose Faint, grassy peat. Lemon grass. Raspberries. Marshmallow. Shortbread.

Body Light but notably smooth. Lightly creamy.

Palate Soft. Creamy. Faintly honeyed. Raspberries. Lemon zest.

Finish Nutty, toffeeish dryness. Very delicate. Gently appetizing.

SCORE 76

KNOCKANDO 18-year-old, 1980, 43 vol
Available mainly in the US.

Colour Medium gold.

Nose More shortbread. Almonds. Nice balance of late lemon.

Body Creamier. Rounder. Very smooth indeed.

Palate Nuttier, spicier, drier. Tightly combined flavours.

Finish Late fruit, lemon grass, and light peat. Very appetizing.

SCORE 78

KNOCKANDO Slow Matured (distilled 1980, bottled 1998), 43 vol
Available mainly in France.

Colour Bright medium gold.

Nose Seems faintly peatier than the version above.

Body Fractionally oilier?

Palate Possibly more lemon and raspberry fruitiness.

Finish Crisp. Shortbread. Late warmth.

SCORE 78

KNOCKANDO Extra Old (distilled 1977, bottled 1999), 43 vol

Colour Medium to full gold.

Nose Soft. Complex. Freshly oaky. Lightly sherryish. Creamy. Faintly smoky.

Body Smooth. Textured.

Palate Nutty. Tightly combined flavours gradually unfold. Late fruit. Raspberries. Strawberries.

Finish Late, nutty dryness. Satisfying. Soothing.

SCORE 79

KNOCKANDO Master Reserve 1977 (bottled 1999), 43 vol

Colour Full gold.

Nose Very complex and elegant.

Body Surprisingly full.

Palate A more sherried version. Delicious interplay of lively flavours: cream, fruit, and nut.

Finish Aniseedy sherry. Warming. Dryish.

SCORE 80

KNOCKANDO Single Cask, 21-year-old, 43 vol

Colour Full gold to pale amber.

Nose Rich for a relatively light malt. Sherryish. Raisiny.

Body Full. Smooth. Rounded.

Palate Yet more sherried. Rich, nutty flavours. Lots of flavour development, with gradual dryness and faint smokiness. Remarkably appetizing.

Finish Aniseedy sherry. Nutty. Faint, fragrant smokiness. Soothing.

SCORE 81

Earlier versions of Knockando

A 1976 edition called Special Selection (bottled 1992) was notably raspberryish and on the dry side. SCORE 77. An Extra Old Reserve from 1968 (bottled 1992) had more assertiveness and depth. SCORE 79. Independent bottlings are very rare indeed. A 1980 bottled by Cadenhead at 12 years old and 58 vol was flowery, honeyish, and sugar-sweet. SCORE 69.

LADYBURN

PRODUCER William Grant and Sons
REGION Lowlands **DISTRICT** Western Lowlands

ADDRESS Girvan, Ayrshire, KA26 9PT

BRIEFLY, AND SOME TIME AGO, Glenfiddich's Lowland partner, at Girvan, in Ayrshire. The owners built a grain distillery there in 1963, and added the Ladyburn malt distillery in 1966. Both distilleries were primarily intended to feed the Grant's blends, but both have also given rise to "official" bottlings as singles. The bottled grain, with a juicily sweet character, is still available in many parts of the world. It is matured in heavily charred casks and marketed as Black Barrel. The official bottling of Ladyburn malt was very briefly available, exclusively in the US. Perhaps wishing to concentrate on the growing success of their better-known products, the company closed the malt distillery in the mid 1970s. In the late 1980s, Cadenhead released a creamy, flowery, surprisingly long 14-year-old. This was followed by the paler, drier version reviewed below.

HOUSE STYLE Perfumy and dry. Aperitif.

LADYBURN 20-year-old, 46 vol, Cadenhead

Colour Very pale, white wine.	
Nose Light, fruity, dry.	
Body Light and soft.	
Palate Light, medium-sweet, quickly becoming perfumy and dry.	
Finish Powerful, dry.	

SCORE 57

LAGAVULIN

PRODUCER UDV (Diageo)
REGION Islay **District** South Shore

ADDRESS Port Ellen, Islay, Argyll, PA42 7DZ
TEL 01496-302730 **VC**

THIS CLASSIC ISLAY MALT, with the driest and most sustained attack of any readily available whisky, has in recent years emerged from relative obscurity to international stardom. Purists regret the demise in the late 1980s of its especially vigorous 12-year-old version, but the more mature 16-year-old still has a tremendous punch. The producers have on occasion denied using sherry wood for this version. Well, perhaps not first-fill, but there is certainly a residual sherry character. The launch in 1997–98 of a version identified as being finished in Pedro Ximinez sherry excited great interest. How would this famously robust whisky live with the most hefty of sherries? Would each cancel out the other, so that the punch was finally restrained? Or would the two combine to produce a superpower? Neither is quite the case. The two elements are like heavyweights punching in a clinch.

Decanter magazine once compared the relationship of Lagavulin and Laphroaig on Islay with that of Cheval Blanc and Petrus in Bordeaux. In name at least, Lagavulin must be the Cheval Blanc, as it contributes malt whisky to the White Horse blends, and the animal decorates the distillery sign.

The well-kept distillery has armchairs for visitors. "We give our guests plenty of our time," says manager Mike Nicolson. "They like a meaningful exchange rather than an audio-visual." The tour includes a look at the rock whence the Lords of the Isles departed to fight the Vikings. The stone frame of the sea gate still stands.

The distillery's water arrives by way of a fast-flowing stream that no doubt picks up plenty of peat on the way there. The maturation warehouses are battered by the sea, and they have their own jetty.

Lagavulin (pronounced "lagga-voolin") means "the hollow where the mill is". There are reputed to have been ten illicit stills on this bay in the mid 1700s. Lagavulin traces its history to 1816.

HOUSE STYLE Dry, smoky, complex. Restorative or nightcap.

When the seas are high, Lagavulin's outer walls are knee-high in salt water.

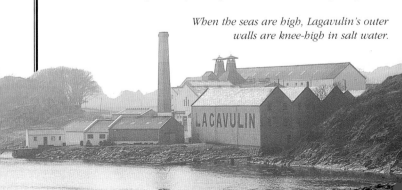

LAGAVULIN 12-year-old, 43 vol

Colour Pale amber.

Nose Sea-salt, peat, intense dryness, sherry.

Body Full, round, syrupy.

Palate Dry, smoky, peaty, salty.

Finish Salty, dry, smoky, with a roaring crescendo. Complex and immense.

SCORE 89

LAGAVULIN 16-year-old, 43 vol

Colour Full amber.

Nose All the elements, but more sherry.

Body Full, smooth, firm.

Palate The dryness is at first offset by the sweetness of the sherry character. As the palate develops, oily, grassy, and, in particular, salty notes emerge. This giant is dignified but full of life.

Finish A huge, powerful, bear hug of peat.

SCORE 95

LAGAVULIN 1979, Double Matured, Distillers Edition, 43 vol
Finished in Pedro Ximinez sherry.

Colour Orange sandstone.

Nose Fresh attack, with hits of peat, tar, sulphur, and salt, soothed with beeswax.

Body Full. Syrupy.

Palate Rich and extremely sweet, then smoky, becoming medicinal, and eventually seaweedy.

Finish Pepper, salt, sand. What it loses in distillery character, it gains in a different dimension of distinctiveness.

SCORE 95

LAGAVULIN 13-year-old (1984), 46 vol, Murray McDavid
Aged in Bourbon wood.

Colour Primrose.

Nose Dry, almost crisp, peaty smoke.

Body Medium, firm.

Palate Crisp, peaty smoke dominates. Like biting into smoky grass. Then oily, a hint of seaweed, and salt.

Finish Dry, big, and warming. Late medicine.

SCORE 87

LAGAVULIN 1979, 40 vol, Murray McDavid

Colour Refractive, pale gold.

Nose Restrained, fragrant smoke. Fresh grass.

Body Medium. Slightly syrupy.

Palate Starts light and grassy-sweet, developing peat, smoke, and pepper.

Finish Peppery. Sandy dryness.

SCORE 86

Earlier versions of Lagavulin
A 14-year-old (1978) at 64.7 vol from Cadenhead was big, oakily dry in attack, becoming sweeter. SCORE 88. Another Cadenhead at 15 years old and 64.4 vol was lighter but saltier. SCORE 87.

LAPHROAIG

PRODUCER Allied Distillers
REGION Islay DISTRICT South Shore

ADDRESS Port Ellen, Islay, Argyll, PA42 7DU TEL 01496-302418 VC
WEBSITE www.laphroaig.com

U NDAUNTED BY THE COMMAND "love it or hate it" (borrowed, without attribution, from a distinguished writer on whisky), ever more devotees commune with this malt. Like hospital gauze? Medicinal, reminiscent of mouthwash or disinfectant, phenolic, tar-like? That is the whole point: the iodine-like, seaweed character of Islay. The famous Laphroaig attack has diminished a little in recent years, unmasking more of the sweetness of the malt, but it is still a very characterful whisky, with a distinctively oily body. Laphroaig has its own peat-beds on Islay, its own dam on the Kilbride river, a floor maltings at the distillery, and relatively small stills. Its maturation warehouses face directly on to the sea. The distillery was built in the 1820s by the Johnston family, whose name is still on the label. In 1847 the founder died after falling into a vat of partially made whisky. In the late 1950s and early 1960s, the distillery was owned by a woman, Miss Bessie Williamson, a glamorous lady, judging from a photograph on the wall. The romance of the place extends to occasional weddings at the distillery, part of which serves as the village hall.

HOUSE STYLE Medicinal. Nightcap.

LAPHROAIG 10-year-old
Versions have been marketed at 40 and 43 vol. The stronger is slightly richer.

Colour	Full, refractive gold.
Nose	Medicinal, phenolic, seaweedy, with a hint of estery sweetness.
Body	Medium, oily.
Palate	Seaweedy, salty, oily.
Finish	Round and very dry.

SCORE 86

LAPHROAIG®

SINGLE ISLAY MALT
SCOTCH WHISKY

Years 10 *Old*

STRAIGHT FROM THE WOOD

The most richly flavoured
of all Scotch whiskies

ESTABLISHED 1815

DISTILLED AND BOTTLED IN SCOTLAND BY
D. JOHNSON & CO., (LAPHROAIG),
LAPHROAIG DISTILLERY, ISLE OF ISLAY

70cl e   57.3% vol

Original Cask
STRENGTH

LAPHROAIG 10-year-old, cask strength, 57.3 vol

Colour Very full gold.

Nose Drier, with "tarred rope" phenol.

Body Medium, with some syrupy viscosity.

Palate Seaweedy. Both salty and sweet. Tar-like.

Finish Medicinal. Tar, phenol, peat, earth.
A wonderfully complex whisky.

SCORE 88

LAPHROAIG®

AGED **15** YEARS

SINGLE *ISLAY* MALT
SCOTCH WHISKY

"The most richly flavoured of all Scotch Whiskies"

ESTD **1815** ESTD

DISTILLED AND BOTTLED IN SCOTLAND BY
D.JOHNSTON & CO .,(LAPHROAIG), LAPHROAIG DISTILLERY, ISLE OF ISLAY

750 ml   PRODUCT OF SCOTLAND **43% ALC/VOL**
L00107   L00108

LAPHROAIG 15-year-old, 43 vol

Colour Pale amber.

Nose Phenol, tar, sulphur.

Body Medium to full, with a soothing oiliness.

Palate A deceptive moment of sweetness and grassiness, then an
explosion of sulphur, burning peat, and Islay intensity.

Finish Round, dry, long, warming.

SCORE 89

LAPHROAIG 1976, 43 vol

Colour Pale amber.

Nose Powerful tar aromas.

Body Medium to full. Firm and smooth.

Palate Coal-tar soap. Lively embrace of dryness and scenty sweetness.

Finish Warming, soothing, soporific, long.

SCORE 89

LAPHROAIG 30-year-old, 43 vol (bottled November, 1997)
Bottled from 123 sherry butts branded with the legend SS *Great Auk*, believed
to be the ship in which they came from Jerez over three decades ago.

Colour Dark orange.

Nose Soft. Polished oak. Fragrant smoke. Roses. Lemony notes.

Body Full, creamy.

Palate Astonishingly fresh. Toasted almonds. Edible seaweed. Briar. Smoke.

Finish Musky. Bittersweet. Beautifully balanced for such a great age.

SCORE 90

Other versions of Laphroaig
Independent bottlings of Laphroaig have largely vanished. A dark 1974, at
55 vol from Signatory, was characterful but lacking balance. SCORE 87. More
recently, a 1987, at 46 vol from Murray McDavid, was in the pale style, with
a light but clean interplay of Laphroaig characteristics. Very long. SCORE 84.

LINKWOOD

PRODUCER UDV (Diageo)
REGION Highlands   DISTRICT Speyside (Lossie)

ADDRESS Elgin, Morayshire, IV30 3RD
TEL 01343-553800

THE MIGRANT BIRDS THAT VISIT this distillery on their journeys south in October and north in April are logged daily by gardener Hilary Lamont. The dam that provides the cooling water is, she notes, a port of call to tufted ducks and goldeneyes – and a seasonal home to wagtails, oyster catchers, mute swans, and otters. In the ten acres of the site, nettles attract red admiral and small tortoiseshell butterflies; cuckoo flowers entice the orange tip variety; bluebells seduce bees. Ms Lamont additionally serves on the panel that noses samples from the still each Friday. She says she often detects the nectar of the meadows, honeysuckle, and peach. Linkwood is by the river Lossie, close to Elgin. It was founded in 1821, and for some years was operated under the name of John McEwan, a subsidiary of DCL, before the creation of United Distillers. The older of its two stillhouses, in the original buildings, is still used for a few months each year. It produces a slightly heavier spirit than the larger stillhouse built in the 1960s and extended in the 1970s. Whisky-writer Philip Morrice recalls that at one stage the management forbade the removal of spiders' webs in case a change in the environment should affect the whisky.

HOUSE STYLE Floral. Rose water? Cherries? Delicious with a slice of fruit cake.

The well-kept lawns and flower-beds at the Linkwood distillery are just one part of the day's work for gardener Hilary Lamont.

LINKWOOD 12-year-old, 40 vol

This John McEwan bottling, now hard to find, is in the heavier style, clearly with some sherry influence.

Colour Full, gold.

Nose Sweet, light-but-definite nuttiness, and some depth.

Body Medium, rounded.

Palate Sweet start, developing to lightly smoky dryness.

Finish Dryish, smooth, confident, lots of finesse.

SCORE 83

LINKWOOD 12-year-old, 43 vol, Flora and Fauna

The first of these bottlings, in the mid 1990s, was very slightly disappointing. Toward the end of the decade, the character seemed richer.

Colour Full primrose.

Nose Remarkably flowery and petal-like. Buttercups. Grass. Fragrant. Clean and sweet. Faint peat.

Body Medium, rounded, slightly syrupy.

Palate Starts slowly, and has a long sustained development to marzipan, roses, and fresh sweetness. One to savour.

Finish Perfumy, dryish. Lemon zest.

SCORE 82

LINKWOOD 1983 (bottled 1997), 59.8 vol, Cask Strength Limited Bottling

Colour Bright gold.

Nose Turkish delight. Pistachio nuts. Cherries. Fudge.

Body Medium to full. Rich.

Palate Fudgy, nutty, moving to flowery dryness.

Finish Flowery. Lemony.
Back to the richness of earlier years, though not quite the complexity.

SCORE 83

LINKWOOD 1974, 22-year-old, cask strength, Rare Malts

Colour Full gold.

Nose Rosewater. Flowers. Some peat.

Body Soft.

Palate Sugared almonds. Cream toffee. Condensed milk. Indian desserts.

Finish Almondy. Firm. Sustained. Long.

SCORE 82

A 1972 version from Rare Malts, bottled in 1995, was bigger, with a more oaky, cedary aroma, a raisiny palate, and a big finish that suggested sugared almonds and parma violets. SCORE 84.

LINKWOOD 1988 (sherry butt No. 2768, bottled 1998), 43 vol Signatory

Colour Bright to full gold.

Nose Fudge, with some leafy, flowery dryness.

Body Light to medium. Very soft and smooth.

Palate Very sweet. Creamy and nutty, but not heavily sherried.

Finish Nice flowery, peaty, balancing dryness.

SCORE 82

Vintage 1975
Single Highland Malt Scotch Whisky
Matured in oak casks for 22 years
Distilled at Linkwood Distillery

LINKWOOD 1975 (bottled 1998), 55.7 vol, Signatory

Colour Pale amber.

Nose Distinct oak. Good wood extract.

Body Medium to full. Rich.

Palate Beautifully rounded. Oak, nuts, cream, rosewater.

Finish Rounded, nutty dryness. Late vanilla and roses.

SCORE 83

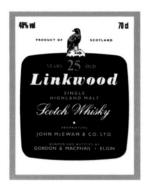

LINKWOOD 25-year-old, 40 vol, Gordon & MacPhail

Colour Amber, with red tinge.

Nose Polished oak. Honeysuckle.

Body Medium. Satiny.

Palate Nutty. Cookie-like maltiness. Hints of grassy sweetness and faint peat.

Finish Lemon zest. Lemon grass. Very long development.

SCORE 83

Earlier versions of Linkwood

A 15-year-old, at 40 vol from the same bottler, was slightly more expressive. SCORE 84. A 14-year-old, at 58.5 vol from Cadenhead, was oakier and sappier. SCORE 83.

LITTLEMILL

Producer Loch Lomond Distillery
Region Lowlands   **District** Western Lowlands

address Bowling, Dunbartonshire, G60 5BG
tel 01389-752781 **VC** Planned to re-open as a working museum

IT IS HOPED THAT THE NEW MILLENNIUM will see a new still-house in the former maltings at historic Littlemill. The intention is that it should be a very small working distillery, with a bottling hall, as well as being a tourist attraction and museum. These plans have long been nurtured by current proprietors Loch Lomond. (They own both the Loch Lomond and Littlemill distilleries, as well as Glen Scotia.) The previous proprietors went into receivership in 1994. An eight-year-old still being bottled was made in stills dismantled in the 1990s. Until the 1930s, Littlemill followed the Lowland practice of triple distillation. The surviving buildings date from at least 1817, but appear to be older. Littlemill was long believed to date from 1772, but more recent evidence suggests that it was already distilling in 1750. It is thus one of the several claimants, each with a slightly different justification, to being the oldest distillery in Scotland.

House style Marshmallow-soft. A restorative, or perhaps with dessert.

LITTLEMILL 8-year-old, 43 vol

Colour Very pale white wine.

Nose Oily. Marshmallow? Perhaps toasted marshmallows.

Body Light, soft.

Palate Malty-sweet, yet not overbearing. Marshmallow again, perhaps powdery icing sugar? More recent bottlings slightly less rounded than in the past, and a little more spirity.

Finish Slight dryness. Coconut?

Score 81

LITTLEMILL 1989 (cask 881/2, bottled 1997), 43 vol, Signatory

Colour White wine.

Nose Toasted coconut.

Body Light, oily, leafy.

Palate Very light. Subtle. Developing distinct coconut.

Finish Icing sugar.

SCORE 78

LITTLEMILL 1966 (25-year-old), 53.5 vol, Cadenhead

Colour Fractionally fuller.

Nose Slightly woody.

Body Lightly creamy.

Palate Coconut. Toasted coconut. Slightly woody.

Finish Surprisingly hot.

SCORE 76

LITTLEMILL 1965 (32-year-old, cask 5275), 49.1 vol, Signatory
10th anniversary series

Colour Primrose.

Nose Distinct icing sugar.

Body Firm, smooth.

Palate Sugary, developing some nutty bitterness.

Finish Nuts. Orange oil. Hot.

SCORE 79

LOCH LOMOND

PRODUCER Loch Lomond Distillery
REGION Highlands   DISTRICT Western Highlands

ADDRESS Lomond Estate, Alexandria, Dunbartonshire, G83 0TL
TEL 01389-752781

THIS MOST IDIOSYNCRATIC malt-and-grain distillery (linked only with its own blending company) was for a time especially identified by its Inchmurrin single malt. It is now giving a greater emphasis both in its products and its company name to its location near Loch Lomond. The distillery can produce half a dozen or more by varying the way in which it operates and combines its pot-stills. The distillery, established in 1965–66, is in a former calico dyeworks, in an industrial location that is, by a thread, across the Highland line. The name Loch Lomond is used on a clearly identified single malt (see opposite), but also a "single blend" (not reviewed). The latter is composed from the distillery's column-still grain whisky, and its various pot-still malts. Four of these are not usually bottled as singles.

These include Glen Douglas, and the progessively more heavily peated Craiglodge, Inchmoan, and Croftengea. With the growing interest in peaty malts, the last may be bottled in the first three or four years of the new millennium. Tasted as a work in progress, at seven years old, it had a sweet, oily, smoky aroma; a bonfire-like palate; with suggestions of fruit wood, briar, and oak smoke; and a lingering length.

HOUSE STYLE Medicinal. Restorative.

OLD RHOSDHU, no age statement (minimum of five years old), 40 vol

Colour Amber.

Nose Scented. A luxurious malt to drink in the bath.

Body Light to medium. Soft, oily.

Palate Dry, perfumy, spicy. Powerful flavours.

Finish Wintergreen? Perhaps not the bath – the sauna.

SCORE 65

INCHMURRIN, no age statement (minimum ten years old), 40 vol

Colour Full gold to amber.	

Nose Eucalyptus. Banana. Mint toffee.

Body Medium.

Palate Smooth, pleasantly oily. Lighter in flavour but lots of development.
Eucalyptus. Very unusual.

Finish Soothing, warming. Sweetish. Scenty.
After a dip in the loch?

SCORE 67

LOCH LOMOND 12-year-old
(To be marketed in Germany. Sampled at cask strength
as a work in progress.)

Colour Greeny-gold.

Nose Leafy. Fruity. Banana.

Body Medium. Slightly syrupy.

Palate Lighter, cleaner, and more rounded. Sweet start, again with
lots of herbal flavour development.

Finish Light but very long. Scenty. Sweet lemons, moving to menthol
and peppermint.

WORK IN PROGRESS

LOCH LOMOND 23-year-old
(Difficult to find.)

Colour Gold to amber.

Nose Mint toffee. Sweet. Appetizing.

Body Medium. Smooth.

Palate Clean. Toffee. Mint toffee. Falling away somewhat.

Finish Seems notably peatier, more assertive, and more warming
than the other Loch Lomonds.

SCORE 69

LOCH LOMOND 1966, 47 vol

Colour Full lemony-gold.

Nose Scenty. Crystallized fruits.

Body Medium to full. Toffeeish.

Palate Mint ice cream. Drying on the tongue.

Finish Leafy. Garden mint.

SCORE 69

LOCHNAGAR

PRODUCER UDV (Diageo)
REGION Highlands   DISTRICT Eastern Highlands

ADDRESS Crathie, Ballater, Aberdeenshire, AB35 5TB
TEL 01339-742716 **VC**

R EPUTEDLY, QUEEN VICTORIA ENJOYED this famously rich malt and used it to lace her claret, thereby ruining two of the world's greatest drinks. The distillery is at the foot of the mountain of Lochnagar, near the river Dee, not far from Aberdeen.

A man believed originally to have been an illicit whisky maker established the first legal Lochnagar distillery in 1826, and the present premises were built in 1845. Three years later, the Royal family acquired nearby Balmoral as their Scottish country home. The then owner, John Begg, wrote a note inviting Prince Albert to visit. The Prince and Queen Victoria arrived the very next day. Soon afterwards, the distillery began to supply the Queen, and became known as Royal Lochnagar. Over the years, the distillery has been rebuilt three times, most recently in 1967. Its whisky has been an important component in the blend VAT 69.

The water flows from the small peak of Lochnagar over peat and heather. The 12-year-old is aged in second-fill casks, while the Selected Reserve has 50 per cent sherry.

HOUSE STYLE Malty, fruity, spicy, cake-like. After dinner.

ROYAL LOCHNAGAR 12-year-old, 43 vol

Colour Full gold.

Nose Big, with some smokiness.

Body Medium to full. Smooth.

Palate Light smokiness, restrained fruitiness, and malty sweetness.

Finish Again, dry smokiness and malty sweetness. The first impression is of dryness, then comes the sweet, malty counterpoint.

SCORE 80

ROYAL LOCHNAGAR Selected Reserve, no age statement, 43 vol

Colour Amber-red.

Nose Very sherryish indeed. Spices, ginger cake.

Body Big, smooth.

Palate Lots of sherry, malty sweetness, spiced bread, ginger cake.
Obviously contains some very well-matured whisky.

Finish Smoky.

SCORE 83

ROYAL LOCHNAGAR Rare Malts, 23-year-old (distilled 1973), 59.7 vol

Colour Bright gold.

Nose Sweet, syrupy, parkin-like.

Body Medium. Very soft.

Palate Very appetizing, fresh, clean sweetness. Very good
flavour development.

Finish Marzipan and nutty dryness.

SCORE 81

ROYAL LOCHNAGAR Rare Malts, 24-year-old (distilled 1972), 55.7 vol

Colour Full, bright gold.

Nose Fresh soda bread. Yeasty.

Body Light to medium. Smooth.

Palate Appetizing, spicy, ginger cake. Lots of flavour
development and complexity.

Finish Cake dusted with cinnamon, nutmeg. Satisfying. Very long indeed.

SCORE 81

LOCHSIDE

PRODUCER Macnab Distilleries (Domecq/Allied)
REGION Highlands   DISTRICT Eastern Highlands

ADDRESS Montrose, Angus, DD10 9AD

ONCE THE FAMOUS JAMES DEUCHAR BREWERY. Lochside, in Montrose, has been a distillery since 1957. Its whisky was the heart of a blend called Macnab's, which was sold in the Spanish market by Distilieras y Crienza, a subsidiary of Domecq sherry. The latter company was acquired by Allied Distillers. The last distillation was in 1992. Since then, the stills have been decommissioned and the warehouses demolished.

HOUSE STYLE Fruity, dry, gentle. Aperitif.

LOCHSIDE 10-year-old, 40 vol
Still available in Spain but very hard to find elsewhere.

Colour Gold.

Nose Some flowering currant.

Body Light to medium, soft, smooth.

Palate Malty start, but not especially sweet. Lots of flavour development. Fruity (blackcurrant?). Becoming dry.

Finish Gentle, not very long.

SCORE 74

Other versions of Lochside
A 1966, bottled at 31 years and 57.7 vol from Signatory, starts with a surprising hint of peat, then becomes sweeter, fruitier, and spicier (licorice?). SCORE 76. An earlier Gordon & MacPhail 1966 at 40 vol was sherryish with a sweet finish. SCORE 73. The Signatory 1966 at 43 vol was drier and slightly oaky. SCORE 71. A Signatory 1959 at 58.5 vol was sherryish and oaky. SCORE 72.

LONGMORN

PRODUCER Chivas (Seagram)
REGION Highlands   **DISTRICT** Speyside (Lossie)

ADDRESS Elgin, Morayshire, IV30 3SJ
TEL 01542-783042

ONE OF THE GREATEST SPEYSIDE MALTS, cherished by connoisseurs but not widely known. Longmorn is admired for its complexity, its combination of smoothness and fullness of character, and from its big bouquet to its long finish. It is noted for its cereal-grain maltiness; oily flavours, reminiscent of beeswax; and estery fruitiness, the last characteristic perhaps deriving from wooden fermentation vessels.

The distillery was built in 1894–95, and has a disused waterwheel and a workable steam engine. It was extended twice during the 1970s. In recent years, the company has begun to market the Longmorn whisky more actively as a 15-year-old. Recent bottlings have been excellent.

HOUSE STYLE Tongue-coating, malty, complex. Versatile, delightful before dinner, and especially good with dessert.

LONGMORN 12-year-old, 40 vol

Colour Full, bright gold.

Nose Complex, firm.

Body Firm, smooth, gentle.

Palate Deliciously fresh, cereal-grain maltiness. Slow, long flavour development, evolving towards a clean, flowery fruitiness.

Finish Clean, smooth, appetizing.

SCORE 85

LONGMORN 15-year-old, 45 vol

Colour Full gold.

Nose Big, slightly oily, barley malt, flowery-fruity notes.

Body Smooth, rounded, medium to big.

Palate Very emphatic, fresh, clean, cereal-grain maltiness.
Suggestions of plum skins.

Finish Tangerines, nuts. Then peppery. Appetizing. Very long.

SCORE 87

LONGMORN 25-year-old, 45 vol, Limited Centenary Edition (1994)

Colour Refractive bronze.

Nose Notably peatier than younger ages, but smokiness is beautifully
rounded, with cereal grain.

Body Smooth, rounded.

Palate Flavours much more tightly combined than in younger ages.
Almost impenetrably complex. A truly urbane whisky.

Finish Sherry, maltiness, nuts, pepper. Both big and long.

SCORE 91

Other versions of Longmorn

Independent bottlings are becoming less available, but Cadenhead released
a remarkably dark, fruity, oak-dominated 1974 (17-year-old) at 58 vol.
SCORE 79. A 1969 (28-year-old), at 56.3 vol from Signatory, is more
conventional in style, but with a notably rich maltiness. SCORE 88.

THE MACALLAN

PRODUCER Macallan (Highland Distillers)
REGION Highlands   DISTRICT Speyside

ADDRESS Aberlour, Banffshire, AB38 9RX   TEL 01340-871471
WEBSITE www.themacallan.com   VC By appointment

T HIS CHÂTEAU OF MALT WHISKY became a part of the Highland Distillers group in 1996. The highly respected group thus inherited a distillery noted for extraordinarily rigorous standards. The progress of Macallan will be watched with eagle eyes by lovers of malt whisky as the distillates of recent years come to maturity in the first decade of the 2000s. Meanwhile, there have been some outstanding new releases, each scoring similarly high points for often quite different attributes.

The character of Macallan has traditionally begun with Golden Promise barley, but this Scottish variety is becoming hard to find. Cultivation has drastically diminished because Golden Promise offers a relatively ungenerous yield of grain to farmers. Its yield to distillers in terms of spirit is also on the low side, but the flavours produced are delicious. Until about 1994, Macallan used only Golden Promise, and this now-precious variety still accounts for about 30 per cent of each infusion.

Macallan's richness is enhanced by the use of especially small stills. When the company has expanded output to cope with demand, it has added more stills, rather than building bigger ones. The number grew from six to 21 between 1965 and 1975. The stills are heated by gas burners. This use of direct flame can impart a caramelization of the malt which steam heat does not.

Most famously, Macallan is known for its loyalty to sherry aging. Other distillers or bottlers may offer editions with more heavy sherry, but none so militantly pursues the wine of Jerez throughout its range. In the course of its history, Macallan has acquired manzanilla, fino, and amontillado casks, but for the past 30-odd years its wood regime has been singular. The distillery buys Spanish-grown oak of the species *Quercus robur*, has it coopered in Jerez, and loans the butts to several bodegas to accommodate at least one season's fermentation of sherry and two season's maturation of dry oloroso. It then imports them as complete casks, thus maintaining sherry character that would diminish if they were knocked down into staves. In the principal versions of The Macallan, 70 per cent of the whisky has been matured in first-fill sherry casks and 30 per cent in second. The remainder of the second-fill casks are used to age whisky for blending.

Sceptics argue that the sherry dominates Macallan, but that is manifestly not true. The whisky has big, bold, beautifully rounded flavours, with touches of peat smoke, the classic Speyside floweriness, and a highly distinctive esteriness that reminds some of

Calvados. In older versions, with less sherry, or perhaps with fino, that apple note metamorphoses into grapefruit, lime, or orange.

Even the seven-year-old malt, bottled exclusively for the Italian market, is full of flavour. One of The Macallan's celebrated adherents, novelist Kingsley Amis, insisted that the ten-year-old version was "the best glass". There is considerable development of character between the ten- and the 12-year-old, while many devotees prefer the 18-year-old. Another novelist, Mordecai Richler, simply nominated "Macallan Single Malt" as his favourite aroma.

The whisky writer Wallace Milroy proposed the 1964 vintage as the stuff of legend. A rival case, so to speak, might be made for the 1950, with its slightly oily, peaty palate and spectacularly long finish. There have been a number of special editions. In 1993, a 60-year-old was bought for £6,400 by a bar manager in Osaka, Japan.

Whisky has probably been made on the Macallan site, on a small hill overlooking the Spey, near Craigellachie, since the late 1700s. A farmer on the hillside first made whisky there from his own barley. A manor house from this period has been restored as a venue for entertaining visitors. An illustration of the house is used on the box that accommodates each bottle of The Macallan. It is intended to convey the sense of a whisky "château", and perhaps to offset the harder lines of what is a functional-looking distillery.

The first licenced distillation at Macallan is said to have taken place in the earliest days of legalized production, in 1824. The business passed in 1892 into the hands of the Kemp family, whose descendant Allan Shiach (also a Hollywood screenwriter under the name Allan Scott) continued to manage it until recently.

Macallan has long been a renowned contributor to blends, notably including The Famous Grouse. In 1968–69, the company decided that single malts would also be an important element of the future. Every whisky lover should be grateful for this decision, though it placed the distillery's independence at stake: Macallan became a public company in order to finance the stock it was laying down for ten years or more as single malt. At the same time, based on tastings of existent stock, the dry oloroso policy was instituted.

HOUSE STYLE Big, oaky, sherried, flowery-fruity. After dinner.

THE MACALLAN 7-year-old, 40 vol
(Italian market only.)

Colour Bright amber.
Nose Sherry, with dry maltiness in the background.
Body Medium to full.
Palate Nutty and sweetish, with buttery malt and fruit coming up behind.
Finish Satisfying, sherryish, malty. A light digestif.

SCORE 81

THE MACALLAN Distiller's Choice, no age statement, 40 vol
(Mainly for the Japanese market.)

Colour Bronze. Paler than most Macallans.

Nose Especially fragrant.

Body Medium. Very smooth.

Palate Lightly buttery and malty. Lively, youthful flavours. Emphasis on classic Speyside floweriness rather than sherry.

Finish Highlights the crisp dryness of Macallan.

SCORE 81

THE MACALLAN 10-year-old, 40 vol

Colour Amber.

Nose Sherry and buttery, honeyish, malt character. Lots of roundness and depth, even at this young age.

Body Full, without being syrupy.

Palate Lots of sherry, without being rich. Plenty of malt. Sweetish.

Finish Satisfying, malty, gingery, becoming dry, with a hint of smoke.

SCORE 87

THE MACALLAN 10-year-old, 57 vol (100° proof)

Colour Amber, marginally fuller.

Nose Sherry still, but drier. A soft whiff of alcohol.

Body Full.

Palate Sherryish. A very clean, rounded fruitness. Intense. Powerful.

Finish Sherry, smoke, alcohol.

SCORE 89

THE MACALLAN 12-year-old, 43 vol

Colour Amber.

Nose Sherry, honey, flowery notes.

Body Full, smooth.

Palate The first hints of flowering currant. Altogether more expressive.

Finish Slightly more rounded.

SCORE 91

THE MACALLAN 15-year-old, 43 vol

Colour Medium amber.

Nose Honey. Distinctly fruity.

Body Full, very smooth.

Palate Toffeeish. Gently fruity and spicy. Hints of peat. A little lacking in dimension.

Finish Grassy. Lightly peaty.

SCORE 92

THE MACALLAN 25-year-old, 43 vol

Colour Full amber-red.

Nose Definite smokiness overlaying the characteristics.

Body Full, firm, round.

Palate The smokiness greatly enhances the complexity.

Finish Dry, complex, very long.

SCORE 95

Some vintages of The Macallan 18-year-old (All at 43 vol)

Most years, The Macallan has released an 18-year-old, at 43 vol, in which some malt lovers find the most robust interplay of the estery whisky and the dry oloroso maturation. These are vatted to offer continuity of character, but inevitably they vary slightly. The following notes emphasize variations that are minimal to the overall character. There is not a full point between any of them. SCORE 94.

1978: Solid orange-amber colour; big bouquet, with some peat; medium to full, soft body; beautifully rounded and complete, with a nutty-sweet sherry accent; firm, smooth, dry, warming finish.

1977: Darker and redder; sherry and restrained fruit on the nose; buttery malt character; sweeter, more sherryish finish.

1976: Bright, full, orange colour; peaty, oaky aroma; firm and smooth; lively flavours of grass, peat, and oak.

1975: More orangey colour; spicy lemon grass and peat in the aroma; fresh, juicy Calvados and flowering currant in the palate; fresh, oaky finish.

1974: Reddish tinge; beautifully balanced peat and malt in the aroma; malty, sherryish sweetness becoming estery and perfumy; sweetness and spice in the finish.

1973: Bright, full amber; very perfumy aroma; very full flavours; sappy oak and vanilla spiciness in a slow, long finish.

1972: Deep orange; oak and peat aroma; very smooth; superb balance between peat and syrupy malt; drying in finish.

1971: Shimmery orange; soft, inviting aroma; oily, perfumy; sherry sweetness.

1970: Full amber-orange; assertive sherry aroma; notably complex; long, vanilla-and-oak finish.

1969: Amber, but paler than usual; peat and malt in the aroma; nutty, sweetish, syrupy; some peat in finish. A restrained edition.

1968: Apricot colour; fudgy, nutty aroma; light on the tongue; slightly syrupy; toffeeish, gently spicy finish.

1967: Tawny colour; very spicy, almost minty aroma; very smooth; buttery malt character; melony finish, with grassy peat.

1966: Bottled "early". This year's edition was a 17-year-old (and labelled as such, of course). Tawny colour; peaty and spicy aroma; oily, nutty, smooth; very restrained peat in the finish.

1965: Tawny-red; nutty, sherry aroma; aniseed, licorice; spicy, oily finish.

1964: Medium orange colour; good balance of peat and malt in the aroma; lightly fruity palate, falling away in the middle; with nutty, sherry sweetness in the finish.

1963: Refractive orange colour; lightly oaky aroma; light, sweet, and sherryish, with a cedary finish.

Some new versions of The Macallan

THE MACALLAN Gran Reserva, 18-year-old (distilled 1979, bottled 1997), 40 vol
(Under this rubric, the whisky will be aged entirely in first-fill casks. The ones chosen in this instance have imparted huge wood extract.)

Colour Distinctively chestnut.

Nose Rich sherry at first. Then malty nuttiness. Raisins, dates. Finally floweriness.

Body Big, oily.

Palate Very dry. Thick-cut, bitter-orange and ginger marmalade on well-done toast. Then buttery, syrupy maltiness, developing to nutty, sherry sweetness. Strictly for the lover of powerfully oaked whiskies.

Finish Richly fruity. Raisiny. Warming.

SCORE 95

THE MACALLAN 30-year-old, 43 vol

Colour Full orange.

Nose Fragrantly fresh. Polished oak. The skin of fresh tangerines.

Body Medium to full.

Palate Despite its great age, no aggressive oakiness or overbearing sherry. Tightly combined flavours. Its great appeal is its mellow maturity. Complex. Just a whiff of smoke.

Finish Dry, warming, soothing, but disappears too quickly.

SCORE 95

Special editions of The Macallan

THE MACALLAN, 40 vol
Commemorating 35 years of the satirical magazine *Private Eye*. (Primarily 12-year-old, but also a cask of 35-year-old, in 5,000 numbered bottles.)

Colour	Yellowy blush.

Nose Very lively and assertive. (Cheeky?) Sweetness, with a flick of fresh leather.

Body Soft, smooth.

Palate Lightly nutty.

Finish Hint of bitterness.

SCORE 92

MACALLAN "The 1874"
(Intended to recall a bottling from that year bought in an auction. The whiskies in the replica version had an average age of just under 18, but included at least one cask of 26 years. A key element was whisky with long maturation in fino sherry casks.)

Colour Orange.

Nose Ginger cake. Caraway. Cumin seeds.

Body Medium. Firm. Smooth.

Palate Dry, with softly orangey notes. Spices. Aniseed. Lemon grass. The most estery of the bigger Macallans. Light peat.

Finish Powerful. Dry. Just a hint of bitterness.

SCORE 95

THE MACALLAN Cask Strength
A new series of single-cask bottlings. The first, cask number 9780, from 1981, was tasted as a work in progress. It has an orangey-red colour; a rich, clean, dryish, sherry aroma; a rounded body; a firm, nutty palate; and a huge, spicy finish, with some oak and peat. A very intense expression of a classic Macallan.

The Macallan Decades series

Like the 1874, this series seeks to replicate, by making vattings from stock, the Macallans of the past. The initial bottlings, intended to evoke the 1920–1950s are identified by social motifs of each period, based on racing cars, trains, boats, and planes.

THE MACALLAN Twenties (racing car motif), 40 vol
A lighter-bodied, drier expression.

Colour Pale walnut.

Nose Sweet, spicy.

Body Quite light and attenuated.

Palate Elegant oakiness. Polished oak.

Finish Oak. Rounded peat. Late, but very light reminder of spiciness and honeyed maltiness.

SCORE 93

THE MACALLAN Thirties (ocean liner motif), 40 vol
A classically delicate, flowery, peaty, lightly phenolic Speysider.

Colour Pale apricot.

Nose Softly but distinctively peaty.

Body Light, smooth.

Palate Deft balance of honeyed maltiness, spicy esters, and fragrant peat smoke.

Finish Long peat, lemon grass, sweetness, and spiciness.

SCORE 95

THE MACALLAN Forties (locomotive motif), 40 vol
In the same flowery-peaty, Speyside style, but drier and less complex.

Colour Primrose.

Nose Nutty, grassy, peaty.

Body Light. Lively.

Palate Light, flowery, grassy. Some sweetness, then peat and smoke.

Finish Deliciously delicate, but definite, fragrant peat smoke.

SCORE 94

THE MACALLAN Fifties (airliner motif)
Closer in style to The Macallan today, but still slightly leaner and drier.

Colour Deep bronze.

Nose Light polished oak. Perfumy.

Body Light but smooth, with some texture.

Palate Well balanced and rounded. Oak, sherry, malt, light spiciness.

Finish Sherry and spices. Long, soothing.

SCORE 93

Rare vintages of The Macallan

THE MACALLAN Millennium 50-year-old (1949), 46 vol

Offered in about 900 Caithness crystal decanters, with a copper insignia made from a retired still at Macallan. Price around £2,000 ($3,000).

Colour Apricot to orange.

Nose Peaty, smoky, almost sooty.

Body Medium, firm, slippery.

Palate Malty, treacly, oaky. The oak is big but never overpowering. A beautifully composed, utterly luxurious whisky.

Finish Like eating hard butterscotch flavoured with root ginger. Tasted as a work in progress.

THE MACALLAN 1948, 46.6 vol

Colour Old gold.

Nose Sherry not obvious - fino? Flowery, leafy, peaty, woody.

Body Light but firm. Smooth.

Palate An altogether more elegant, wistful style. Some sweetness and floweriness, but the outstanding feature is an astonishingly fresh peat-smoke flavour. Great Speyside whiskies once tasted like this.

Finish Gentle but lingering and warming, leaving smoky memories.

SCORE 96

THE MACALLAN 1946, 40 vol

Colour Bright full gold.

Nose Much more estery-fruity.

Body Light, smooth, almost slippery.

Palate Firm, complex flavours. Flowery. Estery, but very delicately balanced. Sweet lime, lemon, and orange. A remarkably seductive whisky for its age.

Finish Bitter orange. Grass. Peat. Again, long smokiness.

SCORE 95

Other bottlings of Macallan

Independents have stayed clear of the definite article. Adelphi has a
nine-year-old, at 58.2 vol, labelled "From Macallan", with a bright, pale
orange colour; a succulent sherry aroma; a buttery maltiness; but a rather
hot finish. SCORE 79. Gordon & MacPhail uses the label "Speymalt from
Macallan Distillery" on a 1990, at 40 vol, with a full, gold colour; well
balanced light sherry and peat in the aroma; a very light, flowery middle;
and a sherryish finish. SCORE 80. The same label has a really excellent 1978,
also at 40 vol, which is much oilier and peatier. SCORE 94. Murray McDavid
employs the formulation Macallan-Glenlivet, on a 1974 at 46 vol, with a
good amber colour; a restrained aroma and palate; but a nice estery
spiciness and balance of flavours. SCORE 92.

Earlier versions of Macallan
J. G. Thomson's "As We Get It" version at cask strength, with no age
statement, was full in colour, sherryish and buttery-malty, but a little spirity.
SCORE 84. A 1969 Inverallen bottling, at cask strength, had a bright, golden
colour, a syrupy body, and a very flowery, perfumy finish. SCORE 84. A
28-year-old from the same house, at 55.7 vol, had a fuller golden colour, a
light-to-medium sherry character and a beautiful balance and complexity.
SCORE 93. A 1965, bottled at 28 years and 55.7 vol, by Signatory, was bright
gold, with peat and perfume. SCORE 92. A 30-year-old, at 52.6 vol, from
Cadenhead was very pale indeed, beautifully flowery, with a touch of peat.
SCORE 88. At the same age from that bottler, a 54.7 version was slightly
fuller in colour, peaty, creamy, and estery. SCORE 90. Without the sherry, it
is not The Macallan, but these paler bottlings showed what a sweet,
flowery nectar this whisky is in any dress.

MANNOCHMORE

PRODUCER UDV (Diageo)
REGION Highlands   **DISTRICT** Speyside (Lossie)

ADDRESS By Elgin, Morayshire, IV30 8FF
TEL 01343-547891

T HE MANNOCH HILLS PROVIDE WATER for several distilleries. This one, south of Elgin, is relatively recent, having been established in 1971–72. Its original role was to provide malt whisky as a component of the Haig blends, augmenting the production of its older neighbour Glenlossie. With the same raw materials and location, the two make similar malts. Mannochmore's seems slightly less complex, but it is very enjoyable nonetheless.

Mannochmore's product became available as a single in the Flora and Fauna series in the mid 1990s, and there has since been a Rare Malts edition. There has also been the curious malt whisky Loch Dhu ("Black Lake"), aimed at "image-conscious young men". Given the fashionability of black among young women, they may feel excluded. The company insists that the colour of the whisky derives from "a secret preparation, involving the double charring of selected Bourbon barrels". The best guess is that the "preparation" – perhaps first a spraying and then a charring – involved caramelization.

HOUSE STYLE Fresh, flowery, dry. Aperitif.

SPEYSIDE
SINGLE MALT *SCOTCH WHISKY*

MANNOCHMORE

distillery stands a few miles *south* of Elgin in *Morayshire*. The nearby *Millnuies Woods* are rich in birdlife, including the Great *Spotted* Woodpecker. The *distillery* draws process *water* from the Bardon Burn, which has its *source* in the MANNOCH HILLS, and *cooling water* from the Gedloch Burn and the *Burn of Foths*. Mannochmore *single MALT WHISKY* has a *light, fruity* aroma and a *smooth,* mellow *taste.*

AGED **12** YEARS
43% vol   Distilled & Bottled in *SCOTLAND.* MANNOCHMORE DISTILLERY, Elgin, Moray, *Scotland.*   70cl

MANNOCHMORE 12-year-old, 43 vol, Flora and Fauna

Colour White wine.

Nose Fresh. Very flowery indeed.

Body Medium, firm, drying on the tongue.

Palate Becoming lightly fruity. Clean. Dry.

Finish Perfumy, light, dry. Faint peat.

SCORE 72

MANNOCHMORE 22-year-old (distilled 1974, bottled 1997), cask strength, Rare Malts

Colour Bright greeny-gold.

Nose Fragrant, flowery, faint peat.

Body Very soft. Lightly smooth.

Palate Oily, wintergreen, peppery fruit.

Finish Robust, hot, faint peat.

SCORE 74

This edition is in a 75cl bottling. Later the same year, a 70cl Rare Malts bottling at the same age seemed much cleaner and rounder. SCORE 76.

LOCH DHU The Black Whisky, 10-year-old, 40 vol

Colour Ebony, with a mahogany tinge.

Nose Licorice, medicinal. Fruity, flowery, whisky aromas very evident.

Body Medium. Softly syrupy.

Palate Light, dryish. Licorice. Hint of cough sweets. Fruit. Scores for initiative, but not for the whisky lover.

Finish Whisky flavours gently emerge. Licorice root. Dryish. Hint of warmth.

SCORE 70

Independent bottlings of Mannochmore
Gordon & MacPhail offer a 1984, at 40 vol, in their Connoisseurs Choice range. This has a bright, buttercup colour; a distinctly buttery, flowery, grassy aroma; a very fat body; and flavours that develop from clotted cream to hard toffee; with nuts and ginger in the finish. SCORE 75.

MILLBURN

PRODUCER DCL/UDV
REGION Highlands **DISTRICT** Speyside (Inverness)

ADDRESS Millburn Road, Inverness, Inverness-shire, IV2 3QX

A S THE TRAIN FROM LONDON finishes its 11-hour journey to Inverness, it glides by recognizable distillery buildings that are now a pub-steakhouse. At least there is still drink on the premises. Millburn is believed to have dated from 1807, and its buildings from 1876 and 1922. It was owned for a time by Haig's. The distillery closed in 1985. A Rare Malts edition was released in 1995.

HOUSE STYLE Smoky, aromatic. Nightcap.

MILLBURN 18-year-old (1975), 58.5 vol, Rare Malts

Colour Greeny-gold.
Nose Oaky and aromatic.
Body Lightly smooth.
Palate Dryish, perfumy, smoky.
Finish Oaky, sappy.

SCORE 74

MILLBURN 1978, 65.6 vol, Gordon & MacPhail Cask edition

Colour Bright greeny-gold.
Nose Dry, lightly peaty, alcoholic.
Body Smooth but drying.
Palate Peaty, vegetal, attack. Becoming sweeter.
Finish Slightly musty. Some medicinal peat. Heady.

SCORE 74

MILLBURN 1974, 40 vol, Connoisseurs Choice

Colour Gold to bronze.

Nose Appetizing peat, perfume, and hint of sherry.

Body Lightly oily.

Palate Lightly malty, quickly becoming perfumy, then peaty.

Finish Slightly aggressive. Dries on tongue.

SCORE 75

An earlier 1971 bottling in this series was fresher-tasting and fuller in flavours. SCORE 76. Its predecessor, the 1966, was peatier and smokier. SCORE 76.

MILLBURN 22-year-old (distilled 1974, bottled 1997, cask 4614), 58.7 vol, Signatory Silent Stills Series

Colour Bright gold.

Nose Lightly peaty.

Body Lightly syrupy. Vegetal sweetness.

Palate Malty, quickly becoming peaty. Hint of woodiness.

Finish Spicily dry.

SCORE 74

MILTONDUFF

Producer Allied Distillers
Region Highlands **District** Speyside (Lossie)

ADDRESS Elgin, Morayshire, IV30 3TQ
TEL 01343-547433

THE BENEDICTINE PRIORY OF PLUSCARDEN, which still exists, was once a brewery – and provided the land on which the Miltonduff distillery stands. Although there is no other connection, the name of the Priory is invoked on the box that houses the Miltonduff bottle. The distillery, established in 1824, south of Elgin, was extensively modernized in the 1930s, and again in the 1970s. Its whisky is very important in the Ballantine blends. The distillery's owners have an arrangement that Gordon & MacPhail will bottle the malt as a single.

For a time, the company also had a Lomond still on the site. This produced a malt with similar characteristics to Miltonduff, but heavier, oilier, and smokier, identified as Mosstowie. That still has been dismantled, but the malt can occasionally be found in independent bottlings. The Miltonduff malt is well regarded by blenders, and makes a pleasant single.

HOUSE STYLE Flowery, scenty, clean, firm, elegant. Aperitif.

MILTONDUFF 10-year-old, 40 vol

Colour Honeyed gold.

Nose Fragrant, flowery. Very faint peat.

Body Light to medium. Firm. Smooth.

Palate Sweetish, firm, clean.

Finish Firm. Lightly nutty. Soothing.

SCORE 75

MILTONDUFF 12-year-old, 43 vol

Colour Soft gold.

Nose Fragrant, dry, flowery, with faint hints of peat and vanilla.
Peatiness more evident when a little water is added.

Body Medium, firm, smooth.

Palate Sweet, very clean and delicately flowery.

Finish Aromatic, soothing, with some malty dryness.

SCORE 76

MILTONDUFF 1968, 40 vol

Colour Amber.

Nose Light sherry and very gentle peat.

Body Medium, textured.

Palate Flowery, honeyish, lightly nutty. Hint of vanilla.

Finish Long, peat-smoke fragrance.
Perhaps better as a light digestif.

SCORE 78

Independent bottlings of Miltonduff

A 17-year-old, distilled in 1981 at 58.4 vol from Signatory, is heavily sherried, with a deep orange colour; a rich body; a marzipan aroma and palate; and oaky finish. Somewhat loses the floweriness and delicacy that is the real point of Miltonduff, but brings out the nuttiness. SCORE 74.
A 13-year-old, distilled in 1978 and bottled at 59.4 vol by Cadenhead, is closer to the house style, though with flowering currant and a touch of woody bitterness in the finish. SCORE 74.

MORTLACH

PRODUCER UDV (Diageo)
REGION Highlands   **DISTRICT** Speyside (Dufftown)

ADDRESS Dufftown, Banffshire, AB55 4AQ
TEL 01313-377373

A RECENT CASK STRENGTH LIMITED BOTTLING and a Rare Malts edition have brought new attention to this classic distillery. All the pleasures of a good Speyside single malt are found in Mortlach – floweriness, peatiness, smokiness, maltiness, and fruitiness – along with a good sherry character in most bottlings. The distilling water comes from springs in the Conval Hills and seems to bring a powerful taste with it. The cooling water is from the River Dullan. Mortlach, the first legal distillery in Dufftown, traces its history to 1823–24. It is very attractive, despite having been modernized in 1903 and 1964. The whisky is an important element in the Johnnie Walker blends, along with Cardhu, Talisker, and many others.

HOUSE STYLE A Speyside classic: elegant and flowery yet supple and muscular. Immensely complex, with great length. After dinner or bedtime.

MORTLACH 16-year-old, 43 vol, Flora and Fauna

Colour Profound, rich, amber.

Nose Dry oloroso sherry. Smoky, peaty.

Body Medium to full, firm, smooth.

Palate Sherryish, smoky, peaty, sappy, some fruitiness, assertive.

Finish Long and dry.

SCORE 81

MORTLACH 1980 (bottled 1997), 63.1 vol, Cask Strength Limited Bottling

Colour Very attractivel, bright orangey-amber.

Nose Distinct peat character. Stalky. Lime skins.

Body Big, rich.

Palate Flowery. Buttercups. Syrupy. Rich sherry notes. Very big in the middle, with lots of flavour development. Soft mint humbugs.

Finish More mint, becoming drier. An outstanding digestif.

SCORE 85

MORTLACH 22-year-old (distilled 1972), 65.3 vol, Rare Malts

Colour Very full gold.

Nose Cereal grains. Fresh baked bread. Some smoky peat.

Body Remarkably smooth, layered.

Palate Hugely nutty. Developing from dryness to sweeter juiciness. Then sweet smokiness.

Finish Complex, with barley-sugar nuttiness and surging warmth. Tremendous length.

SCORE 85

MORTLACH 15-year-old, 40 vol, matured and bottled by Gordon & MacPhail

Colour Bronze.

Nose Appetizingly smoky, with touches of malt and sherry.

Body Medium to full.

Palate Smokiness. Heathery, resiny notes, succulent maltiness, fruitiness (juicy pears), sherry, oak.

Finish Perfumy, long, dry.

SCORE 82

MORTLACH 1969, 40 vol, Gordon & MacPhail

Colour Full orangey-amber.

Nose A floweriness reminiscent of flax or starched linen,
then a lovely interplay of oak, sherry, and peat.

Body Firm, hefty. Light heavyweight.

Palate Oak, cedar. Black chocolate. Mint crisp.

Finish Dry. Toasted almonds. Smoky.

SCORE 83

An earlier bottling, at 21 years, from this company was more
sherryish and less oaky. Perhaps better balanced, but less dramatic.
SCORE 81.

MORTLACH 1988 (9 years old, sherry butt 2626), 43 vol, Signatory

Colour Full gold to bronze.

Nose Raisiny sherry to the fore. Cereal grain and smoke lurking.

Body Medium to full. Well rounded.

Palate Hard-toffee maltiness, then buttery. Finally, nutty sherry.

Finish Lively. Peppermint. Slightly stinging and sharp.

SCORE 82

MORTLACH 1975 (22-year-old, cask 6259), 57.7 vol, Signatory

Colour Bright, refractive gold.

Nose Cleanly flowery and fragrant (coriander leaf/cilantro?).
Lightly peaty. Appetizing.

Body Medium. Rounded.

Palate Sweet at first, then buttery, becoming nuttier and drier.

Finish Very complex. Hit of dry peatiness, then buttery toffee and spicy
warmth. As though all the elements were echoed. A very satisfying and
rounded malt.

SCORE 82

MORTLACH 1980 (19-year-old), 59.3 vol, Adelphi

Colour Amber to tawny.

Nose Flowery. Clean, dry, smokiness.

Body Medium, textured.

Palate Malty. Cookie-like. Becoming buttery. Then toasted
chestnuts and smoke.

Finish Slightly vegetal. Then warming spices and sweetness.

SCORE 81

NORTH PORT

PRODUCER DCL/UDV (Diageo)
REGION Highlands **DISTRICT** Eastern Highlands

ADDRESS Brechin, Angus, DD9 6BE

THE NAME INDICATES THE NORTH GATE of the small, once-walled city of Brechin. The distillery was built in 1820. The pioneering whisky writer Alfred Barnard, who toured Scotland's distilleries in the 1880s, recorded that this one obtained its barley from the farmers around Brechin, and its peat and water from the Grampian mountains. The present-day writer Derek Cooper reports that the condensers were cooled in a stream that ran through the distillery. North Port was modernized in the 1970s, and closed in 1983. It has now been sold for redevelopment.

HOUSE STYLE Dry, fruity, gin-like. Aperitif.

NORTH PORT 19-year-old (distilled 1979, bottled 1998), 61.0 vol, Rare Malts

Colour Bright, pale gold.

Nose Dry, lightly smoky, grassy. Dry fruitiness.

Body Light to medium. Some viscosity.

Palate Light. Leafy. Dried apricot. Dried banana. Toasted marshmallow.

Finish Dry, spirity, sharp. Cedary.

SCORE 68

NORTH PORT 23-year-old (distilled 1971, bottled 1995), 54.7 vol, Rare Malts

Colour Bright gold.

Nose Aromatic, dry, almost sharp.

Body Very light. smooth.

Palate Light, with suggestions of mints, crystallized fruit, and pineapple.

Finish Sharp.

SCORE 67

NORTH PORT-BRECHIN, 1981, 40 vol, Connoisseurs Choice

Colour Full gold.

Nose Perfumy. Fresh bananas.

Body Oily, smooth.

Palate Bananas again. Lightly creamy flavour.

Finish Leafy. Light spiciness. Fades quickly.

SCORE 66

OBAN

PRODUCER UDV (Diageo)
REGION Highlands   DISTRICT Western Highlands

ADDRESS Stafford Street, Oban, Argyll, PA34 5NH
TEL 01631-572004 **VC**

THE WESTERN HIGHLANDS' CAPITAL, Oban, has a whisky label printed with the town's history: settled by Mesolithic cave-dwellers before 5,000 BC, later by Celts, Picts, and Vikings. It was a fishing village, and in the era of railways and steamships became a gateway to the islands of the west, which it still is. Travellers following the muses of Mendelssohn, Turner, Keats, or Wordsworth to Mull or Iona, or Fingal's Cave, return to see a harbourfront centred on the distillery – backed by mossy, peaty hills whence its water flows.

A family of merchants in the town became brewers and distillers in 1794, though the present buildings probably date from the 1880s. The stillhouse was rebuilt in the late 1960s and early 1970s, and there was further work in the last decade. The Oban malt whisky has contributed to Dewar's, and to John Hopkins' "Old Mull".

The whisky already had a following as a single malt when it was presented as a salty-peaty 12-year-old in a Victorian-looking, bevelled "perfume" bottle. That has long been discontinued, and is hard to find. Its firm, dry peatiness perhaps associated it with a vestigial style in the few distilleries on the mainland of the Western Highlands. Oban has become much more widely appreciated as one of the Classic Malts range. In this version, mellowed by even two more years in the wood, and gentler in its peatiness, the salty coastal character is less masked. In 1997, a version finished in Montilla fino was added.

HOUSE STYLE Medium, with fresh peat and a whiff of the sea. With seafood or game, or after dinner.

The ferry town of Oban is a base from which the whisky lover can explore a slice of Scotland: the islands, coast, and Western Highlands.

OBAN 14-year-old, 43 vol

Colour Full gold to amber.

Nose "Pebbles on the beach", said one taster. A whiff of the sea, but also a touch of fresh peat, and some maltiness.

Body Firm, smooth, slightly viscous.

Palate Deceptively delicate at first. Perfumy. Faint hint of fruity seaweed. Then lightly waxy, becoming smoky. Dry.

Finish Aromatic, smooth, appetizing.

SCORE 79

OBAN 1980, "Double Matured", 43 vol, Distillers Edition
Finished in Montilla fino wood.

Colour Amber.

Nose Fragrant. Edible seaweed. Peaches. Very complex.

Body Smooth, bigger.

Palate Salty, nutty, peachy. Sweet in the middle, developing notes of tobacco and seaweed.

Finish The salt comes rolling back like an incoming tide.

SCORE 80

Independent bottlings of Oban
A 1963, bottled at 30 years old and 52 vol by Cadenhead, is powerfully peaty, slightly woody, with a huge, salty finish. SCORE 81. Earlier bottlings (in the late 1980s): a Cadenhead 21-year-old, at 46 vol, was maltier and smoky. SCORE 74. A Connoisseurs Choice 1962, at 40 vol, was more sherried. SCORE 74.

PITTYVAICH

Producer UDV (Diageo)
Region Highlands   **District** Speyside (Dufftown)

address Dufftown, Banffshire, ABB55 4BR

A RELATIVELY NEW and somewhat brutally modern distillery that may have had a brief life. It was built by Bells in 1975. In the late 1980s, enthusiasts for single malts began to wonder whether the product would become available to them. Then independent bottler James MacArthur released a 12-year-old revealing a perfumy, soft-pear house character. The same bottler then added a 14-year-old that more assertively pronounces its dry finish. A bottling of the same age from the Scotch Malt Whisky Society was similar, but seemed to have more spicy dryness on the nose. In 1991 there was finally an official bottling, at 12 years old, in United's Flora and Fauna series. This has all the other characteristics, plus a hefty dose of sherry. There have since been several independent bottlings. The distillery was mothballed in 1993–94. There have been some trial runs there since, but no apparent conclusion as to its long-term future.

House style Fruity, oily, spicy, spirity. After dinner – a Scottish grappa, so to speak.

PITTYVAICH 12-year-old, 43 vol, Flora and Fauna

Colour Deep amber-red.

Nose Sherryish, perfumy, pear skin.

Body Light to medium. Firm. Dry.

Palate Very sherryish. Assertive. Some malty chewiness. Vanilla. Soft, sweet, pear-like fruitiness, moving to a spicy dryness.

Finish Spicy, perfumy, intensely dry, lingering on the tongue.

Score 69

PORT ELLEN

PRODUCER UDV (Diageo)
REGION Islay   DISTRICT South Shore

ADDRESS Port Ellen, Isle of Islay, PA42 7AH

THE RAREST OF ISLAY MALTS, despite a surprising number of independent bottlings. The distillery, founded in 1825, was silent from the 1920s until an expansion in the 1960s, but closed in 1983, and is no longer licensed. Even with the great growth of interest in Islay malts, there has been no talk of its reopening. The distillery's white-painted warehouses are still used, and form an attractive street close to the sea in Port Ellen, one of the principal villages on Islay. Adjoining the distillery is a modern maltings, issuing pungent peat smoke lest anyone requires reminding of the island's preoccupation. The malt is supplied, in varying levels of peatiness, to all of the other Islay distilleries, including those which make a proportion of their own. UDV has two other distilleries on the island: Lagavulin and Caol Ila.

HOUSE STYLE Oily, peppery, salty, smoky, herbal. With smoked fish.

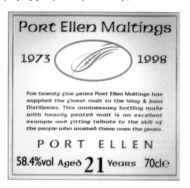

Port Ellen Maltings

1973   1998

For twenty five years Port Ellen Maltings has supplied the finest malt to the Islay & Jura Distilleries. This anniversary bottling made with heavily peated malt is an excellent example and fitting tribute to the skill of the people who worked there over the years.

PORT ELLEN

58.4%vol Aged **21** Years 70cle

PORT ELLEN 21-year-old, 58.4 vol, Anniversary Bottling
A rare "official" bottling, to celebrate 25 years of the maltings at Port Ellen.

Colour Bright gold.

Nose Very medicinal, but clean and firm.

Body Exceptionally oily, creamy.

Palate Smooth and deceptively restrained at first, then the tightly combined flavours emerge: bay leaves, parsley, peppercorns.

Finish Slowly unfolding. Salty, smoky, oaky. Very warming. A subtlety and complexity to which no aquavit or pepper vodka could quite aspire.

SCORE 83

NATURAL
CASK STRENGTH
SINGLE MALT
SCOTCH WHISKY

AGED **20** YEARS
DISTILLED 1978
PORT ELLEN
DISTILLERY
ESTABLISHED 1825
ISLE OF ISLAY
60.90%vol 70cle
PRODUCED AND BOTTLED
IN SCOTLAND
LIMITED EDITION
BOTTLE N° 8525
OCTOBER 1998

PORT ELLEN 20-year-old (distilled 1978, bottled 1998), 60.90 vol, Rare Malts

Colour Gold.

Nose More assertive. Appetizing and arousing. Bay trees. Seaweed.

Body Lightly oily.

Palate More expressive, fruity, dryish flavours. Fruity olive oil.
Parsley. Edible seaweed.

Finish Salty. Smoky. Oaky. Extremely peppery.

SCORE 82

PORT ELLEN 11-year-old, 64.1 vol, Cadenhead

Colour Pale gold.

Nose Leafy, slightly sour.

Body Lightly oily.

Palate Fruity, herbal, seaweedy.

Finish Sweet, parsleyish. Then seaweedy, peppery, warming.

SCORE 79

From the same bottler, an 18-year-old at 62.2 vol is smokier, oakier,
drier, and more peppery, but slightly less complex. SCORE 79.

PORT ELLEN 1980, 40 vol, Connoiseurs Choice

Colour Deep gold to bronze.

Nose Leathery, oaky.

Body Lightly oily.

Palate Oaky, salty.

Finish Oily. Late saltiness.

SCORE 77

PORT ELLEN 1975, 23-year-old, 52.5 vol cask strength, Hart Brothers

Colour Full gold.	
Nose Clean. Lightly medicinal.	
Body Lightly oily.	
Palate Very sweet and parsleyish.	
Finish Peppery.	

SCORE 79

Signatory bottlings of Port Ellen

Without having quite cornered the market, this independent seems to have made something of a speciality of Port Ellen.

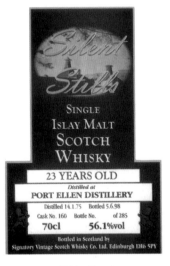

1983, 43 vol
"White wine" colour; flowery aroma; light, oily body; clean hits of sweet, savoury, herbal, then oily. SCORE 77.

1976, 57.9 vol
Similar colour; drier aroma, with a hint of peat; firmer; more seaweed; slightly woody; comes to life in a seaweedy, peppery finish. SCORE 78.

1975, 43 vol
Very pale indeed. Flowery aroma; very light body; fruit and vanilla in palate; peppery finish. SCORE 76.

23-year-old (distilled 1975, bottled 1998), 56.1 vol
Signatory "Silent Stills" series
Greeny-gold; parsley aroma; light, firm body; lightly peaty; peppery finish. SCORE 79.

OLD PULTENEY

PRODUCER Inver House
REGION Highlands   **DISTRICT** Northern Highlands

ADDRESS Huddart Street, Wick, Caithness, KW1 5BD
WEBSITE www.inverhouse.com   **E-MAIL** enquiries@inverhouse.com

MORE READILY AVAILABLE, and much welcomed on the shelves, since a change of ownership. This whisky is nicknamed "The Manzanilla of the North" after the coastal style of sherry. The producers of Manzanilla do supply casks to the Scotch whisky industry, and it is certainly possible that the odd butt has accommodated a charge of Pulteney whisky, but in general this distillery is more inclined towards Bourbon wood. The brininess of the whisky probably owes more to Scotland's sea air. Not only is the Pulteney distillery on the coast, it is the northernmost distillery on the Scottish mainland, at the town of Wick. Part of the town was built by Sir William Pulteney in 1810 as a model fishing port. The Old Pulteney distillery was founded in 1826 and rebuilt in 1959. It has been a contributor to the Ballantine blends. In 1995, it was acquired by Inver House. A whisky with lots of youthful muscle. The new eight-year-old reviewed below is sweeter than a previous bottling at the same age from Gordon & MacPhail.

HOUSE STYLE Fresh, salty, appetizing. Pre-dinner.

OLD PULTENEY 8-year-old, 40 vol, Inver House bottling
Mainly for the French market.

Colour Deep sunny yellow.

Nose Fresh, dry. Very faint peat. Hint of sea air.

Body Light, smooth.

Palate Full of flavours. Lightly peaty, spicy, nutty, both maltily sweet and salty. Extraordinarily lively and appetizing.

Finish Firm, nutty. Again, sweetness and saltiness. Like honey-roast peanuts.

SCORE 78

OLD PULTENEY 12-year-old, 40 vol

Colour Deep yellow.

Nose Dry. Peat, grass, sweet broom.

Body Light, oily.

Palate Light. Still honey and nuts, but oilier.

Finish Oily. Soothing. Very salty.

SCORE 79

OLD PULTENEY 15-year-old, sherry wood (cask 1501, bottle 206), 60.6 vol

Colour Medium oak.

Nose Rich, nutty, raisiny, fudgy. Vanilla.

Body Medium to full. Rich.

Palate Clean, sweet, nutty sherry dominates at first, but the whisky's own character eventually emerges to perform a balancing act.

Finish Peat smoke and salt. Very long. Therapeutic.

SCORE 80

OLD PULTENEY 1964, 40 vol, Gordon & MacPhail

Colour Bronze.

Nose Marshmallow. Toasted nuts. Cookies.

Body Soft. Surprisingly light.

Palate Nutty, cookie-like, toasty, but a little empty.

Finish Oily. Salty.

SCORE 77

Earlier versions of Old Pulteney

A 15-year-old at 40 vol from Gordon & MacPhail had a lovely balance of sherry and saltiness. SCORE 79. A 17-year-old at 52.8 vol, labelled Whalligoe, was lightly smooth and very salty. SCORE 78. A 1961 at 40 vol from Gordon & MacPhail was more sherryish, but still well balanced. SCORE 79.

ROSEBANK

PRODUCER United Distillers
REGION Lowland   DISTRICT Central Lowlands

ADDRESS Falkirk, Stirlingshire, FK1 5BW

I**F A CLASSIC LOWLANDER MUST BE MADE** by triple distillation, as some purists insist, the distinction is today unique to Auchentoshan. Until recently, it was shared with Rosebank, the Lowland favourite of many devotees, though in its floweriness it has much in common with some Speysiders. This pastoral-sounding distillery, at Falkirk, is on the banks (apparently once blessed with roses) of the Forth-Clyde canal. The waterway has long ceased to be an effective means of distribution, and the newer road awkwardly bisects the distillery. Thus, despite origins that may be as early as the 1790s, it was closed in 1993, to much protest. "The decision was painful," conceded United Distillers. There have since been discussions with British Waterways about restoring distillation on the site. This would be as part of a waterfront development dedicated to the district's considerable industrial history.

HOUSE STYLE Aromatic, with suggestions of clover and camomile. Romantic. A whisky for lovers.

ROSEBANK 8-year-old, 40 vol, Distillers Agency
A bottling that is now hard to find.

Colour Amber.
Nose Dry, grassy-flowery, pot-pourri aroma. Hint of dryish sherry.
Body Light, but very smooth.
Palate Dry, flowery, fruity. Becomes much less dry when water is added.
Finish Dry.

SCORE 76

ROSEBANK 12-year-old, 43 vol, Flora and Fauna

Colour Gold.

Nose Grassy-flowery (clover?), light, dry.

Body Light, smooth, slightly syrupy.

Palate At first a malty, sweetish floweriness. Stays flowery, but becomes gingery and dry.

Finish Again grassy and flowery, but crisp (almost sharp) and dry.

SCORE 77

ROSEBANK 15-year-old, 50 vol, Distillers Agency
Another hard-to-find bottling.

Colour Gold.

Nose Flowery.

Body Surprisingly soft.

Palate Light, sweetish, flowery, clean fruitiness. Very appetizing.

Finish Big, soft, long.

SCORE 77

ROSEBANK 1981 (bottled 1997), 63.9 vol, Cask Strength Limited Bottling

Colour Lemony yellow.

Nose Seductively aromatic. Clover. Camomile. Dry.

Body Soft, caressing.

Palate Creamy, lemony, flowery. Buttercups? Pot-pourri.

Finish Fragrant, faintly smoky.

SCORE 78

ROSEBANK 19-year-old (distilled 1979), 60.2 vol, Rare Malts

Colour Vinho verde.

Nose Shamelessly aromatic. Pot-pourri, camomile. Very flowery.

Body Silky. Sensuous.

Palate Delicious, lively flavours. Clover, lavender, fennel.

Finish Very long indeed. Pulsating with sweet and hot flavours. Starts sweet, developing a rounded dryness.

SCORE 81

Some independent bottlings of Rosebank

ROSEBANK 1990, 46 vol, fresh sherry cask, Murray McDavid

Colour Full gold to amber.

Nose Sherry, honey, lemons, buttercups.

Body Light, smooth.

Palate The flowery youth of the whisky and the freshness of the sherry cask achieve an interesting harmony.

Finish Smooth, appetizing. A teasing balance of sweetness and dryness.

SCORE 78

A Murray McDavid bottling of the same age and strength, but from a Bourbon cask, had a good, spearmint-like herbal note, but its flavours held together less well, and it was rather sharp. SCORE 76.

ROSEBANK 1989, 43 vol, Signatory

Colour Lemony yellow.

Nose Very aromatic. Flowery. Honeyed.

Body Creamy.

Palate Creamy, nutty, flowery.

Finish Lemony. Buttercups. Fragrant.

SCORE 77

ROSEBANK 1989, 9-year-old, 58.8 vol Cadenhead

Colour White wine to pale gold.

Nose Assertively flowery. Fragrant. Dry.

Body Light.

Palate Flowery, soft, grassily sweet, moving to very gently dry finish.

Finish Flowery, very lightly nutty, nougat-like.

SCORE 80

ROSEBANK 1988, 40 vol, Connoisseurs Choice

Colour Full gold.

Nose Buttercups, clover, sweet grass, honey, and a tender touch of sherry.

Body Light, soft, smooth.

Palate Flowers softened and sweetened by sherry. Honey, junket, very lightly nutty dryness. A deft balance between the whisky's own character and the sherry.

Finish Candied angelica, honey-coated nuts.

SCORE 79

ST MAGDALENE

PRODUCER DCL/UDV (Diageo)
REGION Lowland **District** Central Lowlands

ADDRESS Linlithgow, West Lothian, EH49 6AQ

THIS SITE ACCOMMODATED A LEPER COLONY in the 12th century, and later a convent, before a distillery was established, possibly in 1765. Production ceased in 1983 and some of the buildings have since been converted into apartments. The distillery has sometimes been known as Linlithgow, after its home town, west of Edinburgh and close to the River Forth.

HOUSE STYLE Perfumy, grassy, smooth. Restorative.

RARE MALTS
SELECTION

Each individual vintage has been specially selected from Scotland's finest single malt stocks of rare or now silent distilleries. The limited bottlings of these scarce and unique whiskies are at natural cask strength for the enjoyment of the true connoisseur.

NATURAL CASK STRENGTH
SINGLE MALT SCOTCH WHISKY

AGED **19** YEARS

DISTILLED 1979

ST MAGDALENE
DISTILLERY
· ESTABLISHED 1765 ·
LINLITHGOW, WEST LOTHIAN
63.80%vol 70cl℮
PRODUCED AND BOTTLED IN SCOTLAND
LIMITED EDITION
BOTTLE N⁰ 0007
OCTOBER 1998

ST MAGDALENE 19-year-old (distilled 1979, released 1998), 63.80 vol, Rare Malts

Colour	Full gold to pale amber.
Nose	Very aromatic. Burnt grass. Rooty. Licorice root. Juicy oak.
Body	Medium to full. Firmly oily.
Palate	Big flavours. Chewy, licorice-like, maltiness.
Finish	Sudden robust hit of peaty, sappy bitterness, rounding out in lively flavours as it develops.

SCORE 78

An earlier Rare Malts bottling of a 1970 St Magdalene had burnt grass, toffee, candy, and exotic fruit. SCORE 77.

ST MAGDALENE 20-year-old (distilled 1978), 62.7 vol
To celebrate the centenary of UDV's Engineering Department.

Colour Chestnut.	

Colour Chestnut.

Nose Polished oak.

Body Big, smooth.

Palate Winey sherry. Juicy oak. Burnt grass.

Finish Nutty, syrupy, smoky. Delicious.

> **SCORE 79**

Some independent bottlings of St Magdalene

ST MAGDALENE 10-year-old, Cadenhead

Colour White wine.

Nose Lightly peaty, slightly phenolic.

Body Lightly syrupy.

Palate Grassy but dry.

Finish Crisp, dry. Light peat. Hint of wood.

> **SCORE 71**

LINLITHGOW 1975, 51.7 vol, Signatory "Silent Stills" Series

Colour Bright full gold.

Nose Clean, light peat.

Body Light to medium. Firm. Smooth.

Palate Grassy, lemony. A true Lowlander.

Finish Perfumy. Linseed oil. Cereal grains. Soothing.

> **SCORE 75**

Other versions of St Magdalene
A 1981, at 40 vol from Connoisseurs Choice, is grassy and sweetish, with exotic fruit. SCORE 67. From Oddbins, a cask-strength 1982 was fruity but with a nice fragrant, smoky balance. SCORE 71. An Oddbins 23-year-old, also at cask strength, was grassier and slightly honeyish, again with a smoky finish. SCORE 70.

SCAPA

PRODUCER Allied Distillers
REGION Highlands   **ISLAND** Orkney

ADDRESS St Ola, Kirkwall, Orkney, KW15 1SE
TEL 01856-872071

I N A LOW-KEY WAY, this is quite a cult whisky, despite somewhat intermittent production. Although the distillery has a functional appearance (despite a restored water wheel), its evocative location helps. Scapa Flow, a stretch of water linking the North Sea to the Atlantic, is famous for its roles in both World Wars. The distillery, near Kirkwall, fails to be the northernmost in Scotland by only half a mile. It was founded in 1885. Two of the original warehouses survive, but most of the present fabric dates from 1959.

The water supply, from a stream called the Lingro Burn, is very peaty, but the distillery uses wholly unpeated malt. It has a Lomond wash-still, which may contribute to a slight oiliness of the whisky. Maturation is in Bourbon casks. Although the whisky is quite light in flavour, it has a distinctive complex of vanilla notes, sometimes suggesting very spicy chocolate, and nutty, rooty saltiness. It has at times been bottled under the name of Allied's subsidiary Taylor and Ferguson. The distillery is now managed by Highland Park.

HOUSE STYLE Salt, hay. Oily, spicy chocolate. After a hearty walk, before dinner.

SCAPA 8-year-old, 40 vol, Gordon & MacPhail
Now hard to find.

Colour Full gold to amber.

Nose Fresh, sea-breeze saltiness, new-mown hay, heather, some Bourbon character.

Body Medium, silky.

Palate Salty, slightly sharp, tangy.

Finish Oily but dry, appetizing.

SCORE 76

SCAPA 10-year-old, 43 vol
Hard to find.

Colour Full gold to amber.

Nose Salt, hay, chocolate, Bourbon. Delicious soft peatiness.

Body Medium, silky.

Palate Smooth, vanilla, chocolate. Rounded. Beautiful balance.

Finish Appetizing bitterness. Rounded peat. Faint salt. Quick warmth.

SCORE 77

SCAPA 12-year-old, 40 vol
The current "official" bottling.

Colour Bright full gold.

Nose Softer. Hay. Warm.

Body Light, smooth, salty.

Palate Clean, sweetish. Vanilla, nuts, salt.

Finish Late salt and pepper, with a hint of peat.

SCORE 76

SCAPA 1988 (casks 176 and 177, bottled 1998), 43 vol, Signatory

Colour White wine.

Nose Salty. Rooty. Faint seaweedy fruitiness.

Body Light but firm, smooth and oily.

Palate With less wood extract, much more peat comes through.

Finish Grassy sweetness. Peatiness. Saltiness.

SCORE 76

SCAPA 1987, 40 vol, Gordon & MacPhail

Colour Full primrose.

Nose Leafy. Slightly sour, herbal note. Peat. Salt.

Body Light but syrupy.

Palate Syrupy, nutty, salty.

Finish Nutty, salty, very long. Appetizing.
A complex, delicate, well-balanced vintage.

SCORE 79

SCAPA 1986, 40 vol, Taylor and Ferguson/Gordon & MacPhail

Colour Full gold to amber.

Nose Hay. Leather. Perfumy.

Body Smooth. Oily.

Palate Nutty. Lemony. Salty.

Finish Lemony. Oily. Long.

SCORE 78

SCAPA 1983, 40 vol, Gordon & MacPhail

Colour Amber.

Nose Salt, hay, chocolate, Bourbon.

Body Medium, silky.

Palate Smooth, vanilla, chocolate. Tangy towards finish.

Finish Chocolate, toffee, licorice, salt. Reminiscent of the salty licorice sold in The Netherlands and Nordic countries.

SCORE 78

Earlier versions of Scapa

A 1963 from Gordon & MacPhail, at 40 vol, was wonderful full-flavoured and complex, from brine to Bourbon to chocolate. SCORE 79. A 24-year-old from Cadenhead (distilled 1965, bottled 1990), at 46.5 vol, was salty and heathery. SCORE 77.

THE SINGLETON

PRODUCER Justerini and Brooks (Diageo)
REGION Highlands   **DISTRICT** Speyside

ADDRESS Mulben, Banffshire, EB55 6XS
TEL 01542-885000

I N 1986, WHEN THE SINGLETON WAS LAUNCHED as a bottled malt, the cynics response was "a designer whisky". The brand name, implying an "only one", was contrived because the producers felt that the name of the distillery, Auchroisk (pronounced "othroysk") was too difficult for the prospective consumer. The Gaelic name means "ford across the red stream". The distillery lies on the Mulben burn, which flows into the Spey. A nearby spring, producing very soft water, was the reason the site was chosen when this handsome distillery was established in 1974. The whisky is sweet, with a hint of aniseed, as evidenced by some Cadenhead bottlings from plain wood under the Auchroisk name. Bottlings as The Singleton have been at ten to 12 years, some with vintage dates. The current version is less sherryish than in the past. This enjoyable Speysider has gone mainly to Japan, but deserves greater availablity.

HOUSE STYLE Softly spicy. Liqueurish. After dinner.

THE SINGLETON 10-year-old, 43 vol

Colour Bronze.

Nose Light sherry, malt, licorice, aniseed. Gently malty. The faintest hint of peat.

Body Medium. Very smooth.

Palate Licorice, aniseed, light sherry.

Finish Liqueurish, with a lightly smoky background.

SCORE 78

SPEYBURN

PRODUCER Inver House
REGION Highlands **DISTRICT** Speyside (Rothes)

ADDRESS Rothes, Aberlour, Morayshire, AB38 7AG
WEBSITE www.inverhouse.com **E-MAIL** enquiries@inverhouse.com

THERE ARE MANY CLAIMANTS to being the most beautifully situated distillery in Scotland, and Speyburn is surely one of them. This handsome Victorian distillery, set in a deep sweeping valley, makes a spectacular sight on the road between Rothes and Elgin. It was built in 1897 and, despite modernizations, has not undergone dramatic change. In the early 1990s, Speyburn was acquired by Inver House, whose ten-year-old has largely superseded the similar 12-year-old released in the Flora and Fauna series by the previous owners. The 21-year-old is a fine Speysider.

HOUSE STYLE Flowery, herbal, heathery. Aperitif.

Set in a hollow in the rolling hills of the Spey valley, the Speyburn distillery produces a characterful malt that is becoming easier to find.

SPEYBURN 10-year-old, 40 vol

Colour Solid gold.

Nose Flowery.

Body Medium, gentle.

Palate Clean, lightly malty. Developing fresh, herbal, heathery notes.

Finish Fresh, very sweet, lightly syrupy.

SCORE 71

SPEYBURN 12-year-old, 43 vol, Flora and Fauna

Colour Pale gold.

Nose Very dry.

Body Medium, smooth.

Palate Slightly sweet and malty, developing a herbal, heathery dryness.

Finish Dry, warming, aromatic, assertive.

SCORE 71

SPEYBURN 21-year-old, 40 vol

Colour Full peachy gold.

Nose Flowery, leafy, peaty.

Body Medium. Gentle. Clean, good, long malt background. Again, fresh, herbal, heathery notes.

Palate Lovely combination of malt, heather, and sherry.

Finish Nutty sweetness, becoming drier. Late peaty warmth.

SCORE 76

Earlier versions of Speyburn

A 1975, from Cadenhead, was greeny-gold, with a leafy aroma, very light flavours, and a peaty finish. SCORE 69. A 1971, from Connoisseurs Choice, had lots of heather honey and malt, with a touch of bitter herbs. SCORE 76.

SPRINGBANK

PRODUCER J. and A. Mitchell
REGION Campbeltown   DISTRICT Argyll

ADDRESS Well Close, Campbeltown, Argyll, PA28 6ET
TEL 01586-552085 VC Summer only by appointment

T HE MOST COMPLETELY TRADITIONAL of all whisky distilleries, protector and protagonist of the Campbeltown style, is also among the most forward-looking. Reviving an old Campbeltown name, the distillery will in 2006 bottle a whisky called Hazelburn, distilled in 1997. This follows another such revival, the release in 1985 of the acclaimed Longrow, distilled in 1973–74. Springbank itself appears in a wide variety of vintages, ages, and woods, the most famous of which is the 1966, distilled from locally grown barley kilned over local peat. After a gap of 33 years, malting barley is again being grown by a local farm – especially for Springbank.

The distillery has its own maltings, which after being silent for more than a decade was restored seven or eight years ago, though using Islay peat. It is a floor maltings and meets all of the distillery's needs. That combination of circumstances is unique to this distillery. Springbank is also unusual in being able to triple distil.

Hazelburn is made from unpeated malt, triple distilled, and is expected to be a relatively light whisky. Springbank uses medium-peated malt, with a trajectory that amounts to two-and-a-half times distillation. Longrow employs heavily peated malt, double distilled. Underlining its commitment to Campbeltown, the distillery has also provided staff in recent years to help care for its sole local rival Glen Scotia (see entry), now reopened under new ownership.

Campbeltown, on the narrow peninsula called the Mull of Kintyre, was more accessible, and commercially important, in the days of steamship travel between neighbouring islands, and actually became more remote with the growth of rail and road transport. "The mist rolls in from the sea," sang Paul McCartney, and it really does, no doubt influencing the flavour of the older whiskies maturing in the earth-floored warehouses numbers one and three at Springbank.

Over the centuries, the town has had about 30 distilleries, some of which ruined their reputations by producing hurried whiskies for the US during Prohibition, and closed soon afterwards. The Hazelburn distillery, believed to have dated from 1796, operated intermittently for about 125 years. It was behind the Springbank buildings. Several distilleries huddled together on a street called Longrow, where one of Springbank's warehouses still stands. The Longrow distillery was founded in 1824, and lasted 70-odd years. After a period of illegal whisky making, a family called Mitchell began the Riechlachan distillery in 1825. The site of their illicit still became Springbank, possibly in 1828, and the company is still owned by this reticent family. The distillery was rebuilt in the 1880s, and is little changed.

As an isolated independent with its own under-utilized bottling line, in 1969 Springbank bought the century-old firm of Cadenhead. This company, formerly based in Aberdeen, has always been an independent bottler. Both Springbank and Cadenhead use the same bottling line, in Campbeltown, but they are run as separate enterprises.

Neither company chill-filters its whiskies, or adds caramel to balance the colour. Being long-established enterprises, they have a considerable inventory of casks. Some Springbank once even found its way into a couple of casks of acacia wood. As awareness of woods has increased in the industry, Springbank has mainly acquired Bourbon barrels, to highlight the character of the whisky itself, but most bottlings are vatted to give a touch of colour and sweetness from sherry wood. If a sherry cask proves particularly good, it may be bottled straight. Without a hierarchy of marketing policy makers, the three or four people who run the business on a daily basis taste regularly and bottle what they think is good and ready.

SPRINGBANK HOUSE STYLE Salty, oily, coconut. Aperitif.

LONGROW HOUSE STYLE Piny, oily, damp earth. Nightcap.

SPRINGBANK C.V., 46 vol
What do the initials mean? The chairman's vatting? A cask vatting? It certainly is that, but the letters actually indicate curriculum vitae. The idea was to embrace a lifetime of Springbanks by vatting examples from eight to 30 years. This is an imaginative introduction to a multi-faceted character but, fearing that it may have created a "definitive" Springbank, the distillery has decided to return to individuality. This short-lived experiment is therefore a collectors' item.

Colour Lime-green to gold.

Nose Very complex. Coconut cream. Coconut fibre. Grain. Salt.

Body Light. Oily.

Palate Extraordinarily lively. Sherbety. Passion fruit. Salt.

Finish Tingly. Iron-like. Dry. Refreshing. Appetizing.

SCORE 84

SPRINGBANK Rum Cask, 10-year-old, 40 vol
Minimum of three years in rum. Release in the year 2000.

Colour Very pale. Greenish.

Nose Distinct mint-toffee.

Body Light to medium. Textured.

Palate Toffee, mint, spices, lemon grass.

Finish Lime-like. Toffee. Hot peppermints. Warm. Smoky peat.
Astonishingly long.

SCORE 88

SPRINGBANK 12-year-old, 46 vol
A new, sherried edition, darker and richer than the previous
Bourbon-wood 12-year-old.

Colour Walnut.

Nose Sea air. Oak. Sherry.

Body Light to medium. Very smooth.

Palate Very salty, lightly oily, with very long development
to passion fruit.

Finish Coconut. Toast. Long, lingering.

SCORE 84

A 12-year-old "100° Proof", at 57 vol, has a darker orange colour; a
wonderfully briny aroma; a very smooth body; a fruity palate; and an
extremely salty finish. A classic Springbank. SCORE 84.

SPRINGBANK 21-year-old, 46 vol

Colour Full amber to dark oak.

Nose Sea air, sherry, oak.

Body Medium. Firm.

Palate Restrained salt, more coconut, passion fruit, nut-toffee.

Finish Salty. Coconut. Fibre. Oak.

Score 87

Special editions of Springbank

SPRINGBANK 25-year-old, 46 vol, Limited Edition

Colour Apricot.

Nose Sea air. Sherry oak. Very clean.

Body Creamy.

Palate Excellent sherry, but held in balance. Walnuts. Restrained esters. Very faint suggestion of banana. Coconut. Salt. Brine. A magnificently complex whisky.

Finish Salty. Some peat. Dry.

SCORE 95

SPRINGBANK 1966 (32-year-old), Cask Strength

Made from local barley and local peat, but matured in Bourbon rather than the sherry of the earlier, "West Highland", version. The stills were fired with local coal. The mine closed soon afterwards.

Colour Distinctively shimmering gold.

Nose Clean, sweet, barley malt. Gently sweet peat smoke.

Body Creamy but firm. Like a rich cookie.

Palate Clean maltiness. Interplay of creamy richness and cookie-like dryness.

Finish Late hit of smoky dryness.

SCORE 94

Very old Springbanks

Available with the 25-year-old in a millennium set

30 years: Full oak colour; huge aroma of brine, oak, and sherry, beautifully balanced; sherryish, very sweet palate; developing restrained, Islay-like phenol; finishing with sweetness, salt, and pepper. Surprising lack of woodinesss for its age. SCORE 94.

35 years: Deep, refractive amber; brine, soft oak, and sherry in the aroma; sweet, smooth, clean sherry in the palate; complex, developing some coconut and seaweed; salt and pepper in the finish. Tightly combined flavours. Very sophisticated. SCORE 95.

40 years: Bright, full gold; very powerful and assertive in its Islay-like aroma, after which its sweet, coconut palate seems something of a surrender. Gentle phenol in the finish. Still great subtlety, but a faded star. SCORE 86.

45 years: Bright gold; peat and seaweed in the aroma, again falling away somewhat in its coconut-like sweetness. SCORE 85.

50 years: Greeny-gold; lightly peaty, burnt grass, and brine in the aroma; coconut-like and syrupy; peppery finish. SCORE 86.

Earlier versions, now hard to find

1980: Full bronze; briny, spicy, medicinal aroma; firm, chewy, malty body; seaweedy palate (more Islay-like); characteristically salty finish. SCORE 90.

1979: Greeny-gold to primrose; gorse-like aroma; sweet, coconut palate; flowery, salty finish. A very delicate vintage, with some complexity. SCORE 85.

1978: Dark orange; oaky, medicinal, briny aroma; smooth, malty body; powerful passion fruit and iron in the palate; pepper and salt in the finish. SCORE 89.

1977: Apricot to orange; sweetish aroma, with some sherry; smooth, oily, very Islay-like; warming, soothing finish. SCORE 88.

1972: Peachy colour; distinctly medicinal, Islay-like aroma; oaky palate, developing phenol, seaweedy sweetness, and pepperiness. SCORE 88.

1967: Bright deep orange; brine, coconut, and oak in complex aroma; relatively sweet, malty, and sherryish in palate; late, very restrained pepper and salt. A very rounded vintage. SCORE 86.

1965: Deep gold; fresh, briny aroma; oily; very sweet, with some coconut; salty finish. Lacks complexity. SCORE 84.

1962: Dark oak colour; charcoal aroma; char-dust in the whisky, but still the pepper, buttery malt, and salt survive. Scores points for being an archaeological experience. SCORE 89.

1958: Bronze to copper; brine and passion-fruit in aroma; very sweet embrace, then sudden, big hit of Islay-like phenol. Nothing between the extremes. SCORE 87.

Longrow

Longrow has been distilled every year since 1990. As from the year 2000, it will be regularly in the range as a ten-year-old. By 2002, the bottlings will have been made with barley from the restored maltings. As from 2014, there will also be a 14-year-old. These promise to be outstanding whiskies.

LONGROW 10-year-old, 46 vol

Colour Pale, bright. Distinctly greeny-gold.

Nose Fresh. Piny.

Body Light, oily.

Palate Sweet. Creamy at first. Coconut. Then peppery and piny.

Finish Pine-log fires. Sudden surge of warmth.

SCORE 88

LONGROW 1974, 16-year-old, 46 vol

Colour Full gold, with green tinge.

Nose Pungent, piny, earthy, peaty.

Body Medium, oily.

Palate Sweet-coconut oiliness, distinctively piny, phenolic, peaty.

Finish Salty, intense, tenacious, distinctive, long.

SCORE 90

The same year's Longrow as an 18-year-old, tasted as a work in progress, seems to have developed more spicy phenol flavours. The same year as a 21-year-old was slightly sweeter, more complex, and longer. Score 91.

Some independent bottlings of Springbank

SPRINGBANK 5-year-old, 61.2 vol, Adelphi

Colour Dark oak.

Nose Chocolate. Coconut fudge.

Body Medium. Silky.

Palate Sweet, fudgy, earthy, smoky. Lacks complexity.

Finish Earthy, salty, long.

SCORE 82

SCOTCH MALT WHISKY SOCIETY, cask 27.43, 8-year-old, 59.3 vol

Finished in port wood.

Colour Almost cerise. Port-like.

Nose Creamy fruitiness.

Body Rich and syrupy.

Palate Cherryish, earthy, then lightly smoky.

Finish Tavel rosé wine. Salted cashews.
An aperitif in its own right.

SCORE 84

SPRINGBANK 1969, 54 vol, Signatory

Colour Full gold.

Nose Light brine and coconut.

Body Light, oily.

Palate Sweetish. Pronounced coconut. Light touch of seaweed.

Finish Smokiness. Sweet then dry. Late salt.

SCORE 85

The same vintage at 46 vol, from Murray McDavid, is similar but slightly drier. SCORE 85.

SPRINGBANK 1967, 46 vol, Murray McDavid

Colour Full gold with greenish tinge.

Nose Briny, leafy, appetizing.

Body Light, oily.

Palate Leafy, sweetish, coconut-like. Lacks complexity.

Finish Leafy, stalky, woody, peppery.

SCORE 84

STRATHISLA

PRODUCER Chivas (Seagram)
REGION Highland   DISTRICT Speyside (Strathisla)

ADDRESS Seafield Avenue, Keith, Banffshire, AB55 3BS
TEL 01542-783044 **VC**

T HE OLDEST DISTILLERY IN THE NORTH OF SCOTLAND. In the 13th century, Dominican monks used a spring nearby to provide water for brewing beer. The same water, with a touch of calcium hardness and scarcely any peat character, has been used in the distillation of whisky since at least 1786. Strathisla, which has also at times been known as Milltown, began its life as a farm distillery. It started to take its present shape from the 1820s onwards, especially after a fire in 1876. In 1950 it was acquired by Chivas/Seagram. As a significant contributor to Chivas Regal, it is now the showpiece distillery for that blend.

Lightly peated malt is used, as well as wooden wash-backs and small stills. Although wooden wash-backs are by no means unusual, Strathisla believes that fermentation characteristics play a very important part in the character of its dry, fruity, oaky malt whisky. The only official bottling is the 12-year-old, but a range of ages is bottled under the distillery's name by Gordon & MacPhail.

HOUSE STYLE Dry, fruity. After dinner.

STRATHISLA 12-year-old, 43 vol

Colour Full, deep gold.

Nose Apricot. Cereal grains. Fresh, juicy oak.

Body Medium, rounded.

Palate Much richer than previous bottlings. Sherryish, fruity.
Mouth-coating. Then Strathisla's teasing sweet-and-dry character.

Finish Smooth and soothing. Violets and vanilla.

SCORE 80

STRATHISLA 1982, 40 vol, Gordon & MacPhail

Colour Full gold.

Nose Dexterous balance of dryish oak, almondy sherry, and light peat.

Body Medium but rich.

Palate Honeyed. Light, dry oak.

Finish Nutty. Slightly woody. Warming.

SCORE 80

STRATHISLA 21-year-old, 40 vol, Gordon & MacPhail

Colour Rich yellowy gold.

Nose Pronounced sherry. Very complex indeed. Some fruit. Good cereal-grain maltiness.

Body Surprisingly light. Soft and smooth.

Palate Astonishingly honeyed, but less complex than the nose suggests.

Finish Very delicate late oak and peat.

SCORE 80

STRATHISLA 1972, 62.6 vol, Gordon & MacPhail "Cask" series

Colour Full gold to bronze.

Nose Sherry. Almonds. Perfume.

Body Medium to full. Syrupy, then drying.

Palate Sherry. Violets, flowery, grassy, woody. Dries on tongue.

Finish Dry. Woody. Hint of peat.

SCORE 79

Earlier versions of Strathisla

Gordon & MacPhail has made many bottlings at 40 vol. An eight-year-old had cereal grain and complexity. SCORE 79. A 15-year-old was smooth and soothing. SCORE 80. A 1980 was honeyed and fruity. SCORE 80. Among several vintage-dated editions, a heathery 1967 was outstanding. SCORE 81.

STRATHMILL

PRODUCER UDV (Diageo)
REGION Highlands   **DISTRICT** Speyside (Strathisla)

ADDRESS Keith, Banffshire, AB55 5DQ
TEL 01542-885000

THE TOWN OF KEITH must once have been a considerable grain-milling centre. The Glen Keith distillery was built on the site of a corn mill. Strathmill, as its name suggests, went one better. It was rebuilt from a corn mill, in 1891, when the whisky industry was having one of its periodic upswings. Three years later, it was acquired by Gilbey, of which Justerini and Brooks became a subsidiary through IDV (now UDV/Diageo). Arguably, it has been in the same ownership for more than a century. Its whisky was for many years central to the Dunhill/Old Master blends (see Tamdhu), but does not seem to have been available as a single until a bottling of the 1980 by the wine-merchant chain Oddbins in 1993. This lusciously sweet version was quickly followed by a similar bottling of the same year from Cadenhead, and now the Signatory edition below. It is time for an "official" bottling.

HOUSE STYLE The whisky world's answer to orange muscat.
With dessert.

Vintage 1985
Single Highland Malt Scotch Whisky
Matured in oak casks for 12 years
Distilled at Strathmill Distillery
on 4.10.85   Bottled 1.98
Butt No. 2330   Bottle No.   of 5058
This whisky has been selected, produced and bottled in
Scotland for and under the sole responsibility of
Signatory Vintage Scotch Whisky Co. Ltd.
Edinburgh EH6 6SW, Scotland
70cl   43%vol

STRATHMILL 1985 (butt 2330, bottled at 12 years old), 43 vol, Signatory

Colour White wine. Very pale indeed.

Nose Sweet. Dessert apples. Orange skins. Resiny. Estery.

Body Medium. Syrupy.

Palate Sweetish. Very fruity. Oranges. Apples. Pears. Seed-like.

Finish Dryish. Apple skins. Pears. Late perfume. Faint hint of cloves.

SCORE 71

TALISKER

PRODUCER UDV (Diageo)
REGION Highlands ISLAND Skye

ADDRESS Carbost, Isle of Skye, IV47 8SR
TEL 01478-640314 **VC**

O NE OF THE MOST INDIVIDUALISTIC OF SINGLE MALTS, with a powerful palate and an emphatic island character. It has a distinctively peppery character, so hot as to make one taster's temples steam. The phrase "explodes on the palate" is among the descriptions used for certain whiskies by blenders at UDV; surely they had Talisker in mind when they composed this. "The lava of the Cuillins" was another taster's response. The Cuillins are the dramatic hills of Skye, the island home of Talisker. The distillery is on the west coast of the island, on the shores of Loch Harport, in an area where Gaelic is still spoken. The local industry was once tweed.

After a number of false starts on other sites, the distillery was established in 1831 and expanded in 1900. For much of its life, it used triple-distillation, and in those days Robert Louis Stevenson ranked Talisker as a style on its own, comparable with the Islay and Livet whiskies. It switched to double-distillation in 1928, and was partly rebuilt in 1960. The distillery uses traditional cooling coils – "worm tubs" – which can make for a fuller flavour than a modern condenser.

Some malt lovers still mourn the youthfully dry assertiveness of the eight-year-old version that was replaced by the current, more rounded version a couple of summers older. There is now, additionally, a 1986 vintage finished in Amoroso sherry.

Independent bottlings seem to have vanished. A long-gone 14-year-old at 64.4 vol from Cadenhead, apparently without sherry, was full of sea air, seaweed, and pepper on the nose, and explosively peppery and salty in palate. A 15-year-old, from the same bottler, at 56.4 vol, was yellowy-brown, heavily sherried, and dominated at first by the cask, but then followed by an astonishingly long development of distillery flavours. A 1955, at 53.6 vol, from Gordon & MacPhail had a brighter, but still deep, amber-red colour. It seemed to have slightly less sherry and more oak, but again had considerable development.

The island is also home to an unrelated company making a vatted malt called Poit Dubh, and a blend, Te Bheag. Both are said to contain some Talisker, and their hearty palates appear to support this suggestion. A dry, perfumy, blended whisky called Isle of Skye is made by the Edinburgh merchants Ian Macleod and Co. The style of whisky liqueur represented by Drambuie is also said to have originated on the Isle of Skye, though its origins actually remain somewhat clouded in Scotch mist.

HOUSE STYLE Volcanic. A winter warmer.

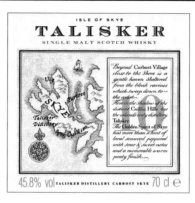

TALISKER 10-year-old, 45.8 vol

Colour Bright amber-red.

Nose Pungent, smoke-accented, rounded.

Body Full, slightly syrupy.

Palate Smoky, malty-sweet, with sourness and a very big pepperiness developing.

Finish Very peppery, huge, long.

SCORE 90

TALISKER "Double Matured", 1986, 45.8 vol, Distillers Edition
Finished in amoroso sherry wood.

Colour Orange.

Nose Toffee, bitter chocolate, and toasted nuts, with late salt and pepper.

Body Full, textured.

Palate Toffeeish, then toasty. The distracting richness of these flavours introduces a shock of contrast when the seaweed and pepper suddenly burst through.

Finish Powerful salt and pepper.

SCORE 90

TAMDHU

Producer Highland Distillers
Region Highlands   **District** Speyside
address Knockando, Morayshire, AB38 7RP

UNTIL MACALLAN JOINED THE HIGHLAND distillers group, that company's principal bottled Speyside malt was Tamdhu. Both of these malts, along with Glenrothes, are important Speyside elements in a proposed Vintage Malt whisky from The Famous Grouse (and, of course, blends under that name). Since 1997–98, Tamdhu has also played an important role in the Dunhill blends.

It is to be hoped that Tamdhu, a mild, urbane whisky, leaning towards sweetness, is not in future overlooked as a single malt. The distillery is in the heart of Speyside, between Knockando and Cardhu. It was founded in 1896, and largely rebuilt in the 1970s. Water comes from the Tamdhu burn, which flows through woodland into the Spey.

Tamdhu has a sizable and impressive Saladin maltings, providing for all its own needs and those of several other whisky makers. A modest reminder of this is the stylized ear of barley that appears on the label of the principal version of Tamdhu. The distillery is impeccably well kept, and has its own touches of tradition, notably its enthusiasm for wooden fermenting vessels.

House style Mild, urbane. Sometimes toffee-nosed. Versatile.

TAMDHU, no age statement, 40 vol

Colour Bright gold.

Nose Flowery. Faintly lemony. Cereal grain.

Body Light, soft.

Palate Clean, sweet. Very slightly toffeeish. An easily drinkable, malt-accented introduction to singles.

Finish Flowery. Very faint hint of peat.

SCORE 74

TAMDHU 8-year-old, 40 vol, The MacPhail's Collection

Colour Gold to amber.

Nose Distinct touch of sherry.

Body Light to medium.

Palate Attractive interplay of sherry and malt, then perfumy.

Finish Light touch of balancing peaty dryness.

SCORE 75

TAMDHU 13-year-old (distilled 1984, bottled 1997, 2144) 61.5 vol, Adelphi

Colour Bronze.

Nose Sherryish. Nutty. Flowery.

Body Treacly.

Palate Intense sweetness but beautifully balanced by perfumy dryness. A good after dinner malt.

Finish Spicy, complex. Surge of warmth.

SCORE 77

TAMDHU 1970 (27-year-old, butt 375, bottled 1997), 49.5 vol, Signatory Cask Strength Series

Colour Deep amber to tawny.

Nose Peaty, buttery, sherryish, oaky.

Body Medium, smooth.

Palate Firm, oaky. Touch of treacly sweetness. Spicy.

Finish Late sweetness and smoky, peaty dryness.

SCORE 76

TAMNAVULIN

PRODUCER JBB
REGION Highlands **DISTRICT** Speyside (Livet)
ADDRESS Ballindalloch, Banffshire, AB37 9JA

O N THE STEEP SIDE OF THE GLEN of the Livet, the river is joined by one of its tributaries, a stream called Allt a Choire (in English, Corrie). This is the site of the Tamnavulin distillery, taking its name from "mill on the hill". The location is more often spelled Tomnavoulin, but such discrepancies are hardly unusual in Scotland.

Part of the premises was formerly used for the carding of wool. The distillery, built in the 1960s, has a somewhat utilitarian look. The whisky is an important component of the Mackinlay blends. Tamnavulin has been mothballed since 1996, shortly after its owners, Invergordon, were acquired by JBB (Jim Beam).

Stocks are such that the 12-year-old is readily available. Among the malts produced in and around the glen of the Livet river, the elegant Tamnavulin is the lightest in body, although not in palate. In taste, it is a little more assertive than Tomintoul, with which it might be most closely compared.

HOUSE STYLE Aromatic, herbal. Aperitif.

TAMNAVULIN 12-year-old, 40 vol

Colour Vinho verde.
Nose Very aromatic. A touch of peat, hay, heather, herbal notes. Slightly medicinal.
Body Very light indeed, but smooth.
Palate Lemon, flowering currant. Winey. Vermouth-like.
Finish Aromatic. Juniper?

SCORE 76

A ten-year-old, now hard to find, was fractionally lighter all round. SCORE 76.

TAMNAVULIN 22-year-old, 45 vol

Colour	Deep amber to copper.
Nose	Almondy sherry, junipery aroma, and oak.
Body	Light but firm.
Palate	Sherry. Lemon pith. Stalky. Aromatic.
Finish	Spicy. Crisp.

SCORE 77

TAMNAVULIN 24-year-old, 45 vol, Stillman's Dram

Colour	Full gold.
Nose	Vanilla pod. Grass. Light peat.
Body	Light but firm.
Palate	Junipery, grassy, lightly peaty. Clearer flavours without the sherry of the 22-year-old.
Finish	Crisp. Lemon and juniper. Appetizing.

SCORE 78

A Stillman's Dram at 27 years old, released in 1996, was sherryish, with a nice balance of nuts and pepper. SCORE 78.

TAMNAVULIN 1988 (bottled 1997) 58.9 vol, Gordon & MacPhail Cask Series

Colour	Bright greeny-gold.
Nose	Grass and juniper.
Body	Surprisingly full and rounded. Oily.
Palate	Grassy, grainy, oaty, creamy.
Finish	Grassy. Stony.

SCORE 77

TEANINICH

PRODUCER UDV (Diageo)
REGION Highlands   DISTRICT Northern Highlands

ADDRESS Alness, Ross-Shire, IV17 0XB
TEL 01349-885001

TWO RARE MALTS BOTTLINGS have brought a little more attention to the malt whisky from this low-profile distillery. Has its whisky been obscured by its tongue-twisting name (Tee'ninick)? Perhaps, but many distillery names are difficult to people who do not speak Gaelic. Has it failed to gain a reputation for its single because it has contributes mainly to blends (in this case, Robbie Burns, Haig Dimple, and VAT 69?). That is not unusual, either. The distillery, founded in 1817 and extended in 1899, the 1960s, and the 1970s, has seen its older buildings and stillhouse masked by new ones, making it look unromantically modern to the passer-by, but is not alone in that respect, either. It should be more widely appreciated. Whisky tourists should note that Teaninich, near Alness, is not far from the Dalmore distillery. Nor is it distant from Glenmorangie.

HOUSE STYLE Robust, toffeeish, spicy, leafy. Restorative or after dinner.

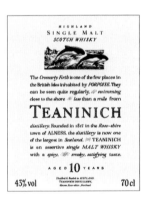

TEANINICH 10-year-old, 43 vol, Flora and Fauna

Colour Pale gold.

Nose Big, fresh aroma. Fruity. Hints of apple, leafy, smoky.

Body Medium, rich.

Palate Fruity, remarkably leafy, lightly peaty. Sparks with flavour. Very appetizing.

Finish Leafy, herbal. Rounded.

SCORE 74

TEANINICH 23-year-old (distilled 1973, bottled 1997), 57.1 vol,
Rare Malts

Colour Bright gold.

Nose Herbal, leafy, oily.

Body Big, smooth, firm.

Palate Leathery. Gunmetal.

Finish Quick, warming, robust.

SCORE 76

TEANINICH 23-year-old (distilled 1972, bottled 1998), 64.95 vol,
Rare Malts

Colour Full gold.

Nose Incense, bergamot, sandalwood.

Body Big.

Palate Rich, toffeeish, nutty, sugared almonds.

Finish Developing some leafy, slightly woody, bamboo-like dryness.

SCORE 75

TEANINICH 24-year-old (distilled 1973, bottled 1997), 56.6 vol, Adelphi

Colour Distinctly greenish tinge.

Nose Honeydew melons. Leafy. Slightly leathery.

Body Big, firm.

Palate Leathery, grassy, peaty.

Finish Spicy, mustardy, peaty.

SCORE 75

Earlier versions of Teaninich

A 17-year-old Master of Malt, at 43 vol, was herbal, earthy, and peaty.
SCORE 72. A 1982 Connoisseurs Choice, at 40 vol, was more toffeeish
and creamy. SCORE 76.

TOBERMORY

PRODUCER Burn Stewart
REGION Highlands   **ISLAND** Mull

ADDRESS Tobermory, Isle of Mull, Argyllshire, PA75 6NR   **TEL** 01688-302647 **VC**
WEBSITE www.wallace-malt.co.uk

I F THE ART OF DISTILLATION was brought from Ireland over the Giant's Causeway, it must have arrived on Mull. The island's sole current distillery is in the harbour village of Tobermory. The village was once known as Ledaig ("Safe Haven", in Gaelic). The distillery traces its origins to 1795, but has a much interrupted history and many owners. The proprietors during the period 1972–75 made some particularly fine whisky.

Various owners have at times used the name Tobermory on a blend and a vatted malt, but it now appears on a clearly labelled single malt, produced after the distillery reopened in 1989–90. This version has a peatiness, albeit light, derived entirely from the water. The barley malt is not peated. The name Ledaig has, for some years, been used for older versions of the whisky employing peated malt. Ledaig is now being made again, and its peatiness gradually being increased. A two-year-old sampled as a work in progress in 1999 had a grassy start followed by a surge of smoky peatiness.

The maritime character of the whiskies was diminished when the warehouses were sold by previous owners to make room for apartments. The whisky is now matured on the mainland by the current proprietors, Burn Stewart, at their Deanston distillery.

HOUSE STYLE Faint peat, minty, sweet. Restorative.

TOBERMORY 10-year-old, 40 vol
Colour Full gold.
Nose Light but definite touch of peat. Some sweetness.
Body Light to medium. Very smooth.
Palate Faint peat. Enjoyable interplay of malty, nutty dryness, and toffeeish, faintly minty sweetness. Slightly weak in the middle, but recovers well.
Finish Light, soft, becoming sweeter.

SCORE 69

LEDAIG, no age statement, 42 vol

Colour Gold.

Nose Appetizingly peaty, then lightly spicy and sweet.

Body Fuller, creamier, oilier.

Palate Firm, appetizing dryness. Hint of burnt grass. Toast. Nutty malt character. Sugared almonds.

Finish Very minty.

SCORE 72

LEDAIG "Over 15 years"), 43 vol
(The preposition is superfluous; all ages on labels represent the youngest whisky in the bottle.)

Colour Gold to bronze.

Nose Soft, full peatiness.

Body Light but smooth.

Palate Slightly thin. Toffeeish, then spicy.

Finish Sweet, smoky, full peatiness. A hint of the sea in this one.

SCORE 73

LEDAIG 1979, 43 vol

Colour Pale gold.

Nose Stony, lightly grassy, and peaty.

Body Light to medium, smooth.

Palate Grassy, lightly smoky sweetness. Hint of burnt grass. Some peat coming through.

Finish Vanilla, grass. Delicately peaty.

SCORE 72

LEDAIG "Over 20 years", 43 vol

Colour Pale amber.

Nose Slightly musty.

Body Creamy.

Palate Dull start, but some burnt grass, cream, and mintiness develops.

Finish Late peatiness.

SCORE 71

LEDAIG 1974, 43 vol

Colour Pale gold.

Nose Clean, crisp, dry peatiness.

Body Light, smooth.

Palate Clean toffee.

Finish Minty, grassy, very lightly peaty.

(Tasted as a work in progress, therefore not scored.)

Earlier versions of Ledaig

There have in the past been some very good independent bottlings of this malt. An 18-year-old, at 55.2 vol from James MacArthur, bottled in the mid 1990s, was full of island character. SCORE 79. A 1973, at 40 vol from Gordon & MacPhail, was intensely peaty and phenolic. SCORE 76. Also in the mid 1990s, a bottling at 60.2 vol from the Scotch Malt Whisky Society had a peaty, perfumy leatheriness, with some sweetness. SCORE 75. A version at 43 vol, from Oddbins, was similar, with a hint of the sea.
SCORE 75.

TOMATIN

PRODUCER Takara, Shuzo and Okura
REGION Highlands   **DISTRICT** Speyside (Findhorn)

ADDRESS Tomatin, Inverness-shire, IV13 7YT   **TEL** 01808-511444 **VC**
E-MAIL info@tomatin.co.uk

THIS DISTILLERY, AT 1,028FT (315M) on the upper reaches of the river Findhorn, was the first in Scotland to be wholly owned by a Japanese company. Tomatin was established in 1897, but saw its great years of expansion between the 1950s and the 1970s. During this period, it became the biggest malt distillery in Scotland. It is just a little smaller than Suntory's Hakushu distillery, in Japan.

As a large distillery, Tomatin produced a broad-shouldered malt as a filler for countless blends during the boom years. It is neither the most complex nor the most assertive of malts, but it is far tastier than is widely realized. For the novice wishing to move from lighter single malts to something a little more imposing, the climb to Tomatin is well worthwhile. As a step on the way, there is now the famous old blend The Antiquary, recently acquired by Tomatin.

HOUSE STYLE Malty, spicy, rich. Restorative or after dinner.

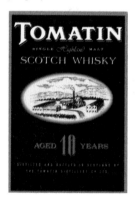

TOMATIN 10-year-old, 40 vol

Colour Full gold.

Nose Appetizingly fresh and clean, with a light, malty sweetness, and a hint of dry, perfumy smokiness.

Body Medium, soft, smooth.

Palate Sweet, but not overpoweringly so. Dips slightly in the middle, then develops an attractive balance of gingery, perfumy dryness.

Finish Slightly chewy. Nutty. Very faint peat.

SCORE 75

TOMATIN 12-year-old, 43 vol

Colour Full gold to bronze.

Nose Malty. Lightly raisiny. Spicy, perfumy. Hint of aniseedy sherry?

Body Medium. Buttery.

Palate Clean, sweet. Malty. Fudgy. Nutty. Very well-rounded.

Finish Soothing, warming. Spicy. Gingery.

SCORE 76

TOMATIN 30-year-old, 43 vol
Edition for centenary of distillery (1897–1997).

Colour Walnut.

Nose Juicy, nutty sweetness.

Body Full. Rounded.

Palate Complex. Tightly combined flavours. Fudgy, nutty. Lightly peaty.

Finish Cigar-like, smoky fragrance.

SCORE 79

Earlier versions of Tomatin
An "official" 25-year-old, at 43 vol, was spicier, with some bergamot. SCORE 78. A Cadenhead 13-year-old, at 60.4 vol, was sharper and drier. SCORE 74. A Connoisseurs Choice 1968, at 40 vol, was fruity and orangey. SCORE 75. A 1964 in that same range was even fruitier but drier. SCORE 74. A Signatory 1966, at 43 vol, was aromatic, perfumy, and toffeeish. SCORE 75.

TOMINTOUL

PRODUCER JBB
REGION Highlands   DISTRICT Speyside (Livet)

ADDRESS Ballindalloch, Banffshire, AB3 9AG

THE VILLAGE OF TOMINTOUL (pronounced "tom in t'owl") is the base camp for climbers and walkers in the area around the Rivers Avon and Livet. Nearby, Cromdale and the Ladder Hills foreshadow the Cairngorm Mountains. It is about eight miles from the village to the distillery, which is on the edge of forest, close to the river Avon. The distillery was built in the 1960s and is modern in appearance. Its whisky contributes to the Whyte and Mackay blends. The wildness of the surroundings contrasts with the elegance of the district's malts. Tomintoul is the lightest among them in flavour, though it has a little more body than its neighbour Tamnavulin.

HOUSE STYLE Delicate, grassy, perfumy. Aperitif.

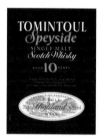

TOMINTOUL 10-year-old, 40 vol

Colour Full, sunny gold.	
Nose Grassy. Lemon grass. Orange flower-water.	
Body Light, smooth, slippery.	
Palate Sweetish. Crushed barley. Pot-pourri.	
Finish Lively and lingering gently. Nutty. Lemon grass.	

SCORE 77

This replaces a 12-year-old, which seemed less fruity. SCORE 76.

Other versions of Tomintoul

A hard-to-find "official" 24-year-old, at 40 vol, is sweetly sherryish, but still flowery. SCORE 78. A 23-year-old, at 54.3 vol from Adelphi, is greeny-gold, faintly herbal, but nutty and sweetish. SCORE 77. A 26-year-old, at 55.5 vol from the same bottler, is fuller in colour, with a suggestion of sherry and a surprising peatiness. SCORE 78.

TORMORE

PRODUCER Allied Distillers
REGION Highlands   **DISTRICT** Speyside

ADDRESS Advie by Grantown-on-Spey, Morayshire, PH26 3LR
TEL 01807-510244

THE MOST ARCHITECTURALLY ELEGANT of all whisky distilleries. With a musical clock, belfry, and ornamental curling lake, it looks like a spa offering a mountain-water cure. In a sense, it does: the water of life, *uisge beatha*. Tormore, among the Cromdale Hills, overlooking the Spey, was designed by Sir Albert Richardson, president of the Royal Academy, and erected as a showpiece in 1958–60, during a boom in the scotch whisky industry. It was the first completely new malt distillery built in the Highlands in the 20th century. The whisky was originally intended as a component of Long John, and later became an element of Ballantine's. Admirers find it aromatic, sweet, and easily drinkable, but the more cautious deem its firmness "metallic." It has not been much marketed as a single malt in recent years. Nor does the distillery have tours, which seems a wasteful denial of its original purpose as a visual celebration.

HOUSE STYLE Nutty. Firm, smooth. Versatile. Perhaps best as a restorative.

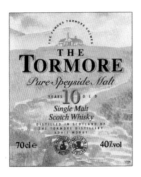

TORMORE 10-year-old, 40 vol

Colour Full gold.

Nose Notably nutty. Almondy.

Body Medium, smooth, firm, textured.

Palate Soft, beautifully balanced, with honeyish sweetness and toasty dryness.

Finish Full, well rounded.

SCORE 76

TULLIBARDINE

PRODUCER JBB
REGION Highlands   **DISTRICT** Midlands

ADDRESS Blackford, Perthshire, PH4 1DG

NEAR GLENEAGLES IS THE MOOR OF TULLIBARDINE, on the Ochil Hills. In this area, the village of Blackford is the source of Highland Spring bottled water. The hills and their springs have provided water for brewing since at least the 12th century. In 1488, a Tullibardine brewery brewed the ale for the coronation of King James IV at Scone. A former brewery site accommodates the distillery. There may have been whisky making there in the late 1700s, but it was not until 1949 that the present distllery was erected. It was built by Delmé Evans, a noted designer of distilleries, whose functional styling can also be seen at Glenallachie and Jura. The whisky from Tullibardine has contributed to blends such as Scots Grey and Glenfoyle, but the distillery has been mothballed since 1995. It is in the Highland region, though south of Perth and half way to Stirling.

HOUSE STYLE Winey, fragrant. With pre-dinner pistachios. More sherried versions with a honeyish dessert (baclava?).

TULLIBARDINE 10-year-old, 40 vol

Colour Bright gold.
Nose Soft, lemony, malty, sweetish.
Body Medium, firm, oily, smooth.
Palate Full, with clean, grassy-malty, buttery sweetness. Only medium-sweet. Develops to a fruity, almost Chardonnay-like wineyness.
Finish Sweetish, fragrant, appetizing, big. Vanilla-pod spiciness.

SCORE 76

TULLIBARDINE 27-year-old, 45 vol
An "official" bottling, now hard to find.

Colour Full gold to bronze.

Nose Touch of sherry. Then expressive, scenty, luscious, inviting.

Body Medium, smooth, clean.

Palate Softened by the sherry. Still grassy, but slightly nuttier.

Finish Lemon grass. Honeyed but dry. Nutty.

SCORE 77

TULLIBARDINE 30-year-old, 45 vol, Stillman's Dram

Colour Amber.

Nose Dry honey.

Body Medium to full. Rounded.

Palate Honey, butter, nuts, sherryish wineyness.

Finish Sherryish. Sweet. Nutty. Spicy.

SCORE 77

TULLIBARDINE 1972 (22-year-old), 53.5 vol, Signatory

Colour Bright primrose.

Nose Fresh. Grassy. Herbal.

Body Light. Firm. Oily.

Palate Grassy. Lemony. Hint of straw.

Finish Drying. Grassy. Slightly woody.

SCORE 76

Vatted Malts

A new interest in this style of whisky is being evinced among owners with big-name brands of blended Scotch. Examples include Chivas Brothers' Century (containing 100 whiskies) and Johnnie Walker ("Green Label") Pure Malt.

For all the rounding that the 100 elements provide, Century (Score 79) most obviously showcases the flowery-fruity nuttiness, firmly creamy maltiness, and fragrance of the classic Speyside malts owned by Chivas brothers.

Johnnie Walker Pure Malt (Score 80) tries to be gentle and smooth but cannot altogether hide its maritime flavours: its salt and pepper, its seaweed, exotic spices, lemons, and almonds. A dissembling counterpart to the more robustly aggressive blend Black Label.

Whyte and Mackay's parent JBB has a vatting containing malts from each of the four main regions, under the name The Corriemhor Cigar Reserve. This is smoky but lighter and more restrained than Dalmore's Cigar Malt (from the same company).

Being neither singles nor blends, vatted malts come and go. There have been many. Some of the best are vatted to highlight the malts of a particular island or region, sometimes by merchants or supermarkets. One merchant, Loch Fyne Whiskies, has gone further by constantly topping up a cask, as though it were in a solera system. This has produced some richly sherried but salty whiskies, a constant work in progress, under the label The Living Cask.

Grain whisky

Grain whisky is made in eight industrial-scale distilleries, most of which are in the urban central belt. Girvan is an exception, being in the far south, and it offers a single grain with a lot of wood extract: the sweet, juicy Black Barrel (Score 71). Two more offer singles. Invergordon, in the far north, has a ten-year-old single grain, very light-tasting, with a hint of vanilla (Score 70). Cameron Bridge, in Fife, has a single grain, with sherry and caramel notes (Score 70). Enthusiasts may find the others in independent bottlings, but grain whisky is really for blending. A rare single from outside Scotland is a Schwäbischer Whisky made from barley and ecological wheat at the Gruel distillery, of Teck, Germany: syrupy, with apple and fresh oak (Score 63).

SOME MALT WHISKIES FROM OUTSIDE SCOTLAND

A growing number of nations are offering malt whiskies. Some of the newer entrants are, inevitably, less polished than examples from old-established whisky countries such as Ireland or Japan.

Australia

Cradle Mountain Malt Whisky, 43 vol, distilled in Ulverstone, Tasmania: white wine colour; earthy-fruity (apple core?) aroma; and a grainy dryness. SCORE 61. This whisky is vatted with Scotland's Springbank to create the livelier, salty Antipodean Double Malt (54.4 vol). SCORE 66.

Sullivan's Cove Single Malt, 40 vol, distilled in Hobart, Tasmania: full gold; smooth; leathery and dry. SCORE 63.

Czech Republic

King Barley Malt Whisky, over 12 years old, 43 vol, from Dolany: peachy colour; a hint of peat in a grassy, nutty aroma; a clean, syrupy, malty sweetness; and a spicy finish. SCORE 67.

Germany

Sonnen Schein, 40 vol, was produced from Scottish malt in a modified column still, at Witten, south of Dortmund, for release as a ten-year-old in 2000. It is bright greeny-gold, with a smoothly peaty, faintly medicinal aroma; a creamy, oily body; a hugely estery, fruity, pears-and-peat finish. Tasted as a work in progress.

Ireland

Bushmills Malt, ten years old, 40 vol: gold; sweet aroma; fudgy palate; and creamy, oily, linseed finish. SCORE 75.

Bushmills Malt, 16 years old, 40 vol: more of a burnt-toffee character, with suggestions of toasted almonds. Bushmills aged in first-fill Bourbon barrels and an equal proportion from sherry butts are married in port pipes for six to 12 months. SCORE 83.

Bushmills Millennium is distinctly citrussy and spicy, though each cask is slightly different. The whisky was distilled in 1975 and re-casked in the early 1990s in first-fill Bourbon. It is sold by the cask, at natural strength. SCORE 83.

(Bushmills, in County Antrim, is a malt distillery. The whisky called simply Bushmills, and the premium label Black Bush, are malt-accented blends. Their grain component is distilled at Midleton, County Cork.)

Coleraine Single Malt, 57.1 vol, now hard to find, is a 34-year-old from this long-gone distillery. Some toffee, fruit and spice, but with a gritty, sunflower-seed dryness. Score 77.

Connemara, 40 vol, is an oily, perfumy, pronouncedly smoky, sweetly grassy whisky made in Cooley from peated Scottish malt. Score 81.

Knappogue Castle 1991, 40 vol, also from Cooley: clean, satin-like; slightly oaty-tasting and very sweet. Score 75.

Locke's Malt, 40 vol (which has a sister blend), is a toasty, peachy vatting from the same distillery. Score 76.

Tyrconnell, 40 vol, also from Cooley, is grainier, with a hint of charcoal. Score 74.

Japan

Kirin Seagram 20th anniversary Pure Malt Whisky (40 vol), no age statement: peachy colour; softly flowery aroma; light, buttery-malty palate; dusty dryness and fragrance in finish. Lightish, especially in the middle, but elegant. Score 75.

Kirin Seagram Fuji-Gotemba Single Barrel (Number 56182), 20-year-old: orangey colour; marmalade and toast in the aroma; oily maltiness beautifully balanced by a crisply peaty finish. Score 78.

Nikka Single Malt Whisky, 10-year-old, 43 vol: warm gold colour; dry, appetizing aroma; clean, spicy palate; and a robustly peaty background. Score 76.

Nikka Miyagikyo 12-year-old, from the company's distillery in the city of Sendai: fractionally fuller colour and firmer, nuttier sherry note. Score 77.

Nikka Hokkaido 12-year-old, 43 vol, from Yoichi: bronze-red; nutty sherry and chewy malt, with an earthy peatiness that seems to crumble in the mouth. Remarkable interplay. Score 78.

Nikka Single Cask 10-year-old (distilled at Yoichi, 1998), 62.3 vol: full orange colour; very sherried and raisiny-sweet, gingery spice, and late smoke against a relatively light body. Very lively. Score 78.

Nikka Cask-strength whiskies available at the Yoichi visitor centre: less than 1-year-old: very pale, greeny-gold; spirity but nutty and fruity. Score 65. 5-year-old: bright gold, cleanly malty and sweet, with a touch of spicy dryness in the finish. Score 71. 10-year-old: peachy colour; elegant interplay of malt and fragrant smoke. Score 76. 15-year-old: bronze; perfumy, sherryish, beautifully balanced. Score 79.

Suntory Pure Malt Series

10-year-old from the Yamazaki distillery, 40 vol: soft, full gold; fresh, clean aroma; crisply nutty, malty palate; very gentle grassiness in the soothing finish. SCORE 76.

10-year-old from the Hakushu distillery, 40 vol: bright gold; drier in aroma and firm entrance, but slightly richer in malt character, with a hint of marshmallow; very lightly peaty finish. SCORE 76.

12-year-old from Yamazaki, 43 vol: full gold to bronze; appetizing grassiness in the aroma and palate, gently balancing the malty sweetness all the way to a dryish, warming finish. SCORE 77.

12-year-old from Hakushu, 43 vol: bright, full gold; appetizingly peaty aroma; lively interplay of malty and spicy flavours. Very appetizing. SCORE 78.

18-year-old from Yamazaki, 43 vol: orange-amber colour; clean oak, toast, and sherry in the aroma; lightly syrupy; more toastiness and spice. Restrained but complex. SCORE 79.

Two Suntory editions now hard to find

1981 Kioki Jikomi, from Hakushu East, "distilled by direct flame and fermented in Douglas fir": bright gold; rounded, with peat, malt, and epsecially fruity flavours that are almost refreshing. SCORE 78. 1991 Kodaru Jikomi, vatted from Yamazai and the main Hakushu distillery, "filtered through bamboo charcoal": full orange-amber colour. Sweetish, with a slight, ash-like dryness and warming finish. Somewhat lacking in the middle. SCORE 73.

New Zealand

Lammerlaw Single Malt, 43 vol, no age statement, from Dunedin: sunny-gold; light, clean peat, grass, and apricot in the aroma; firm, maltiness; warm finish, with peat returning. SCORE 70.

Pakistan

Murree Single Malt, 43 vol, no age statement (8–10 years): pale greeny-gold; grassy, flowery aroma and finish, with sugary, "boiled sweets" character, vanilla, and some syrupy maltiness. SCORE 62.

United States

Old Potrero Single Malt, 62.3 vol, from San Francisco. Made in a pot still, entirely from rye (but all malted), in an effort to replicate the earliest American whiskeys. Bright deep orange; nutty oak and orange marmalade in the aroma; honey, dates, mint-tea; hugely powerful. Originally bottled at one-year-old. Tasted at three years as a work in progress. This is produced at the Anchor Steam Brewery. Several other small breweries and distilleries on the West Coast are exploring distillation.

STORING AND SERVING MALTS

Whisky cannot improve in the bottle, but it can lose its freshness if mishandled. Store bottles upright, away from direct light or extremes of temperature. After three or four years, whisky in a bottle that is less than half-full can oxidize and begin to disintegrate.

The aroma of whisky is heightened in a copita or snifter, rather than a tumbler. An especially rich whisky will best express its textures if it is not diluted, though the alcohol can numb the tongue. The smallest drop of water will heighten the bouquet.

MALT WHISKY WITH FOOD

Even with water, whisky is a strong drink to serve with food, but the combination can work well. Seaweedy, peppery, salty malts are a natural accompaniment to sushi. In London's Mitsukoshi restaurant, chef Yoshihiro Motohashi, who has cooked for the Emperor of Japan, offered the salty Oban with eggs of flying fish, the tea-like Lagavulin with cod in caramelized miso, and the peppery Talisker with raw tuna. In the same city, chef Andy Barber, at The Fulham Road restaurant, presented oysters with the lightly peaty Dalwhinnie and a dill-marinated salmon with the herbal-tasting Cragganmore.

Another typical Scottish shellfish, scallops, featured with the gently grassy Auchentoshan in a dinner at the James Beard House, in New York, presented by Oregonian chef Christopher Zefiro. Salty, smoky whiskies are an equally logical accompaniment to smoked salmon or gravadlax. Aberdeen Angus beef and Scottish game require richer malts. Zefiro presented quail and chicory with the ferny Bowmore and herb-crusted beef (Aberdeen Angus?) with the heathery Highland Park. At a dinner at the Museum of the University of Pennsylvania, venison was served with raspberries (typical in Perthshire) and Blair Athol whisky. Any creamy dessert, but especially butterscotch, will be very happy with a richly sherried malt.

MALT WHISKY WITH CIGARS

And the after-dinner cigar? This is a natural partner to a smoky whisky or richer post-prandial malt. The Dalmore's Cigar Malt is designed to do its job with some versatility, being both rich and smoky. At a cigar-and-malts tasting at the London Hilton, the flowery Rosebank was offered with a creamy Macanudo, the perfumy Glendullan with a spicy Santa Damiona, and the leafy Teaninich with an aromatic Cohiba Coronas Especiales. A study for *Whisky Magazine* proposed the smokier Ardbeg with a piny Cohiba Robusto, the richer Talisker Amoroso Finish with a cedary Romeo y Julieta, and Glenfarclas 21-year-old with a hot, peppery Bolivar Corona Gigantes. As with food and wine, it is a choice of complement or contrast.

USEFUL ADDRESSES

RETAILERS

England

London

Cadenhead's Whisky Shop
3 Russell Street
Covent Garden
WC2B 5JD
tel 0171 379 4640

La Reserve
56 Walton Street, SW3 1RB
tel 0171 589 2020

Milroys of Soho
3 Greek Street, W1V 6NX
tel 0171 437 2385
www.milroys.co.uk

The Vintage House
42 Old Compton Street
W1V 6LR
tel 0171 437 2592
www.sohowhisky.com

Midlands

The Wee Dram
5 Portland Square
Bakewell
Derbyshire, DE45 1HA
tel 01629 812235
www.weedram.co.uk

East

The Whisky Shop
87 Bailgate
Lincoln, LN1 3AR
tel 01522 537834

Scotland

Edinburgh

Cadenhead's Whisky Shop
172 Canongate, Royal Mile
EH8 8DF
tel 0131 556 5864

Peckham & Rye Ltd
Waverley Station
EH1 1BB
tel 0131 557 9050

Glasgow

Peckham & Rye Ltd
61-65 Glassford Street
G1 1UJ
tel 0141 553 0666

Highlands

Cairngorm Whisky Centre
Inverdruie, Aviemore
Inverness-shire
PH22 1QU
tel 01479 810574

Loch Fyne Whiskies
Inverary
Argyll, PA32 8UD
tel 01499 302219
www.lfw.co.uk

USA

New York City

Park Avenue Liquors
292 Madison Avenue
NY 10017
tel 212 685 2442
www.parkaveliquor.com

Chicago

Sam's Wine & Spirits
1720 North Marcey
Il 60614
tel 1 800 777 9137
www.sams-wine.com

San Francisco

The Cannery Wine Cellars
2801 Leavenworth
Fisherman's Wharf
CA 94133
tel 415 928 4340
www.cannerywine.com

INDEPENDENT BOTTLERS

Adelphi Distillery Ltd.
3 Gloucester Lane
Edinburgh, EH3 6ED
tel 0131 226 6670

Gordon & MacPhail
George House
Boroughbriggs Road, Elgin
Moray
IV30 1JY
tel 01343 545111
www.gordonandmacphail.com

Hart Brothers (1988) Ltd.,
85 Springkell Avenue
Glasgow, G41 4EJ
tel 0141 427 6974
www.hartbrothers.co.uk

James MacArthur
20 Knights Templar Way
High Wycombe
Bucks
HP11 1PY

Murray McDavid
56 Walton Street
Knightsbridge
London
SW3 1RB
tel 0171 823 7717
www.murray-mcdavid.com

The Master of Malt
96a Calverley Road
Tunbridge Wells
Kent
TN1 2UN
tel 01892 513295
www.masterofmalt.co.uk

The Scotch Malt Whisky
Society Ltd
The Vaults, 87 Giles Street
Edinburgh
EH6 6BZ
tel 0131 554 3451
www.smws.com

Scott's Selection
Speyside Distillery Co. Ltd.
Duchess Road
Glasgow
G37 1AU
tel 0141 353 0110
www.speysidedistillery.co.uk

Signatory Vintage Scotch
Whisky Company Ltd
7&8 Elizafields
New Haven Road
Edinburgh
EH6 5PY
tel 0131 555 4988
www.signatory.com

INDEX

FURTHER READING

The World Guide to Whisky
Michael Jackson (1993, 1991, 1987)

Scotch Missed
Brian Townsend (1993)

The Whisky Trails
Gordon Brown (1993)

A Taste of Scotch
Derek Cooper (1989)

Whisky and Scotland
Neil M Gunn (1988, 1977, 1935)

The Whiskies of Scotland
R J S McDowall, revised by
William Waugh (1986, 1967)

The Schweppes Guide to
Scotch *Philip Morrice* (1983)

Whisky *Gavin D Smith* (1993)

The Making of Scotch Whisky
Michael Moss and *John Hume*
(1981)

Earlier Classics

Scotch Whisky *David Daiches*

Scotch *Sir Robert Bruce Lockhart*

The Whisky Distilleries
of the United Kingdom
Alfred Barnard

ACKNOWLEDGMENTS

My thanks again to all the people whose assistance was acknowledged in earlier editions of this book, and to the following:

Dominique Anderson, Takahiro Asano, Kathy Badrick, M. P. Bhandara, Trisha Booth, David Boyd, Derek Brown, Andrew Carney, Neil Clapperton, Jim Cryle, Robin Dods, Gavin J.P. Durnin, Leslie Duroe, Rachel Dutton, Hans Jürgen Ehmke, Mike Green, Malcolm Greenwood, Christian Gruel, Robert Hicks, Sandy Hislop, Ian Kennedy, Cathy Law, Bill Lumsden, Nicola Mackinlay, David MacLennan, James MacPherson, Fritz Maytag, Anthony McCallum, Jim McEwan, Nina McKellar, Gerry McSherry, Jim Milne, Euan Mitchell, Gordon Mitchell, Shuna Mitchell, Petr Mlíka, Rainer Mönks, Sarah Moody, Nick Morgan, B.A. Nimmo, Richard C. Paterson, Lucy Penrose, Donna Pitwell, Steve Poore, Lucy Pritchard, Rebecca Richardson, David Robertson, Mr. Alex W. Ross, Tadashi Sakuma, Charlie Sharpe, Jacqui Stacy, David Stewart, Iain Stothard, Dr Jim Swan, Andrew Symington, Linda Thomson, Stuart Thomson, Jim Turle, Gordon Wright, Vanessa Wright.

Countless other people in the industry have helped me over the years, and their assistance is much appreciated.

Dorling Kindersley would like to thank Steve Gorton for photography, Jane Bolton for editorial assistance, Margaret McCormack for the index, and Lovell Johns Limited for the maps.

Photography by Ian Howes, except half title and title page, Steve Gorton; page 11, United Distillers; pages 13, 15, 25, 39, 155, 161, & 244, Michael Jackson; page 14, bottom left, Glenmorangie Distillery Ltd.; page 67, Gordon & MacPhail; page 122, Campbell Distillers Ltd.; page 208, Glenturret; page 220, Charles Tait Photographic. Extra label and bottle photography by Steve Gorton.